Environmental Governance through Partnerships

NEW HORIZONS IN ENVIRONMENTAL POLITICS

Series Editor: Arthur Mol, *Chair and Professor in Environmental Policy, Director, Wageningen School of Social Sciences, Wageningen University, The Netherlands, Professor in Environmental Policy, Renmin University, Beijing*

The New Horizons in Environmental Politics series provides a platform for in-depth critical assessments of how we understand the many changes in the politics of nature, the environment and natural resources that have occurred over the last 50 years. Books in the series question how the environment is (re)defined, debated and protected; explore differences between countries and regions in environmental politics; analyse how actors do and do not collaborate around environment and natural resource conflicts; describe who wins and who loses and in what ways; and detail how to better study, analyze and theorize such developments and outcomes.

The series is designed to promote innovative cross-disciplinary analysis of the contemporary issues and debates influencing the various dimensions of environmental politics. Covering a diverse range of topics, the series will examine the political, economic and ethical aspects of environmental policy, governance and regulation. It brings together cutting edge research on environmental politics worldwide in order to shed light on, and explain current trends and developments.

With oversight from the Series Editor, Professor Arthur Mol – a noted specialist in the field of environmental politics at Wageningen University, The Netherlands – the New Horizons in Environmental Politics series comprises carefully commissioned projects from experts in the field including both academics and professionals. The audience for the series is global, and books in the series are essential reading for students, academics and professionals – in short, anyone with an interest in understanding the vital issues affecting environmental politics in the 21st Century.

Titles in the series include:

Subnational Partnerships for Sustainable Development
Transatlantic Cooperation between the United States and Germany
Holley Andrea Ralston

The Politics of Climate Change Negotiations
Strategies and Variables in Prolonged International Negotiations
Christian Downie

Russia and the Politics of International Environmental Regimes
Environmental Encounters or Foreign Policy?
Anna Korppoo, Nina Tynkkynen and Geir Hønneland

American Environmental Policy
The Failures of Compliance, Abatement and Mitigation
Daniel Press

Environmental Governance through Partnerships
A Discourse Theoretical Study
Ayşem Mert

Environmental Governance through Partnerships

A Discourse Theoretical Study

Ayşem Mert

Centre for Global Cooperation Research, Käte Hamburger Kolleg, University Duisburg-Essen, Germany

NEW HORIZONS IN ENVIRONMENTAL POLITICS

Cheltenham, UK • Northampton, MA, USA

Published by
Edward Elgar Publishing Limited
The Lypiatts
15 Lansdown Road
Cheltenham
Glos GL50 2JA
UK

Edward Elgar Publishing, Inc.
William Pratt House
9 Dewey Court
Northampton
Massachusetts 01060
USA

A catalogue record for this book
is available from the British Library

Library of Congress Control Number: 2014954956

This book is available electronically in the **Elgar**online
Social and Political Science subject collection
DOI 10.4337/9781782540052

MIX
Paper from
responsible sources
FSC® C018575

ISBN 978 1 78254 004 5 (cased)
ISBN 978 1 78254 005 2 (eBook)

Typeset by Servis Filmsetting Ltd, Stockport, Cheshire
Printed and bound in Great Britain by T.J. International Ltd, Padstow

Contents

Foreword

Frank Biermann

Public–private partnerships for sustainable development are today widely seen as the most prominent outcome of the 2002 World Summit on Sustainable Development in Johannesburg, South Africa. At that time, governments could not agree on major new legislative initiatives to mitigate global environmental change and to advance sustainable development. Instead, they opted to focus on the implementation of existing policies and on the support of partnerships between governments, civil society, business and other societal actors. These partnerships were eventually registered with the United Nations and became known as the 'type-II outcomes' of the Johannesburg Summit, as opposed to the traditional 'type-I' outcomes such as treaties or other major intergovernmental initiatives, which were not achievable then. Several hundred of such 'partnerships for sustainable development' have been agreed before, during and in the few years after the Johannesburg Summit.

While the idea of public–private partnership at the global level was not new in 2002, the high number of the newly agreed partnerships, as well as the prominence and, in parts, enthusiasm that surrounded this mechanism of global governance, was surely unprecedented. Recently, the Voluntary Initiatives for Sustainable Development Goals and International Cooperative Initiatives in the context of post-2015 climate governance have made these governance mechanisms even more prominent.

Yet, the eventual role and relevance of partnerships remain open to debate till today. Some observers view the new emphasis on public–private partnerships as problematic, since voluntary public–private governance arrangements might privilege more powerful actors, in particular 'the North' and 'big business', and consolidate the privatization of governance and dominant neo-liberal modes of globalization. Also, some argue that partnerships lack accountability and (democratic) legitimacy. Yet others see public–private partnerships as an innovative form of governance that addresses deficits of interstate politics by bringing together key actors of civil society, governments and business. In this perspective, public–private partnerships or similar governance networks for sustainable development are important new mechanisms to help resolve a variety of current governance deficits. In many of these normative debates the rather broad concept of partnership (and various articulations thereof) is necessarily reduced to a few particular meanings and cases in order to make sense of the complex reality.

It is precisely this problem that Ayşem Mert's important contribution to the study of partnerships addresses. Instead of examining particular articulations and examples of partnerships, it aims to take in all their meanings for various actors and their function for several governance practices and discourses. On the one hand, it places the concept of partnership in its various historical contexts such as business and public administration, international relations, transnational governance, globalization and legal studies. On the other hand, it uses a large-*n* database, expert surveys, and in-depth interviews to examine in detail what partnership and the United Nations partnership regime mean for various parties involved in their social construction and international negotiation. By doing so it reveals why the concept is so attractive to decision-makers and policy practitioners alike. In the final analysis this book provides a detailed theoretical examination of these novel governance arrangements.

In this sense, this volume is a major contribution to the Netherlands Shifts in Governance research programme and a follow-up to the Partnerships for Sustainability project at the VU University Amsterdam, which started in 2005. In the earlier work of this project, detailed empirical analyses were conducted regarding specific questions of the emergence, influence and legitimacy of sustainability partnerships. Notably, our 2012 analysis of the more than 300 partnerships for sustainable development agreed around the 2002 Johannesburg Summit showed that while partnerships have been portrayed by the United Nations as mere implementation instruments for global sustainability goals, they have also a strong political dimension. The negotiations that resulted in partnerships were marked by profound contestations over partnerships between different governments, business representatives and civil society delegations. This process resulted in a definition and operationalization of the partnership idea that was heavily influenced by powerful actors such as the United States or business interests. While the resulting institutional framework for partnerships was sufficiently vague to allow for the inclusion of many divergent interests, the insufficient monitoring and reporting requirements placed limits on the effectiveness of partnership governance from the very beginning. Analysing the Johannesburg partnerships as the outcome of a political bargaining process rather than the functional answer to various governance demands, opens up the possibility of addressing the question of performance and broader impacts beyond a narrow focus on problem-solving effectiveness. This timely book follows up on these results by asking crucial critical questions, for instance how and why partnerships have become the designated governance mechanism to solve environmental problems, what conflicts have settled into the logic of the partnerships regime, and how they normalize and legitimize certain rationales, symbolic orders, or modes of organization over others. Thus, the hegemonic struggles during their negotiations are key to this analysis.

In addition to highlighting the political nature of the United Nations partnership regime, our earlier research also addressed the question of functional and geographic distribution of partnerships for sustainable development. Here we found that – in contrast to many functionalist accounts – partnerships are not necessarily filling functional gaps. They also do not necessarily emerge in the geographic spaces where the demand for partnerships is greatest. Policy network theories go a long way in explaining the geographic dimension of emergence, with partnerships emerging in countries that are member to many international organizations. However, network theories do not seem to be applicable to the participatory dimension of partnerships. While the representation of non-state actors is considerable, most partnerships are still led by traditional actors in international relations. Some evidence for an institutional explanation for partnership distribution can be found in the fact that partnerships are often active in issue areas that are already densely populated by international law and agreements. However, no prevailing organizational model or best practice could be identified for the overall process around partnerships. Mert now fundamentally problematizes the existing win–win narrative and positive connotations of partnerships by exposing the roots of the concept in liability in business law and the relationship it has with the concept of corporation in the globalizing world political economy. As an explanation, she argues that certain transformations that are taking place in global politics is reflected in partnerships, and that these can be traced when seen as discursive practices.

Finally, with regards to the question of legitimacy, our earlier research inquired whether public–private partnerships can be regarded as democratic, and whether they fulfil core democratic values, such as participation, accountability, transparency and deliberation. We have concluded that their democratic credentials are weak in terms of incorporation of core democratic values, that they consolidate rather than transform asymmetrical patterns of participation between North and South, between established and marginalized groups, and between state and non-state actors. While Johannesburg partnerships appear to encourage user participation, it remained unclear how substantial the involvement of local stakeholders in decision-making has become. Mert continues this line of inquiry by adding the numerous democratic imageries that the partnership regime is embedded in. She asks which discourses mediate our understanding of partnerships, and how participatory democracy has been one of the dominant discourses in developmental and environmental governance architectures. The promise of democratic participation, as she convincingly argues, legitimizes numerous problematic practices such as inclusion of contested technologies into the sustainability debates. Our finding (that the implications of technological improvements are not straightforward, as different technologies have varying implications for the autonomy, flexibility and self-reliance of communities) is the basis of her analysis of developmentalism.

In sum, this volume is an important and timely step forward in our understanding of the emergence and legitimacy of public–private partnerships for sustainable development. The book's contribution is both theoretically refreshing and innovative and empirically well-grounded in a deep analysis of major global discourses. Given the still ongoing discussions on multisectoral partnerships in the UN system, this book offers important new perspectives on this partnership idea that will be valuable for both political theorists and policy practitioners.

Frank Biermann
VU University Amsterdam, the Netherlands;
Lund University, Sweden

Acknowledgements

The research presented in this book was generously funded by the Netherlands Organization for Scientific Research (grant number 450-04-313), where it was part of the larger Netherlands-based research programme on 'Shifts in Governance'. The final stages of editing have taken place at the Käte Hamburger Kolleg/Centre for Global Cooperation Research, University of Duisburg-Essen. Permission to use the image on page 135 (Figure 6.1) has been granted by MIT Press. Permission to use the image on page 161 (Figure 6.3) as well as the various quotations from the novel *The Monkey Wrench Gang* has been granted by Lippincott Williams & Wilkins and Penguin Books Ltd. Special thanks go to Alex Pettifer, Alison Hornbeck, Aisha Bushby, Jane Bayliss and Victoria Litherland of Edward Elgar Publishing; they accommodated my reasoning and guided me throughout the publication process.

I would like to thank my colleagues and project team for their cooperation, insights and critique. My sincere thanks must go to Sander Chan (Deutsches Institut für Entwicklungspolitik), Frank Biermann, Philipp Pattberg, and Henk Overbeek (VU University Amsterdam) and Daniel Compagnon (Sciences Po Bordeaux). Their support made this arduous process of critical reasoning possible. The final version of this book has benefited extensively from the critique and advice provided on the earlier versions by Bas Arts of Wageningen University; Jason Glynos and David Howarth of University of Essex; Maarten Hajer of the University of Amsterdam, and Steven Bernstein of University of Toronto. They generously gave their time to offer me valuable comments toward improving my work.

Finally, I would like to thank my friends and family who have been a constant source of curiosity, strength, and intellectual courage. There are no proper words to convey my deep gratitude to Eric Deibel for being a source of endless inspiration and my most valued critic throughout the process of thinking, writing, and most importantly 'being'.

This book is dedicated to the memory of my grandmother, Hüsniye Özcan. Her aspirations inspired me and her devotion to transform her country empowered many women.

Abbreviations

CEO	Chief Executive Officer
CGIAR	Consultative Group on International Agricultural Research
CIP	Communal Infrastructure Project
CSR	Corporate Social Responsibility
DDT	Dichlorodiphenyltrichloroethane
ECOSOC	Economic and Social Council
EU	European Union
G8	Group of 8
G77	Group of 77
GITSI	Global Initiative towards a Sustainable Iraq
GSPD	Global Sustainability Partnerships Database
HGM	Hybrid Governance Mechanism
HSS	Hegemony and Socialist Strategy
IAEA	International Atomic Energy Agency
IGO	Intergovernmental Organization
IMF	International Monetary Fund
IR	International relations
IUCN	International Union for Conservation of Nature and Natural Resources
JPOI	Johannesburg Plan of Implementation
MDGs	Millennium Development Goals
MEA	Multilateral Environmental Agreement
NGO	Non-governmental organization
ODA	Official Development Assistance
OECD	Organisation for Economic Co-operation and Development
PrepCom	Preparatory Committee Meeting
PRSP	Poverty Reduction Strategy Paper
UN	United Nations
UN CSD	United Nations Commission on Sustainable Development
UN DESA	United Nations Department of Economic and Social Affairs
UN NGLS	United Nations Non-Governmental Liaison Service
UNCED	United Nations Conference on Environment and Development

UNCHE	United Nations Conference on the Human Environment
UNDP	United Nations Development Programme
UNEP	United Nations Environment Programme
UNFIP	United Nations Fund for International Partnerships
UNICEF	United Nations Children's Fund
US	United States
USAID	United States Agency for International Development
USD	United States dollars
WCED	World Commission on Environment and Development
WNU	World Nuclear University
WSSD	World Summit on Sustainable Development
WTO	World Trade Organization
WWF	World Wide Fund for Nature
WWII	World War Two

PART I

Setting the scene

1.   Introduction

Discourses [are] practices that systematically form the objects of which they speak.

(Foucault 1972: 49)

1.1   PARTNERSHIPS IN ENVIRONMENTAL GOVERNANCE

The objects this book speaks of, and thereby contributes to the formation of, are called *partnerships*. In social science and policy studies literature, partnerships are often sectorally specified, such as *public–private* partnerships, *private–private* partnerships, *United Nations (UN)–business* partnerships, *business–science* partnerships and most recently *public–social–private* partnerships. In other contexts, the area on which the partnership operates is emphasized. Then, they may be called *development* partnerships, *health* partnerships, or *water* partnerships. Sometimes they are named on the basis of their organizational structure. Then, a partnership may be called a network, an alliance, a commission or initiative. These categories are not mutually exclusive, therefore researchers refer to them under either of these previous terms, or as a general category: *governance networks*.

This book investigates a specific subgroup of partnerships working on sustainable development and operating at a transnational level, called *sustainability partnerships* or *Type-II outcomes*. This last name is a reference to the story of their origin, how they came to be regarded as the (secondary but only) outcome of the World Summit on Sustainable Development (WSSD), held in Johannesburg in 2002. International agreements (Type-I outcomes) over the negotiated sustainability issues have not been reached in the Preparatory Commission Meetings (PrepComs) of the WSSD. The lack of legally binding agreements put the limelight on Type-II outcomes, making them critical for global environmental governance. The partnerships that were endorsed in the Johannesburg Summit and its follow-up are the specific sample this book uses to investigate global environmental governance networks.

Secondly, this book is mainly concerned with transnational and global governance, wherein the interactions of non-state actors across national boundaries are the focus (Dingwerth 2007: 2–3). For this study, it is critical to make the differentiation between transnational and other levels of governance since partnerships are assumed to operate differently at these different levels. When a government or a municipal authority decides to provide public services through outsourcing service provision and choose for building partnerships, they make a decision from among the various policy options they have. The execution of these projects remains in the realm of various actors, often the private sector. Nevertheless,

- from the perspective of the public authority in question, partnerships are political decisions;
- from the perspective of the private sector (service provider), partnerships are a promise and contract (Andersen 2008);
- from the perspective of the public, the partnership's success or failure is linked to the accountability of the *public* authority while the legally binding contract protects the public from suffering losses.

The accountability of the public authority is not, however, guaranteed at the transnational level. Where there is no shadow of hierarchy, partnerships could remain as mere promises. Moreover, there is no legal authority to petition in case there are undesired consequences for the communities involved. Hence, it is necessary to study their practices at the transnational level, without regard to the generally positive assumptions made at other levels of operation.

In sum, this book is about transnational partnerships that work on sustainable development, their introduction into global environmental governance, their negotiation into a partnerships regime by nation states, their endorsement by the United Nations in 2002 as a legitimate governance mechanism, and their mainstreaming by the hundreds of partnerships initiated since then. Accordingly, special attention is paid to the UN processes which have been instrumental in the expansion of partnerships as a governance mechanism.

1.2   BACKGROUND: GOVERNANCE 'AT THE END OF HISTORY'

While the UN institutions have provided *the fora* for the transformation of partnerships to a transnational regime, *the timing* of this transformation coincided with conceptual changes in environmental governance.

At the global level, this was a time when the intrinsic value of nature was seldom evoked as a reason for its protection. It has become increasingly difficult to comprehend nature without reference to humanity's influence on it, and *the environment* (as opposed to nature) has become a function of developmental goals in governance platforms. This new and mediated understanding of nature had its impacts: if nature was to be protected from the economic activities of human societies, the logics of cooperation and competition in and among public and private sectors had to be resolved. Partnerships emerged as a tool of environmental policy at this point when both sides of the political spectrum had to respond to this new outlook. Various philosophers reflected on the death of nature (Merchant 1998), post nature (Curry 2008) and *after Nature* (Strathern 1992; Escobar 1999). The term refers not only to our species' inability to maintain natural cycles, it also reflects the difficulty of understanding and representing nature in an age of such unprecedented intervention in nature. An ontology addressing this situation is the subject of Chapter 3 on 'discourses and institutions *after Nature*'.

As for world politics in general, this was a time of increasing involvement of non-state actors (particularly business actors) in decision-making and policy implementation at all levels. At the national level, since the 1980s many public services have been outsourced to the private sector in the rich countries. This trend was also growing in the so-called developing countries, and its global application required the formation of institutions that could carry out the same idea. It is in this sense that transnational partnerships comprise a *regime*: they have become a globally accepted norm, translated into legitimate institutional arrangements across the world and at various levels. As is documented in Chapter 4 of this book, negotiations of sustainability partnerships have included criteria to transform these loosely organized arrangements into a more specialized set of activities. It is therefore reasonable to understand sustainability partnerships as a *partnerships regime*, in line with Stephen Krasner's (1983: 1) definition of the term as 'implicit or explicit principles, norms, rules and decision-making procedures around which actors' expectations converge in a given area of international relations'.

The UN's endorsement of sustainability partnerships took place at a time global regulatory arrangements were losing their popularity, firstly because they were proven to be ineffective in many areas of environmental governance during the previous decades. Implementation of international treaties has been limited without the consent and contribution of business actors. Secondly, after the Cold War, environment was no longer the obvious area for collaboration between otherwise antagonistic political systems. The 'end of history' narrative that emerged just before the end of the Cold War was the background wherein the positive bias towards partnerships emerged.

The political atmosphere towards (and after) the end of the Cold War allowed for such extreme announcements as 'the end of history', with liberal democracy the victorious ideology. It was the approaching fall of the Soviet Union that inspired Francis Fukuyama's famous phrase as early as 1989. Five years later, one of the greatest proponents of the partnership concept, UN Secretary-General Kofi Annan (1997) put forth a clear vision of governance in a unipolar world: 'Today, market capitalism has no rival. [. . .] In today's world, the private sector is the dominant engine of growth; the principal creator of wealth. [. . .] This is why I call for a new partnership among governments, the private sector, and the international community'.

In the following years, various forms of cooperation among countries or between state and non-state actors were called 'partnership'. What Ann Zammit (2003) calls the 'proliferation of partnerships' or what Jens Martens (2007: 4) termed 'the new mantra shaping the UN discourse on global politics' was this spread in the use of the term 'partnership' to represent any arrangement from development projects to international security agreements. Within ten years of Annan's speech, the UN had already 'facilitated grants for 365 projects implemented by 39 UN agencies [. . .] for the benefit of 123 countries' under the heading of partnerships (UNFIP 2006).

Apart from their unpopularity due to their perceived ineffectiveness, international environmental agreements were also suffering from a general turn towards neo-liberal globalization. The *partnerships regime* was a part of the transformation from predominantly regulation-oriented solutions towards predominantly voluntary, market-based solutions. The emergence of partnerships thus coincided with the decline in the number and scope of the global environmental agreements (Mitchell 2010; Quental et al. 2011).

This transformation has not been without contestation. Various groups within the UN system such as The South Centre, the affiliated civil society groups, as well as workers and trade unions disagreed with and resisted it. These contestations are important sources of information for a political scientific inquiry into the partnerships regime because they reveal the changes in the power distribution by the shift towards market-based governance. Secondly, they indicate conflicts that still exist: while some of the issues regarding new governance mechanisms have been resolved, others, the later chapters argue, have sedimented into the logics of these new practices called partnerships. Understanding these conflicts could reveal the structural limitations of such institutions or solve some of the underlying challenges. This study aims to achieve the former through a number of methods, detailed in Chapter 2.

The 348 partnerships registered by the UNCSD make a sizeable and well-documented sample to study the partnerships regime as they comprise an interesting and opportune set for researchers. As a body of partnerships their official establishment took place at the last global summit on environment and development; the negotiations were official and public, and the contestations can still be traced. They have become the main implementation mechanisms of sustainable development policies (particularly that of the Millennium Development Goals, MDGs), but they are registered with a commission with very limited power. The Commission on Sustainable Development has the functions of information gathering, advising member nations and making recommendations as a part of Economic and Social Council (ECOSOC). Its decision-making power is limited to the recommendations it makes to the General Assembly through the ECOSOC. And yet, the CSD embodies the largest number of partnerships focusing on sustainable development. The narrations and counter-narrations, the mainstreaming and normalizing effects of partnerships through sheer numbers, the discourses employed and abated can all be studied through this large and diverse sample.

To determine such variability, one should keep in mind that various partnership groups are clustered on the basis of different premises, despite their numerous similarities. This is important because of the generally positive bias towards partnerships in policy science and international relations (IR) literatures. Some of the earlier studies on partnerships in general (cf. Visseren-Hamakers and Glasbergen 2007) and the partnerships regime in the UN system in particular (cf. Witte et al. 2002) display a highly positive outlook on the future of these projects as well as their influence on environmental governance. Partnerships are generally expected to have a desirable effect on achieving sustainable development, although this optimism is often linked to certain conditions (such as screening and oversight). Noticing this tendency, Andersen (2008: 1) suggests that partnerships unite the political centre and the political left by overcoming 'the dilemma between public shared responsibility and independent social criticism' (including the critical potential of civil society). Moreover they solve the dilemma between the logics of cooperation and competition in and among public and private sectors, which became the major uniting principle for more conservative groups and business actors. He concludes that this positive bias is undeserved: '[E]ven though partnerships are defined in almost completely positive terms, they often fail. Social partnerships collapse into indifference, or become dissolved in conflicts' (ibid.: 1).

This study does not take the existing belief in partnerships and the partnerships regime for granted. It focuses as much attention on their origins as on their results. Rather than evaluating their problem-solving capabilities, it examines their discursive influences and ideological effects within and outside the UN system. It thus takes a step back and puts partnerships into focus rather than taking the assumptions already made by the system that produced the partnerships regime. For this reason, although *the results of the partnerships regime* are interesting for this study, they are not understood as a test of their success or failure: existing literature reveals that some studies find the same results successful, while others interpret them as failure.

The success of partnerships as a form of governance is not determined by outcomes: partnerships are fast expanding to most environmental issue areas; they are already successful in this mimetic sense. But the recognition that there is no consensus on the success or failure of the *partnerships regime* should not be understood as an attempt to relativize such endeavours away. Rather, it is an attempt to understand the role and capabilities of social science differently, as the following section aims to establish. After all, as Jacques Derrida (2002) warns us, although deconstruction does not produce general rules or methods, it is constantly aware of contexts; and our methods must be adjusted to each case without resorting either to relativism or empiricism. Hence, it is necessary to ask what kind of transformations the replication of this form of governance foreshadows.

1.3   RESEARCH QUESTIONS: AN INQUIRY INTO MEDIATING DISCOURSES

Concepts social scientists use to describe processes and phenomena are abstractions, indicating the common element in these singular events and phenomena. Inversely, we know about singular events and phenomena through filters of theory and imaginary that contextualize them to our pre-existing mental categories. In this sense, abstraction and narration are deeply related. Concepts such as democracy, globalization or environmentalism are *narrations*, made up of various storylines, as much as abstractions.

In their study of globalization, Cameron and Palan (2004: 3) argue that when abstract concepts are articulated, we often react to these storylines, which they call *mediating discourses*:

> Policy-makers, CEOs, NGOs, anti-capitalist protesters and new social movements do not react to 'globalization' as such [but] to a mediating discourse which tells them what globalization is, how it affects their lives and, most

crucially, how it will affect them in the future. The aggregate reaction and response to the mediating discourse, in turn, is an important component shaping the 'reality' of globalization itself.

Thus, mediated concepts and mediating discourses mutually constitute one another, in an ongoing, circular process. The argument, for instance, that globalization is a 'myth' would make no difference to Cameron and Palan's (ibid.) understanding:

> The issue here is not simply whether or not a given theory is true in the conventional sense – that is, an empirically testable proposition – but whether the stories contained within [the narration] are believed by sufficient numbers of people prepared to invest serious time and money in them. If enough such people exist, and if they command sufficient economic, political, social and cultural resources, then any myth, however outrageous or outlandish, to some extent becomes a 'reality'.

Similarly, there are narrations about partnerships (how they came to be, what they are, how they affect our lives and how they will do so in the future) that mediate our understanding of them. Andersen (2008: 1) recognizes this aspect when he suggests

> Partnerships are much praised, but often without great accuracy regarding their actual content. Most of us know partnerships as a loose metaphor, which we can inscribe any meaning to. We nod our heads and smile at each other in mutual affirmation of the fact that partnerships represent the way forward. But no one sees that we may in fact be speaking from entirely different perspectives and about entirely different concepts, or at least not until the project fails and the partnership does not turn out as desired.

Studying the mediating discourses is significant as they influence what is understood by partnerships and influence the reactions of policy-makers, experts, civil society groups, or corporations. In turn, the aggregate reaction to these mediating discourses is an important component that shapes partnerships. As the increasing number of partnerships indicates, the amount of temporal, financial and human resources invested in partnerships certainly assure their continued presence. They command various types of resources, and many careers depend on their perceived success. For the foreseeable future, partnerships are likely to be central to environmental governance.

To demonstrate the idea of this cyclical co-constitution between narratives and phenomena, imagine the establishment of a partnership. Various audiences perceive this event through the mediation of discourses operating like filters: from a legal perspective a contract is signed; from a political perspective an institution is initiated; from an economic perspective a transaction process is started; from a sociological perspective an event is performed and so forth. Receiving all these different narrations from a variety of communicative subsystems allows audiences of policymakers, experts, civil society groups or corporate executives to interpret factual information (for example when and where the partnership was established, who the partners were, what the aim of the partnership was for those partners) such that they

> construct a picture of its significance, place it in an historical context, and frame it in a more or less coherent narrative of social development. [. . .] Out of this welter of observations, performances, interpretations, and predictions certain collective stories then emerge [which in turn inform the society] about itself, and prepare [its members] for future action. (Ibid.: 5)

This book aims to reveal different narrations about partnerships and examine whether they are necessary or desirable institutions. Their influence is more relevant to their desirability than their effectiveness. The platforms wherein they emerged and the political language they transform are analytical components to understand their influence. The research questions therefore can be listed as:

1. How and why did partnerships become the designated governance mechanism to solve environmental problems?
2. How and why did this process prescribe the resulting manifestations of partnerships as opposed to others?
3. Do partnerships normalize or legitimize certain rationales, symbolic orders, or modes of organization, over others?
4. Which discourses mediate our understanding of partnerships? Are there any conflicts between them? If so, is it possible to reveal some of the paradoxes that sedimented into the logics of the partnerships regime through a historical study of these discourses?
5. Inversely, what kinds of shifts do partnerships reflect about the changes taking place in global politics and ideologies, environmental governance and democracy?
6. In what aspects are these shifts able to transform the existing practices, power structures and orders of meaning in global governance?

The first two questions are about the emergence of partnerships, the history and contestations around their negotiation as global environmental governance mechanisms, whereas the third one concerns the existing and possible implications of the partnerships regime. These are addressed in the first empirical chapter (Chapter 4). The fourth and fifth questions comprise the body of this research, analyzed in Chapters 5 to 7, which focus on the discourses of private governance, sustainable development and participatory democracy respectively. The final question frames the conclusive chapter.

1.4 MAIN ASSUMPTIONS: CO-CONSTITUTION AND CIRCULARITY

This book provides a circular narration of partnerships and global governance. My aim is to reconstruct debates and symbolic contexts related to partnerships as private governance institutions, as environmental projects and as tools of participation in global governance. Through investigating partnerships certain transitions in the global order are also explained. One side of this circle reveals the influence and sedimentation of certain discourses into sustainability partnerships. The other side of the circle reveals how partnerships in turn contribute to, exemplify and/or transform the existing discourses and power structures. On the one hand, partnerships often exacerbate these discursive shifts. On the other hand, partnerships themselves change and adapt to these newly constructed realities, too. As Bäckstrand and Lövbrand (2006: 50–51) aptly put it, sustainability partnerships represent a 'microcosm of competing and overlapping discourses' that reflect debates in international relations and environmental governance. Accordingly the main assumptions of this study are that partnerships can be used as analytical mirrors that reflect certain transformations in the discourses of global governance; and that through a study of discourses that mediate our understanding of partnerships, these different symbolic orders can be linked for a fuller analysis and understanding of partnerships.

The circular relationship between partnerships and governance discourses parallels the 'retroductive' method used in this book which is detailed in Chapter 2. It understands social inquiry as a constant cycle between evidence, its interpretation, theorizing, reflection and reappropriation of all these in the light of ontological presuppositions of the particular analysis (Glynos and Howarth 2007: 33–34). The focus of the next section is an initial problematization based on the research questions.

1.5 INITIAL PROBLEMATIZATION: DISCOURSES AND INSTITUTIONS

Partnerships bring certain unlikely principles together. This is reflected in their official definition by the UNCSD (2007), which refers to them as 'voluntary multi-stakeholder initiatives which contribute to the implementation of inter-governmental commitments in *Agenda 21*, the Programme for the Further Implementation of *Agenda 21* and the Johannesburg Plan of Implementation'. This official definition fixes and delimits the nature and the sphere of partnerships.

Regarding their nature, it is emphasized that

- they are voluntary agreements (as opposed to more traditional regulatory mechanisms);
- they are multi-stakeholder initiatives (as opposed to initiatives only among/by state actors).

Regarding the sphere of partnerships, it is stated that

- their goal is to implement intergovernmental commitments (as opposed to participation in the decision-making of these commitments);
- they work on sustainable development issues (as opposed to other issues that might be immediately relevant to the well-being of the environment and people, such as war and peace, or human rights, governance of technologies and so on);
- they act to implement intergovernmentally agreed sustainability goals (as opposed to sustainable development goals that governments cannot agree on or so far have not agreed on, or setting more ambitious or new goals for conservation).

This definition reflects the internal conflicts of the partnerships regime. Firstly, the emphasis on multi-stakeholder participation is balanced by the claim that partnerships are implementation mechanisms. Non-state actors are invited to participate but their participation is restricted to carry out decisions already made by governments. Without non-state participation in decision-making, the partnerships regime appears to depend on a list of principles, the realization of which the governments could not agree on.

Secondly, the most conventional mechanism in the UN system to tackle environmental and social problems is international regulation (that is internationally binding agreements that rest on state regulation and enforcement). Partnerships are operationalized on a different principle, which emphasizes voluntariness. Yet, the issues on which they can work are restricted to existing intergovernmental agreement. It is possible to argue that this is a precaution against unilateral corporate action on issue areas where national interests are divergent. But even then, it represents a greater dilemma: global environmental regulation aims to limit the harmful effects of human activity on the ecosystems of the planet, most often caused by industrial activity. To assume that harmful industries will voluntarily agree to reduce or transform their activities (with no governmental enforcement) is to leave regulation to the irregular influence of environmental activism on the operations of these sectors. A similar argument could be made regarding the global developmental focus of partnerships: if developmental inequalities were the cause of problems partnerships are expected to remedy, then the corporations that (at least to some degree) have caused these inequalities are given a major role, and assumed to be neutral if not benevolent actors.

Finally, the goal determined by the official definition of partnerships rests on an earlier dilemma: 'achieving sustainable development would require broad-based participation and partnerships with non-governmental actors' (UN 1992b: para. 23.1). Why, then, would governments agree to targets that they could neither reach on their own (through binding regulations enforced upon all stakeholders) nor include all stakeholders in the decision-making thereof (which indicates that there are conflicting interests of different stakeholders and little or no agreement among them)? Moreover, this conceptualization sets sustainable development, a discourse that brings together the often conflicting aims of environmental protection and economic development, as an ultimate goal.

But how could all these conflicting statements, assumptions and demands end up in the official definition of a new governance mechanism after long negotiations? This question has to be answered at two levels. Empirically, the discourses mentioned must be studied in greater detail. The mediating discourses on partnerships were selected for this study, accordingly: voluntariness points towards privatization, multi-stakeholderism points towards non-state actor involvement (both in terms of participation and privatization), and the sustainable development is set as the goal for all CSD partnerships. Therefore, it needs to be scrutinized how such conflicting discourses can merge in an official definition, starting with an initial theorization on the relationship between discourses and institutions.

Maarten Hajer (1995: 61) defines discourse as 'a specific ensemble of ideas, concepts, and categorizations that is produced, reproduced, and transformed in a particular set of practices and through which meaning is given to physical and social realities'. If these sets of practices are deeply established and socially agreed upon, it is more difficult to change them. Thus, the more a discourse structures our understanding and articulations, the deeper it lies in the consciousness of the society and the more normal it feels; hence, the more difficult it would be to politicize and change it. Hajer calls this process 'discourse structuration' (ibid.: 60). A successful discourse, Hajer argues, almost always solidifies into an institution, or is translated into institutional arrangements, a process he calls 'discourse institutionalization' (ibid.: 61).

In a more theoretical vein, the relationship between institutions and discourses is established via the concept of *sedimentation*. According to David Howarth (1995: 132) post-structuralist discourse theory does not account for institutions 'as referring to trans-historical and objective laws of historical development, or [. . .] as unified subjects or agents endowed with intrinsic interests and capacities [but as] discourses which, as a result of political and social practices, have become relatively practical and durable'. Both of these approaches to the relationship between institutions and discourses are detailed in the following chapters. For the initial problematization, my aim is to highlight their common approach to sedimentation and conflict: neither of these descriptions excludes the possibility of conflicting discursive elements, storylines, or practices to sediment into the logics of the same institution. In a more recent article, David Howarth writes more explicitly about the inevitability of inconsistencies and the possibility of conflict in policy regimes, linking them to discourse theory through Derrida's concept of 'undecidability':

> Poststructuralist discourse theory stress[es] the *radical contingency* and *structural undecidability* of discursive structures. All systems of meaning are in a fundamental sense lacking or incomplete, [and any] policy regime or practice will exhibit inconsistencies or tensions, as well as various exclusions or negations, which cannot be captured by any essential set of rules or principles. [. . .] Discourses thus exhibit moments of *structural undecidability*, in which the argumentative logic of the text is poised between two equally plausible lines of development. In Derrida's words, these moments of undecidability require the taking of 'ethico-theoretical decisions' that exclude certain possibilities. (Howarth 2009: 312)

The empirical chapters trace such moments wherein ethico-theoretical decisions were made in the history of partnerships. This is important to reveal that allegedly neutral, technical stances in fact conceal highly normative commitments. Examination of the agents that fulfil these positions further discloses the political consequences of such decisions (Hajer 1995: 55). Secondly, these conflicts and their sedimentation into the partnerships regime remains a focal point throughout this analysis. The *sedimentation of conflict* in international relations has so far not been examined in detail. Mainstreaming this idea with the general discourse theoretical framework is one of the theoretical pursuits of Chapter 3, after the main theoretical premises and ontological presuppositions are discussed.

1.6   ORGANIZATION OF CHAPTERS

This book is organized into two parts. The first part continues with two chapters on methodological and theoretical reflections that have guided the research and writing process. It concludes with the first empirical chapter, based on the Global Sustainability Partnerships Database (GSPD), developed at the Institute for Environmental Studies, VU University Amsterdam. This chapter compares the aims of various stakeholders during negotiations of Type-II outcomes with the actual partnerships regime. Part II comprises the analysis of three mediating discourses, resulting in the conclusions.

After this introductory chapter, Part I continues with 'Methodological reflections: studying change within continuity'. This chapter explains the tools and methods for a circular narration that analyzes and embeds partnerships. Discourse theory and eco-criticism are powerful methods, but they also must be grounded in ontological presuppositions guiding their use and interpretation. Such ontological presuppositions and the analytical concepts are mainly established in Chapter 3. 'Theoretical reflections: discourses and institutions *after Nature*', reveals the antiessentialist theoretical foundation of this book, wherein nature is no longer considered in opposition to or the exclusion of society.

The first empirical chapter (Chapter 4) focuses on the 'story' of CSD partnerships, from the first time they have been mentioned in an official UN document to their negotiations and official enactment. Titled 'Partnerships as sedimented discourses: the emergence of Type-II outcomes', it details how the partnerships regime emerged, what role Type-II outcomes were given in governance, and whether actual partnerships contradict these goals.

In Part II, each chapter studies one of the mediating discourses, both historically and in relation to sustainability partnerships. Chapter 5 contextualizes partnerships to their economic background, to observe how the term evolved from a form of business ownership to an institution of transnational governance. It focuses on the discussions around *privatization of governance* in terms of the shifts in the perception of corporations and rights of ownership. More generally, it establishes the framework of globalization and the increasing influence of capital markets on governance. In Chapter 6, the discourse of sustainable development is examined, to place CSD partnerships in their political context. Bringing together the unlikely ideas of environmental protection and economic development, sustainable development has been an exceptionally successful UN discourse, since 1987. To look into this dual origin of the term, a history of environmentalism and one of developmentalism are constructed and linked. Through this nexus, global environmental governance and its various contemporary institutions can be understood in their historical setting. Chapter 7 examines the participation deficit in governance and the proposition that partnerships address this problem. Participation is an ideal that is often employed to justify and legitimize partnerships. Studying participatory discourses historically reveals what kind of democratic inclusion partnerships can deliver.

Chapter 8, 'Conclusions', begins with the empirical, theoretical and methodological results of this study. However it also aims to take another step – as Andersen observed, partnerships are a promise to address the dilemmas between the political centre and left and between the logics of cooperation and competition among public and private sectors. The implication of this observation for global and transnational governance is the extension of democracy to the global level and the promise of inclusion. Thus, the concluding chapter reflects on the potential of partnerships for democracy and environmental governance.

2. Methodological reflections: studying change within continuity

The first author of Speech was God himselfe, that instructed Adam how to name such creatures as he presented to his sight; For the Scripture goeth no further in this matter. But this was sufficient to direct him to adde more names, as the experience and use of the creatures should give him occasion; and to joyn them in such manner by degrees, as to make himselfe understood; and so by succession of time, so much language might be gotten, as he had found use for; [. . .]

But all this language gotten, and augmented by Adam and his posterity, was again lost at the tower of Babel, when by the hand of God, every man was stricken for his rebellion, with an oblivion of his former language. And being hereby forced to disperse themselves into severall parts of the world, it must needs be, that the diversity of Tongues that now is, proceeded by degrees from them, in such manner, as need (the mother of all inventions) taught them; and in tract of time grew every where more copious. (Hobbes 1651 [1985]: 100–101)

2.1 THE WORLD OF THINGS AND THE REALM OF WORDS

The tower of Babel represents a movement from unison to division. Humanity spoke a shared language once; they regarded their civilization so advanced that they wanted to build a city with a tower that reaches heavens. They reasoned, 'let's make a name for ourselves; otherwise we shall be scattered abroad upon the face of the whole earth' (NASB, Genesis 11: 4). By making a name and an artefact that symbolizes that name, they aimed to resist division. Displeased with their hubris, God confused their languages and scattered them across the world. With the loss of a universal language and perfect unity, difference and conflict started among men. This was the mythical origin of politics.

Thus are nativity myths of language and political science intertwined: Thomas Hobbes, the first philosopher to call himself a political scientist starts his philosophical inquiry into the state of nature by looking into the myths of origin of language and politics.[1] Hobbes wrote *Leviathan* in a time of great crisis, during the English civil war. He sought to construct a novel myth of unity outside of the divided religious realm. This unifying factor would be the Sovereign, whose rule is absolute; and his will is the unified will of all that are ruled by him. The content of the social order provided by the Sovereign is not relevant for Hobbes since the order of *any* Sovereign is better than radical disorder (Laclau 1996: 62, 2005a: 88). When he wrote about the tower of Babel, he was replicating such radical dislocation in which all social structure is irreversibly damaged; men talk but do not understand one another.

To establish the severity of this situation, Hobbes argued that the most immediate functions of speech are *remembrance, understanding* and *communication*. Only through words can we remember things, or even determine what we think, and then use this signification for communication. The primacy of language is most obvious when Hobbes (1651 [1985]: 100) states at the beginning of his theory of social contract that it is speech 'whereby men register their Thoughts; recall them when they are past; and also declare them one to another for mutuall utility and conversation; without which, there had been amongst men, neither Common-wealth, nor Society, nor Contract, nor Peace, no more than amongst Lyons, Bears, and Wolves'. Therefore, the destruction of the tower of Babel symbolizes not only the loss of civilization but also that of 'identity', as neither remembrance of the past, nor its communication is possible without common language. The relationship between identity and language is important for post-structuralist discourse analyses, like this one. While identity formation is tackled in the next chapter, this chapter focuses on the relationship between language, society and method.

For Hobbes (ibid.: 100–106), language is the precondition of society, as (1) *the social* can only be produced through shared and reproduced social narratives; (2) complex social narratives can be understood, remembered and communicated only with the mediation of language. Accordingly, he claims 'there being nothing in the world Universall but Names; for the things named are every one of them Individual and Singular' (ibid.: 102).

The implication of this primacy is that Hobbes was 'perfectly aware of the epistemological gap between the world of things and the realm of words [and that] we are discussing not the real in any unmediated or unreflective way, but rather "universalls" – names or abstractions' (Cameron and Palan 2004: 6). To address this epistemological gap, Hobbes (1651 [1985]: 115) suggests to rely not on sense or memory, but on reason and industry to produce first definitions and then

> a good and orderly Method [...] till we come to a knowledge of all the Consequences of names appertaining to the subject in hand; and that is it, men call Science. [If we know] how any thing comes about, upon what causes, and

by what manner; when the like causes come into our power, wee see how to make it produce the like effects.

Hobbes performs a dual operation by first demonstrating his awareness of the gap between the world of things and the realm of words and then separating *knowledge* from *science*: whereas knowledge depends on the senses and memory, pertaining to the things past, science focuses on the future, which can be predicted through careful definition of names and methodological study of their connections and effects. Hence he directs political science towards a knowledge of the consequences (of names and their connections) and prediction of the future. The implication is that things we sense and remember do not constitute science: science is an operation of abstraction; defining the meaning of names geared towards their *future* signification.

By directing science towards the prediction of future signification, Hobbes does not address, but rather circumvents the problem (that is the epistemological gap between the 'Universall' names/abstractions and the 'singular' things and events). The same epistemological gap can be addressed in several other ways, particularly in the Hegelian and Marxist traditions. Hence, possible ways of addressing the epistemological gap between abstractions and events is a necessary starting point for methodological considerations, as the following subsection aims to do.

2.1.1   The Cycle of Politics

The predictive potential of science Hobbes put forth is based on the assumption of an almost mechanical, if not identical, repetition of effects. Against this mechanical understanding of repetition, Karl Marx uses Hegelian dialectics and introduces the dynamic of time to show that repetition is never the reproduction of *identical* results. On the contrary, the passing of time and the simple fact that a similar event has happened before already influences the results of the 'very same' causes. Thus, social dynamics cannot be reproduced through prediction and repetition. This feature of Marx's work is clearest in *The Eighteenth Brumaire of Louis Bonaparte*, where he studies Napoleon III in the context of his uncle's legacy: Marx shows both 'that rewritten history can be re-rewritten', and that his method (as reflected in his language) is 'to repeat in order to produce difference' (Said 1983: 116–124). Said further observes that 'language itself, while genealogically transmitted from generation to generation, is not simply a fact of biological heredity but a fact as well of *acquired identity*' (ibid.). *Generation* involves struggle, and with struggle, difference as well as repetition is *generated*. In a sense, these are the two sides of the same coin that constitutes human history: 'the unchanging, the universal, the constant, the repeatable, on the one hand, and on the other an interest in the original, the revolutionary, the unique and contingent' (ibid.).[2]

Several manifestations of the dialectical relationship between change and continuity (or the social reproduction of sameness and difference) have been focal for Marxist philosophers, although until recently it has remained undertheorized. Hannah Arendt's differentiation between work and labour is one of the most original considerations of the matter, even if it does not evolve into a methodology. Foucault's archaeological method can study change in repetitive practices, but he too, 'lacks a proper theory of permanence and change [leaving a conceptual gap between] the *epistèmes* of [his] early work that mysteriously governed processes of discourse formation, and the contingency of the power effects that is evident in his later work' (Hajer 1995: 52).

Hajer (ibid.: 55–56) addresses this problem by introducing positioning theory, which explains continuity among different discursive elements by social memory or 'the historical references that people draw upon in new *speech situations*'. He focuses on the performative aspect of speech situations by using the concept of *storylines* to explain why one or the other historical reference is taken up: actors (who are not totally free but are the holders of specific positions) have routinized cognitive commitments to a certain framework. Thus, in any speech situation, an actor reproduces a certain storyline that is both consistent with his position and comprehensive (and preferably appealing) to others. Moreover, 'even [to challenge] the dominant story-line, people are expected to position themselves in terms of known categories', simply to be understood (ibid.: 57). This requirement for being comprehensible is partially linguistic, and creates a tension with performativity.

Performative power is in fact an important factor on actors' choices. Narrators choose examples, metaphors, figures of speech and so forth from among various sets of references; and most often, the references which attract the attention of and please their audience are preferred and repeated (Gabriel 2000: 9–10). The relevance of performativity to environmental politics is perhaps most obvious in the non-violent direct actions of environmental groups. These actions seek to direct public attention towards environmental problems by highlighting less immediate 'news' through staging demonstrations around symbolic events, situations and artefacts. While civil disobedience is based on performative power of what is being 'staged', the tension between repetition and generation reveals itself here as well: modes of behaviour, expression, activism that is 'too radical' for most of the society does not generate sympathy for a cause.

As Hajer (ibid.: 57) notes, 'environmental movement is haunted by the dilemma of whether to argue in terms set by the government or to insist on their own mode of expression'.

This dilemma represents the similitude between 'change *versus* continuity', and 'difference *versus* sameness'. In order to create change, a certain amount of difference needs to be socially reproduced, but this should also be balanced by social reproduction of sameness so as to ensure continuity as opposed to radical dislocation. As Said observed, the pendular movement between generation and repetition constitutes history. *Reflection* over this movement is what constitutes politics as such. Thus, the formation of identities of 'us' and 'them', the polarization of social space over issues that generate these identities, actors' choices to mainstream their revolutionary ideas to expand their appeal, their concern that these choices might suggest co-option, and attempts to re-radicalize some other issues can be called the *cycle of politics*. Ernesto Laclau is probably the foremost contemporary philosopher who pays ongoing attention to repetition and change, as well as this reflective component of politics. His conception of *the political* is based solely on the dynamics of contingency and continuity, both in meaning and in identity formation. By doing so, Laclau equates the two pairs ('change/continuity' and 'difference/identity') for the analysis of the political. The following subsection explains how his work underlies the methodology of this study.

2.1.2 The Linguistic Turn and Discourse Theory

In 1985, Ernesto Laclau and Chantal Mouffe published their seminal work *Hegemony and Socialist Strategy* (henceforth HSS). The book developed a post-Marxist project without the class-based reductionism or economic determinism of structural Marxism.[3] Following Laclau's early work (focusing on non-reductionist Marxist theories and Gramscian theory of hegemony), HSS based its post-Marxist project on a historical study of Marxism, followed by a re-reading of Gramsci's theory of hegemony. Following Mouffe's work on democratic theory, HSS argues for radical democracy to become the new strategy of the Left, contesting the neoliberal and neo-conservative understandings, hegemonic in contemporary democratic systems.

HSS was critical both in its suggestion that post-structuralist thought could be employed as a tool for political analysis and in its contribution to the *discursive turn* in the social sciences (Critchley and Marchart 2004: 4–5). It served as the foundation of a post-structuralist theory of discourse, also known as discourse theory, and the *Essex School*. Focusing on populism, identity formation and the role of antagonisms in politics the Essex School has produced a new outlook to the study of politics, the concepts of which are the focus of the following chapter on theoretical underpinnings of this study.

The *linguistic* or *discursive turn* in philosophy and the influence of constructivism in social sciences have generated several schools of thought that distance themselves from a Hobbesian approach to politics and social science. Despite their differences, these schools separated themselves from managerial and/or technocratic approaches to politics and public management as well as exclusively (or predominantly) quantitative methods. In IR, these influences have particularly been useful in the study of transnational movements, institutions and processes, but also have been employed in foreign policy analysis (Wæver 2005), security studies (Hansen 2006) and so forth.

With the linguistic turn, critical studies within political science have parted ways with the objectives Hobbes set for the discipline. Nevertheless, his observation regarding the cognitive operation of naming remains critical (and became even more central): just as names are abstractions while the things they name are individual and singular, concepts social scientists use to describe processes and phenomena we 'observe' are abstractions as well. For this study, the challenge is to strike a balance between understanding the substantively diverse singular examples of individual partnerships and representing the concept of *sustainability partnerships* as an abstraction.[4] The diversity of individual examples necessitates that some of these partnerships are failures; some are success stories relative to these; some are more active than others; some have undesirable consequences, while others can be deemed effective on a different scale. Studies of governance institutions often focus on questions of effectiveness/utility and legitimacy/acceptability in order to categorize and make sense of such diversity. Their results can, at times, reveal which factors make an institution different than others on defined criteria (more successful, more effective, more legitimate and so forth). While these inquiries are interesting for a different intellectual and political project, they are limited to the sample their abstraction is bound to. Such information could be useful for policy purposes, for instance, in understanding what different organizational models mean in different issue areas. It could tell us that more or less institutionalized formations are useful in increasing the amount of plastic recycled, or more decentralized or flexible models would enable more sustainable electricity production. However the use of such methods would be limited in explaining why the partnerships regime is popular in environmental governance, or to follow the examples above, regarding how partnerships could deliver on their promise, if the envisaged future comprises less plastics or electricity.

Moreover, effectiveness-oriented approaches have little reflexive capacity regarding their own role in the society. It is important to recognize that research that aims to solve the problems of existing institutions has difficulty in suggesting their demise. In other words, problem-solving is necessarily place- and time-bound to the problem. The definition of a problem is determined by the necessities of the current society, and restricted to what can or cannot change according to the existing worldviews. Robert Cox (1996: 88–89) criticizes the problem-solving approach since it 'takes the world as it finds it, with the prevailing social and power relationships and the institutions into which they are organized' and assumes impartiality while often serving the interests of the winners of the prevailing power structures. Post-structuralist discourse analysis is *problem-driven*: it prioritizes neither the concerns motivated by data-gathering techniques (as *method-driven* research), nor the vindication of a particular theory (as *theory-driven* research) over the empirical phenomena and its independent problematization (Glynos and Howarth 2007). Thus, an object of study is constructed by the constitution of disparate empirical phenomena as a problem, and by locating it at the proper abstraction level.

To conclude, the main theoretical framework of this study, post-structuralist discourse theory, regards politics as the constant circular movement between change and continuity in societies, which addresses the epistemological gap Hobbes circumvented between the abstraction and the event through a theory-driven approach to methodology. The main concepts and arguments of discourse theory are introduced in Chapter 3, with a particular emphasis on continuity and change as the main constitutive elements of *the political*. Similarly, sustainability partnerships represent both a transformation in global environmental governance and an institutionalization of certain discourses. The methods employed for their analysis must also include linguistic and discursive components as well as indicators of their institutional characteristics. This chapter focuses on the methodological implications of studying change within continuity, and the next section elaborates its application to CSD partnerships.

2.2   SAMPLING AND HISTORY AS A MEANS TO ENLARGING SAMPLE SIZE

As Cox (1996) observed, the assumption of impartiality is a political act on the side of the researcher, whether it is intentional or not. Just as politicians strive to dominate the symbolic order with their own meaning, researchers, too, perform a political act by normalizing their values and mind-set, often by emphasizing the neutrality, the normality, or the inevitability of their concepts. This study aims not to take the existing belief in partnerships for granted. Moreover, it aims to fill the lacuna in literature on the historical and discursive origins of partnerships. This is based on a paradox that needs attention: whereas partnerships are often understood as 'the way forward', the reason for this belief is often delinked from their success in solving the problems they aim or claim to solve. Many studies (Zammit 2003; Andonova 2005; OECD 2006; Biermann et al. 2007) revealed that the partnerships regime has so far been rather unsuccessful in achieving its goals. In sum, partnerships appeal to decision-makers for reasons other than their success.

Some of the earlier studies of the CSD partnerships regime (Witte et al. 2002), as well as various respondents I have interviewed, agreed on 'the great potential' or 'the promise of partnerships' in environmental governance: if they were well-defined, accompanied by strict corporate social responsibility (CSR) requirements and if there were a monitoring process in place, partnerships would have been an effective and desirable governance instrument. Obviously, this assumption is difficult to put to test, since it concerns a hypothetical situation. Yet, a historical study of the discourses that sedimented into *the partnerships regime* can reveal not only some structural limitations of these institutions, but also their potential, so that the reason for this 'belief' in partnerships can be explored.

In their various historical precedents, sustainability partnerships embodied multiple potential actualizations. The resulting governance institution is only one such actualization and is certainly not a final and unchangeable version of the partnerships regime. By looking into the histories of the discourses that make up partnerships, one can reveal and learn from this plurality and potential, and even reverse it. Inversely, knowing the possibilities left out of their actualization could remedy some problems. Understanding the reasons underlying the belief in partnerships could help produce newer and better governance institutions in the future. An inquiry into the historical origins and discursive components of partnerships can enhance the 'sample' from which our abstractions originate. This takes place through the reconstruction of historical debates and contexts related to partnerships, and by linking them to symbolic orders which are related, albeit concealed by long stretches of time, space, or various rationales.

The common element that binds specific projects to the partnership concept is neither explicit nor constant. Discourse analysis is particularly helpful in finding common elements and points of flux in abstraction. Yet, its historical dimension depends on the analysts' choice. It is my contention that the historical uses of the term, the way it was narrated, imagined and popularized can help us understand what is common and what is in flux about partnerships. This contention conforms to Marx's (1939 [1981]: 85) description of the narratives of production:

> Whenever we speak of production, [we mean] production at a definite stage of social development – production by social individuals. [. . .] However, all epochs of production have certain common traits, common characteristics. Production in general is an abstraction, but a rational abstraction in so far it really brings out and fixes the common element and thus saves us repetition. Still, this general category, this common element sifted out by comparison, is itself segmented many times over and splits into different determinations. Some determinations belong to all epochs, others only to a few. [. . .] the elements which are not general and common must be separated out from the determinations valid for production as such, so that in their unity [. . .] their essential difference is forgotten.

If we follow Marx's suggestion, in its most general conceptualization the subject of inquiry (in this case 'sustainability partnerships' as such) is in fact an abstraction; its value depends on the extent to which it 'brings out and fixes the common element' in its various manifestations. While this common element can be sifted through the comparison of many examples, my search for it remains somewhat obscured if this inquiry focuses *only* on CSD partnerships: drawing similarities of the concept of partnerships from different epochs renders the current usage of partnerships in global environmental governance much more intelligible.

This is also the case for the discursive components of partnerships: an historical study of the discourses that played a critical part in their formation reveals various common and differentiated elements, such as their specified sustainability goals, the way they insinuate broader democratic participation in governance, or earlier uses of the term partnership as a form of business ownership. An inquiry into the historical context of partnerships is therefore a significant building block of this analysis. The contestations in various histories that have generated fragments of the partnerships discourse and the mind-set that produced the partnerships regime are particularly intriguing. Assuming that partnerships are here to stay, as a concept that will institutionalize in various, ever-changing ways, it is important to go beyond critique of the existing partnerships regime and reformulate more desirable ways of organization. This position, too, has methodological reasons and consequences.

In a 2004 article focusing on the function and future of critique, Bruno Latour reflects on the question, 'Why Has Critique Run out of Steam?'. His reasons to believe that this is the case are twofold. The first one is the abuse of critical approaches to scientific inquiry. Critical and constructivist methods have relentlessly shown in the last two decades that knowledge, institutions, technologies and rationales all lack scientific certainty and are means to construct 'facts'. They are also linked with power: Knowledge produces (the facts for) power as much as power produces (the need for) knowledge (hence the Foucauldian term power/knowledge). But it has been increasingly the case, recently, that this perception is employed by public figures that 'aim at fooling the public by obscuring the certainty of a closed argument'. Latour rightfully asks what has become of critique, in relation to the following story run by *The New York Times* (2003):

> Most scientists believe that [global] warming is caused largely by manmade pollutants that require strict regulation. Mr. Luntz [a lobbyist for the Republicans] seems to acknowledge as much when he says that 'the scientific debate is closing against us'. His advice, however, is to emphasize that the evidence is not complete. 'Should the public come to believe that the scientific issues are settled', he writes, 'their views about global warming will change accordingly. Therefore, you need to continue to make the lack of scientific certainty a primary issue'.

Such 'artificially maintained scientific controversies' are the first reason why Latour (2004) approaches critique critically. Secondly, he recognizes the increasing tendency both within the academia and outside of it towards disbelief and conspiracy:

> Of course, we, in the academy, like to use more elevated causes – society, discourse, knowledge/power, fields of forces, empires, capitalism – while conspiracists like to portray a miserable bunch of greedy people with dark intents, but I find something troublingly similar in the structure of the explanation, in the first movement of disbelief and, then, in the wheeling of causal explanations coming out of the deep Dark below.

More recently, Latour (2011: 4) refined his position on critique by suggesting that it 'did a wonderful job in debunking prejudices, [. . .] but it ran out of steam because it was predicated on the discovery of a true world of realities lying behind a veil of appearances'. The power of critique in reassembling is limited compared to its power in deconstructing, which results in frustration as manifest in the tendency towards disbelief. Against it, he conceives 'compositionism':

> [Critique] has all the limits of utopia: it relies on the certainty of the world *beyond* this world. [What is the use of poking holes in delusions, if nothing more true is revealed beneath?] By contrast, for compositionism, there is no world of beyond. It is all about *immanence*. The difference is not moot, because *what can be critiqued cannot be composed* (ibid.).

Therefore, Latour (ibid.: 5) argues, social science requires a transformation; to move away from 'debunking from a *resource* [. . .], to a *topic* to be carefully studied'. Using partnerships as a resource, global environmental governance and the most recent institutions with private and hybrid compositions could in fact be critiqued. On the other hand, if partnerships are here to stay, it is also necessary to go beyond critique and reformulate more desirable partnerships. This requires a different approach than the traditional effectiveness and problem-solving focus of most governance studies that regard the aim of partnerships external to the organization of these institutions.

In the following chapters, my aim is not to go so far as 'suspending the critical gesture', as Latour advocates. After all, since Type-II outcomes were endorsed in 2002, there is little improvement, if any, in terms of the already unambitious developmental and environmental indicators. Yet, it seems reasonable to reflect on the possibility that deconstructing partnerships can be a limited aim. This is why not only a history of partnerships but also *a history of the contestations in epistemologies* is necessary. To compose, one has to understand what has been eliminated in the selective process we call politics.

Conceptual fragments of partnerships are found in the three discourses analyzed in Part II. These fragments previously belonged to different semantic constellations. To study what has been eliminated from these constellations and which fragments 'survived', tells us about earlier contestations (what has not happened, the roads not travelled, the fights that were lost). Thus the study of contestations and exclusions are important for discourse analysis. Hansen and Sørenson (2005: 96) note,

> Many approaches to the study of inclusion and exclusion in governance processes focus on 'who' are excluded from/included in the processes of political decision-making. In comparison, discourse analyses focus not only on who is included or excluded, but also more basically on 'what' is being included or excluded. Discourse analysts ask: 'what forms of meaning are discursively excluded and included?' and read those processes as essentially political, that is, antagonistic.

During their formation and negotiation various conceptions of partnerships were eliminated. In the most immediate sense, politics of partnerships reside in these contestations studied in Chapter 4. Analyses of the discourses in Part II reveal what was selected and eliminated even earlier than the emergence of the partnerships regime. Debates and symbolic contexts related to partnerships are reconstructed so as to understand various fragments of the partnerships concept (as private governance institutions, as sustainable development projects, as tools of participation).

These three discourses were selected for a number of reasons. First, as the introduction chapter demonstrates, the official definition of partnerships puts emphasis on *sustainable development* objectives and *multi-stakeholder* formation. Secondly, partnerships have been a way to include the private sector in governance earlier, at the national level; *participation* and *privatization* have been at the core of partnership debates since the 1980s. Thirdly, during the fieldwork these three discourses emerged as most relevant, and were discussed by respondents and policy documents. Although it is difficult to argue that no other discourse could be analyzed, these three are the most prevalent and central to the debates around partnerships.

Latour's compositionist perspective allows for the analysis of these discourses with a focus on partnerships. It helps focus on the discursive changes (even across long stretches of time) most relevant to the study by tracing some key concepts and story-lines. 'Much of the actual textual work is about tracing the development of a few key concepts, their historical origins, their transformations, and not least their constitutive relationship to other concepts [because] discourse is seen as a system, and some elements [. . .] are central to this system' (Wæver 2005: 36). The retroductive explanation model involves a continuous 'to-and-fro movement' between the subject of inquiry and the explanations put forth. The historical study of the discourses under scrutiny reveals how their sedimentation into CSD partnerships has led to a certain formation of the partnerships regime rather than its alternatives. This formation and the circumstances under which it has emerged are important to understand how partnerships reflect current transformations in governance.

The focus on the historical dimension of the three discourses does not suggest historical causality or determinism. On the contrary, the method tries to reveal the unexamined conventions that govern partnerships, as a result of which the problem can be redefined and a range of solutions can arise. As James Tully (1995: 110–116) reflects (following Quentin Skinner's perspective on 'historical linguistics'), language is a 'vehicle for handing down fairly stable vocabulary of characteristic concepts but [words don't] perennially keep the same meaning'. To understand 'the range and depth of original meanings and intentions' as well as their transformation, 'a certain amount of historical knowledge of context is a prerequisite' (ibid.).

Finally the historical reworking of the three discourses requires the study to follow diverse literatures. Although these discourses of governance also interact on other issue areas, it is beyond the scope of this book to include them. The next section lists the methods employed for this construct, the justification of their use and how potential problems are circumvented.

2.3   THE METHODS EMPLOYED

'Partnerships for sustainable development' is a general term, an abstraction. What common traits does this abstraction signify regarding all partnerships that concern themselves with sustainable development? The answer to this question is ambiguous in several ways. First of all, various issues are packed in the term sustainable development. Since its initiation in the 1980s, sustainable development covered increasingly more issues. By now, it can refer to any interaction among actors that defines its core business as environment or development. Secondly, various institutions are packed in the term sustainability partnerships. Different, even incommensurable projects are listed by international agencies as partnerships. Furthermore there are partnerships working on sustainability projects, but that require no such recognition and therefore exist outside of these formal lists. Finally, sustainability partnerships are constantly formed between public and private institutions in various levels of governance. The level of governance in which a partnership operates and the type of actors involved matter greatly in their operations. In short, the variation in the scope, organization and goals of these partnerships is substantial.

Focusing this study on partnerships registered with the UN Commission on Sustainable Development remedies some of these problems. Regarding the level of governance, it specifies partnerships at the global and transnational levels, where the shadow of hierarchy is largely absent. Regarding their goals, the CSD partnerships represent a more coherent set than other possible samples, as their main goals have been identified by UN documents. Moreover, the symbolic/political significance of the endorsement that CSD partnerships received as Type-II outcomes of the Johannesburg Summit make them a turning point in the history of environmental governance. This is not only the first recognition of partnerships in global environmental governance, but also places them squarely in the context of IR as they were the result of intergovernmental negotiations which recognized the presence and necessity of non-state authority. Accordingly, most CSD partnerships are either examples of trans-border cooperation, and/or their membership extends to non-state actors. Finally, they present a coherent set of partnerships that are regarded by governments and non-state actors as a mechanism of environmental governance. If the aim is to understand the *partnerships regime*, rather than individual partnerships, the CSD partnerships encompass a clear sample of choice.

Nevertheless, CSD partnerships in turn manifest very few common traits, as their definition and registration are not guided by binding criteria. Parts of the inquiry into the variety and similarities of CSD partnerships is thus based on a large-n research programme that evolved around the

Global Sustainability Partnerships Database (GSPD) produced at the Institute for Environmental Studies, VU University Amsterdam. This has been particularly useful in determining the extent to which partnerships that are 'out there' are actually operational; whether they actually reflect the UN criteria, which actors are involved as partners; and most importantly in generating a profile of *the partnerships regime* in global environmental governance.

The use of GSPD in this study is descriptive in nature, unlike earlier large-n studies. A first and important step towards such a quantitative study programme has been done by Andonova and Levy (2003) with their early analysis of Type-II partnerships as a potentially innovative governance mechanism. Their work was limited to a relatively small set of variables and it has been largely discontinued after the publication of first results. Other large-n studies mostly used the CSD's own database, which provides information on the basic characteristics of each partnership. These information pages on partnerships are not necessarily accurate, up-to-date, or complete. Many of the details seem to be interpreted differently by each partnership. GSPD included the data provided by the CSD after comparing them with partnership websites, correcting and updating them when necessary. Other sources of information were reports and other publications by partnerships; partners contacted when information was unclear, and a set of surveys with 'experts' conveyed throughout 2007–2008. Respondents to these surveys were representatives of partnerships, major groups, UN officials, diplomats, and academics that work on partnerships or the CSD. While the general descriptive data provided by the GSPD was useful in generating a preliminary landscape for analysis, the main body of data for this research has been the official documents and unofficial narratives provided by the respondents. The formal texts analyzed were expert reports and official texts of UN Conferences, partnership websites or that of major donors and partners.

The foundational statement of Derrida 'there is nothing outside of text' [*il n'y a pas de hors texte*] (1967 [1976]: 158–159) gives only a partial answer to the 'which text should I read?' question, but to accept this premise is critical. On the one hand, any relevant text will reveal 'the structure' it is the product of, as long as one studies it long and closely enough (Wæver 2005: 40). On the other hand, as David Harvey (1996: 80) cautions us, it is dangerous to reduce it to statements like 'everything is text and can be understood as such'. Discourses are not the same as text, but they are how the world is perceived and understood, and therefore the structure (of one's understanding of the world) is necessarily reflected in the text one writes.

Working on public texts has its advantages and challenges. Discourse analysis has a critical advantage when it comes to studying international negotiations through reading public texts (Wæver 2005: 35):

> What is often presented as a weakness of discourse analysis – 'how do you find out if they really *mean* it?', 'what if it is only rhetoric?' – can be turned into a methodological strength, as soon as one is scrupulous about sticking to discourse as discourse. Such questions or critiques derive from a confusion of discourse analysis with psychological and cognitive approaches, or it just assumes commonsensically that 'real' motives *must be* what everybody is interested in, with texts only a means to get to this. Not so: structures within discourse condition possible policies.

While the number and variety of official texts studied throughout the book are rather large, they are but one type of data, and must be contextualized and supplemented. The shortcomings of official texts are that they:

1. often present a schematic description of the discursive framework;
2. result from processes of negotiation and compromise that provide little information about existing discursive patterns of conflict;
3. often have a formalized nature that delimits the informal and more spontaneous expressions of existing discourses;
4. must be contextualized so as to figure if they are emblematic (Hansen and Sørenson 2005: 99).

Formal texts are results of official processes which are the first background to which the resulting documents must be contextualized. It is also necessary to inquire about the mind-set that guided the production of these texts. The text analysis employed here has two dimensions. First, metaphors, rhetorical strategies, uses of imaginaries, and etymology of selected terms are studied to shed light on the frames of mind and of reference that produced them. Secondly, the lines of thought that have produced these terms, metaphors, or fragments of these mind-sets are traced historically in scientific, literary, philosophical and political contexts. This iterative process is informed by a 'literary' or 'cultural' analysis most notably employed by ecocriticism, as well as feminist and (some) Marxist criticism.

In its narrow sense, ecocriticism is defined mainly in relation to literature as 'the study of the relationship between literature and physical environment. Just as feminist criticism examines language and literature from a gender-conscious perspective, and Marxist criticism brings an awareness of modes of production and economic class to its reading of texts, ecocriticism takes an earth-centred approach' (Glotfelty 1996: xix). She explains that among the foci of this method are questions regarding how nature is represented in a text, how related concepts change over time, the relationship between science and literary analysis, and an inquiry into the potential cross-fertilization between disciplines. These foci make ecocriticism an 'avowedly political mode of analysis, [tying its] cultural analysis explicitly to a "green" moral and political agenda [and] environmentally oriented developments in philosophy and political theory' (Garrard 2004: 3).

Although it has originated from the discipline of literature, ecocriticism is inherently an interdisciplinary inquiry. This broader, cultural dimension of ecocriticism is presented in Richard Kerridge's (1998: 5) description of its aim, as tracking 'environmental ideas and representations wherever they appear, to see more clearly a debate which seems to be taking place, often part-concealed, in great many cultural spaces. Most of all, ecocriticism seeks to evaluate texts and ideas in terms of their coherence and usefulness as responses to environmental crisis'.

Another relevance of ecocriticism for this study is its interest in changes in meaning, style, and imagery. For instance, Garrard (2004: 7) understands culture as 'the production, reproduction, and transformation of large-scale metaphors [with] specific – though sometimes ambivalent – political effects or [that] serve particular social interests'. This makes the study of metaphors enabling as it relates use of language to a wider social context: metaphors are not 'fixed entities but develop and change historically' (ibid.: 7–8). When merged with discourse theory, with its emphasis on language, identity formation and politics, ecocriticism becomes a powerful tool for supplying the various backgrounds of worldviews and frames of reference. Moreover, it provides the background for the rationales that underlie the political processes and produce these texts and institutions.

Sustainability partnerships are regularly understood as institutions of *environmental governance*, although they are geared towards a broader development agenda defined by the MDGs. One could wonder, then, whether ecocriticism would be an appropriate method for this inquiry. As my analysis of the sustainable development discourse aims to show, developmental and environmental goals and agendas are intertwined both historically and institutionally. The purpose of ecocriticism, when juxtaposed to this background, is to keep the focus of this analysis on nature and the politics of environment, without assuming developmental goals should be addressed simultaneously, or through the same processes and institutions. Moreover, it helps reveal the way nature is perceived and implicated in developmentalist discourses, sustainable or otherwise.

While this approach remedies some of the problems raised by Hansen and Sørenson, informal and more spontaneous expressions of existing discourses are still important for understanding the conflicts and contestations and adding further dimensions to the analysis. For this reason, a total of 40 in-depth interviews were held with respondents representing various viewpoints, mostly involved in the WSSD process, the CSD, or both: government delegates, NGO observers, or major group representatives to the PrepComs to WSSD, the WSSD Conference itself, officials from the CSD and Department of Economic and Social Affairs (DESA), representatives of partner organizations of CSD partnerships. In a few cases representatives of environmental NGOs, of partnerships not registered with the CSD, or politicians and business people were interviewed.

These interviews provided first- and second-hand narrations of the process that defined CSD partnerships: starting from the first formation of the partnerships concept during the preparations of the WSSD till their endorsement at the Summit. These narrations have been the most clarifying set of data regarding the abstraction that is sustainability partnerships. The length of the interviews varied from twenty minutes to two hours. Most interviews were held during the CSD-16 and 17 meetings at the UN Headquarters, New York.

These narrations provided several accounts of disagreement, ambiguity, and contestation regarding the nature and politics of partnerships. While the formal documents analyzed concealed the hegemonic struggles that took place (in the negotiation and actualization of the partnerships regime), these accounts and observations pointed towards the ambiguities in the texts, and the reasons embedded in the history of partnerships. These accounts were used together with analyses of formal texts. They created an external intersubjectivity to the fieldwork, and helped decide when to stop the snowballing of respondents, and cross-check the factual proximity of what is told.

While ecocriticism and discourse analysis provide a suiting combination, they must be juxtaposed to antiessentialism. 'Ecocriticism *after nature*' requires the critic to relinquish an essentialist conception of nature, which is the starting point of the theoretical considerations that follows.

To conclude: The 'reality' discussed in this book is not only mediated but it is also an abstraction, due to the epistemological gap between the world of things and the realm of words. Even with the use of the methods discussed in this chapter, it may be impossible to 'come to a knowledge of all the Consequences of names' appertaining to partnerships, as Hobbes (1651: 115) would prefer. It does nonetheless embed partnerships in a fuller background. To do this, Hobbes' suggestion to start with producing definitions is necessary, which is the purpose of the next chapter.

NOTES

1. I am aware that Hobbes is not supported in this claim by historians of political thought, and that it is Montesquieu who is credited as the *founder of political science*, and early Greek philosophers for establishing the concepts of the discipline. For a discussion of methodological and theoretical reasons for this consensus see Althusser (1965 [2005]: 13–30). Nevertheless, Hobbes was the first to consider political science as an independent discipline and claim to be a political scientist.
2. Jean Baudrillard (2000: 49) notes that as Marx's depiction of 'Napoleon III as a grotesque copy of Napoleon I [represents] a form of dilution, of historical entropy: history self-repeating becomes a farce. The fake history presents itself as if it were advancing and continuing, when it is actually collapsing'.
3. This should not be understood as a refusal of Marxism. Laclau and Mouffe (1985: 4) explicitly state that their project is *post*-Marxist, but also ultimately post-*Marxist*. HSS strengthens the Gramscian tradition and weakens deterministic assumptions within Marxism.
4. In this sense, partnerships as a governance practice can be seen as the micro-level focus of this book, while the partnerships regime is the macro-level focus. The macro-micro contrast is connected to the distinction between regimes and practices as Glynos and Howarth (2007) employ the term, as a pragmatic and not an ontological distinction. For heuristic purposes, we can fix the notion of regime at the level of transnational governance by studying UNCSD partnerships.

3. Theoretical reflections: discourses and institutions *after Nature*[1]

What is in crisis here is the Symbolic order, the conceptualisation of the relationship between nature and culture such that one can talk about the one through the other. Nature as a ground for the meaning of cultural practices can no longer be taken for granted if Nature itself is regarded as having to be protected and promoted.

After Nature: modification of the natural world has become consumption of it, in exactly the same way as modification of the world's cultures (through colonialisation) has become consumption of them by the international tourist. The old double model for the production of culture – society improves nature, society reflects nature, no longer works. The individual consumes cultural and natural products alike, but in consuming them him or herself reproduces only him or herself. So consuming the world is turning it to already anticipated ends: the pleasures of the closed circuit (Haraway 1985: 8–9), the body as the place of private satisfaction that completes its own desires. [. . .] A crisis perceived as ecological contains all.

We are still After Nature: still act with nature in mind. But I have suggested that the concept that grounded our views of individual consciousness and symbolic activity on the one hand and a relational view of human enterprise and society on the other has been transformed. And because it is ground that is transformed, an equally devastating effect is of triviality. Insofar as the plasticlass person of the late twentieth century also perceives him or herself as a consumer of it, nature seems turned into a mere artefact of consumer choice. Its image may be borrowed here and there, slapped on to products as a new dimension, a kind of marketed contextualisation that reinvents human responsibility as a matter of discriminating between products – even where the greater responsibility might be not to buy at all. But nature as a superadded dimension to human products makes the point nicely. The idea of autonomous form seems old-fashioned. (Strathern 1992: 177–198)

3.1 AFTER NATURE: ANTIESSENTIALIST POLITICAL ECOLOGY

Marilyn Strathern suggests that humanity has entered an era defined by a sense of being 'after Nature', pointing not in the least to our species' recent inability in maintaining the ecological balances that supports life on Earth. More critically, she pointed to how understanding and representing nature has become increasingly difficult at the age of such unprecedented intervention to nature, both in micro (for example further genetic interventions and nanotechnology) and in macro (for example geo-engineering) levels. Donna Haraway (1985), has noted that with this 'artificial production of nature', it becomes impossible to perceive Nature as an independent domain of intrinsic value and authenticity: an unmediated, pristine concept of Nature outside of human intervention is no longer possible even in our minds. These scholars are not suggesting nature has little value or that there is *nothing* natural about Nature any more, although some environmentalists misconceived their work as such (cf. Soper 1996). In contrast, they are preoccupied with the formation of a new, antiessentialist ontology for social sciences that could represent nature and society without making them the binary opposition they have been since (before) the Enlightenment.

Antiessentialism emerged as an objection to the general assertion of essentialism, that entities have (at least some) essential properties that define them. The premise of antiessentialism in relation to the environment would be that nature is always constructed through humanity's discursive processes of giving meaning: every conception we have about nature is also cultural and social. As Latour (1993) and Escobar (1999) recognized, nature is at once real, collective and discursive (fact, power and discourse) and must be naturalized, sociologized and deconstructed accordingly.

In his seminal article titled 'After Nature: Steps to an Antiessentialist Political Ecology', Arturo Escobar (1999: 2) noted that an antiessentialist theory of nature would entail the simultaneous articulation of the biophysical basis of the concept on the one hand, and its culturally constructed and socially produced dimensions on the other. Two important intellectual sources for political ecology are *feminist* and *post-structuralist political thought*, with the antiessentialist conceptions of identity they produced. Rather than assuming an unchanging and pre-existing core (that is an essence), both theories highlight the constant and differential constitution of identity, its radical openness and incompleteness. Escobar also regards 'this critique of essentialism arising out of poststructuralism, the philosophy of language, and hermeneutics as a sine qua non for radical social theory [and] social struggles' and explores whether it can be applied to 'nature' (ibid.: 3):

> Is the category 'nature' susceptible to this kind of analysis? If seemingly solid categories like society and the subject [even so entrenched a category as *the capitalist economy* is subject] to antiessentialist critique, why has nature proven so resistant? [. . .] The poststructuralist rethinking of the social, the economy, and the subject [. . .] suggests ways of rethinking nature as having no essential

identity. As in the case of the other categories mentioned, the analysis would have a double goal: to examine the constitutive relations that account for nature – biological, social, cultural – and to open the way for revealing ethnographically or imagining discourses of ecological/cultural difference that do not reduce the multiplicity of the social and biological worlds to a single overarching principle of determination ('the laws of the ecosystem', 'the mode of production', 'the knowledge system' [etc.]).

Hence, *political ecology* is neither deterministic nor causal: it is the study of articulations wherein historical and biophysical are implicated with each other in order to provide new articulations of the biophysical, the cultural and the technoeconomic, which are 'realizable today, and conductive to more just and sustainable social and ecological relations' (ibid.: 4). Hence, the project is clearly aware and reflexive of its political origins and stance, unlike the articulations found in natural sciences. *After Nature* does not imply a causal relationship between human behaviour and the deepening ecological crises and possible solutions. It emphasizes that *society* and *nature* is conceptually co-constitutive: Nature has always been a concept that defines social institutions and is used to legitimize and construct new ones. On the other hand, various meanings of nature were produced throughout history by socio-political developments.

This is the reason for Escobar to refer particularly to the poststructuralist political theory of Laclau and Mouffe, as the most conducive approach in critical social research with the greatest potential in the search for a non-essentialist understanding of nature. The antiessentialist position of discourse theory can be understood as a stance against causal explanations of social phenomena through which facts and events are tied to universal laws (Howarth 2000: 131). Therefore, its application, discourse analysis, cannot be a method that mechanically applies a neutral set of rules to empirical phenomena (Howarth 2005: 317). Furthermore, on the basis of its philosophical foundations, discourse theory rejects the strict separation of ontological and epistemological (or theoretical and methodological) considerations (Phillips and Jørgensen 2002). It aims to construct new interpretations of the social world, either by revealing phenomena previously unidentified by existing theories, or through the articulation of alternative interpretations by problematizing existing analyses (Howarth 2005: 320). In sum, the aims of political ecology and discourse theory are identical: political ecology has a more specific ecological focus, while discourse theory has a preferred set of concepts and rather well-established ontological presuppositions.

This chapter aims to introduce some discourse theoretical concepts, and to build on and through them the theoretical foundations of my analysis of sustainability partnerships. Although inspired by post-structural discourse theory, I also try to appropriate it for the necessities of this inquiry. In other words, the chapter serves as a theoretical platform on which issues of international relations, environmental and developmental politics in the realm of transnational governance, and particularly the novel mechanisms of governance such as partnerships can be discussed. In this sense, it could be seen as an attempt to bring together the aims of political ecology and the means of discourse theory. The next section focuses on some definitions and assumptions of discourse theory, particularly about language and politics. My goal is not to *summarize* discourse theory, so it does not assume completeness. Furthermore some of the concepts explained below have no generally agreed interpretation (which points to their richness, more than their complexity, in my opinion) so these explanations are my understanding and preferred interpretation of them. The final section focuses on institutions, the sedimentation process mentioned in the earlier chapters, and their relation to these concepts. By doing so, I suggest looking into international negotiations from a new angle: as platforms of conflict sedimentation.

3.2   DISCOURSE THEORETICAL CONCEPTS

Academic literature on sustainable development and private governance, and to a lesser extent stakeholder participation, is full of critical studies that are conscious of the constitutive character of these discourses in IR (Sachs 1992a; Cleaver 2001; Hall and Biersteker 2002). Yet, despite abundant and well-written critique, none of these heavily criticized discourses and practices wither away. This is to some extent because hegemonic struggles over meaning take place in a more subtle fashion at global and transnational levels of governance, particularly in discourses produced by and reproduced within global institutions. Actors with their perceived positions are more dispersed than that of local and national contexts, and change is not imminent or immediate. This is what Oran Young (1989) refers to when he calls international institutions 'sticky'.

From a rationalist, actor-oriented approach it is difficult to analyze how transformation in institutions takes place, as it is often slower than in other agents and yet the whole of the change is bigger than the acts of each actor. Discourse theoretical concepts prove helpful in dynamic analyses of politics, which can account for 'change within continuity'. Concepts such as *empty* and *floating signifiers*, the political logics (*the logics of difference* and *equivalence*) as well as main concepts of discourse theory such as the *hegemonic struggle* and even slower processes such as *institutionalization of discourses* comprise a dynamic understanding of the political, even within institutions.

This dynamism that characterizes discourse theory results from certain fundamental assumptions. Foucauldian discourse analysis examines how meaning is governed by specific rules, such that it often demonstrates how seemingly opposing articulations are in fact governed by a system that defines what can be meaningfully said. For instance, in the contestation regarding the efficacy of carbon markets as a governance mechanism to mitigate climate change, all parties agree that climate change does happen, that it can indeed be mitigated, that it can be mitigated through the reduction of greenhouse gases and that carbon dioxide is one of them. They also agree that these negotiations require an international platform such as the United Nations Framework Convention on Climate Change. Therefore, while at the level of manifest politics these different articulations oppose each other, agents articulating these viewpoints in fact share a common code through which they relate to each other; they struggle, but they struggle over the *same* issues, and opponents try to establish their hegemony, again, over the meaning of the same points (Laclau and Mouffe 1985).

In other words, politics is interplay between demands to change or maintain the existing system; yet these demands constitute a continuum, being incrementally different from one another. Politics takes place in the dynamic sphere of continuity and change. Similarly, Wæver (2005: 36–38) conceives international relations as composed of layered structures of successive depth-levels. His metaphor of placing Foucauldian boxes in each other ideates a dynamic analysis that can specify 'change within continuity':

> Change is not an either–or question, because we are not operating at one level only. The concept of a 'dominant' discourse becomes relative, too. That something is in 'opposition' or even 'marginalised' means only that it is 'outside' and 'different' at the level of manifest politics, while it probably *shares* codes at the next (deeper) level of abstraction. [. . .] The depth-levels [refer] to *degrees* of sedimentation: the deeper structures are more solidly sedimented and more difficult to politicise and change, partly because they are more abstract and thereby logically implied across a wide spectrum. But, principally, change is always possible [. . .]. When pressure builds up in a system and discourse does not easily handle a problem anymore ('dislocation'), it is possible first to make 'surface changes' which keep all the deeper levels intact. This can become increasingly uncomfortable and unstable, however, and at some point a deeper change might happen.

As the dominant power structures operate, resistance emerges at several points, and challenges the status quo. Sometimes these challenges can be domesticated and managed by making surface changes in the discourses of the existing power structure. When this is not possible, paradigmatic shifts might take place, affecting the deeper layers. Therefore, society is never a fully fixed entity; it is always contingent.

The more a discourse structures (or governs) our understanding and articulations, the deeper it lies in the consciousness of the society and the more normal it feels; hence, the more difficult it would be to politicize and change it. Inversely, 'if the credibility of actors in a given domain requires them to draw on the ideas, concepts, and categories of a given discourse', then they are likely to employ these common categories and meanings[2] (Hajer 1995: 60–61). An obvious example of *discourse structuration* would be our conviction that time is linear, or the earlier conviction that the Earth was flat and the centre of universe. Discourse institutionalization, on the other hand, refers to the sedimentation of a certain discourse into repetitive social practices and institutional arrangements. When discourse structuration coincides with discourse institutionalization, Hajer suggests, the discourse can be regarded as hegemonic.

Nonetheless, (even hegemonic) discourses are never fully fixed; they are always contingent and therefore subject to radical alteration (Laclau 1983: 24; Howarth 2000: 122). In principle, change is always possible at any depth-level, as these structures are all socially constituted. *Dislocations* refer to these changes that take place when the existing system of meaning can no longer provide the common categories, solve problems or resist pressure; or inversely, in cases of partial or total disruption of the existing symbolic order. In case of a great dislocation deeper layers of the social imaginary can become open to change as well: this is when 'the system makes a "jump"' (Jeffares 2007: 50), rather similar to Thomas Kuhn's conception of 'paradigm shifts' in his theory of scientific discourses. Laclau (1990: 66) suggests that the greater the dislocation is, the more the 'basic principles' of a group will have been shattered and hence the more prone the social structures would be to radical alteration.

3.2.1 Discourse

Discourses are 'practices that systematically form the objects of which they speak' (Foucault 1972: 49). Any social situation embodies a strategic selection of meanings: while some opinions are voiced and some codes of conduct regarded as normal, others are precluded. This process of strategic selection defines and constitutes objects and simultaneously the boundaries of what is socially acceptable. Building on the Foucauldian conception of discourse, discourse theory understands all social practices to 'take place against a background of historically specific discourses' (Torfing 2005: 14). It regards discourses as systems of meaning that are constitutive of social practices as opposed to the narrower conception of discourse as 'text'.

This does not suggest that there is no material reality, but that our understanding of material reality is necessarily embedded in and conditioned by a discourse (Laclau and Mouffe 1985). This break with the discursive/extra-discursive dichotomy entails, ontologically, that there is no meaning beyond discourse, or objective truth. Discourse theory relies on Lacanian notions of *reality* (the world we convince ourselves that we live in, constructed through language) and *the real* (the material dimension of existence beyond language and thus expression). We are so dependent on our understanding of *reality* that when *the real* surfaces, it radically disrupts our symbolic order.

Discourses are not continuous and consistent articulations, either; although such features can significantly increase their credibility (Hajer 1995). Nor is their tactical function in politics stable or uniform (as in dominant/dominated, hegemonic/repressed discourses); the interplay of various discursive elements form different political strategies (Foucault 1976 [1990]: 100–101):

> It is this distribution that we must reconstruct, with the things said and those concealed, the enunciations required and those forbidden, that it comprises; with the variants and different effects – according to who is speaking, his position of power, the institutional context in which he happens to be situated – that it implies; and with the shifts and reutilizations of identical formulas for contrary objectives that it also includes. [. . .] Discourse can be both an instrument and an effect of power but also a hindrance, a stumbling-block, a point of resistance and a starting point for an opposing strategy. Discourse transmits and produces power; it reinforces it, but also undermines and exposes it, renders it fragile and makes it possible to thwart it. In like manner, silence and secrecy are a shelter for power, anchoring its prohibitions; but they also loosen its holds and provide for relatively obscure areas of tolerance.

This means discourses are not instruments that actors consciously employ in order to shape and transform the world to their liking. On the contrary, discourses provide social agents with subject positions they can identify with (Laclau and Mouffe 1985: 115). Inversely, any individual has various subject positions, determined for instance by their economic class, gender, ethnic identity and so on. In their discussion of the 'multiple forms by which agents are produced as social actors' Howarth and Stavrakakis (2000: 13–14) conclude that 'the political subject is neither simply *determined* by the structure, nor does it *constitute* the structure. Rather, the political subject is forced to take decisions – or identify with certain political projects and the discourses they articulate – when social identities are in crisis and structures need to be recreated'.

Another significant feature of this conception of discourse is its radical openness: Discourses are in constant transformation and can never be fully fixed, as long as the process of articulation continues (Laclau 1983:

24; Howarth 2000: 122). Accordingly, the job of the discourse analyst is to study the processes of articulation (revealed in narratives, story-lines, metaphors, rhetorical strategies, and so forth, each with a separate list of functions it can fulfil) in order to understand the conditions that make a particular discourse possible, viable and/or appealing. In Foucauldian terms, the occupation of the analyst is to understand the 'multiplicity of discursive elements' in the context of existing interrelationships of meaning, the power position of the subject, the social and institutional context and so on. This radical openness results from partial fixation of meaning, inspired by structural linguistics: for a moment, a signifier corresponds to a signified (for example in the Netherlands, currently, 'the war' still refers to the Second World War). This fixation of meaning is always open to modification ('the war' can refer to the US occupation of Afghanistan if, for instance, the involvement of the Dutch army brings terrorist attacks into the country). This dynamic understanding of signification and meaning is consistent with the conception of the political as an interplay between continuity and contingency. On the one hand, the intersubjective reality and partial fixation of signification constitutes the realm of the social, on the other, this fixation is in a constant state of modification through *the political logics* of equivalence and difference: the demands to change and maintain the existing symbolic order (see below).

3.2.2   The Social, the Political and the Phantasmal

In the domain of the *social*, repetitive practices resulting from rule-following, form patterns or relatively fixed meanings. In the domain of *the political*, these meanings, articulations and identities are instituted and challenged; hegemonic struggles, contestations, resistance and dislocations take place. Laclau (2005: 154) suggests that '*all* struggles are, by definition, political' because any struggle over meaning would question and challenge a social practice, politicize it so as to change it. It is critical that Laclau's conception of the political includes both the contestation and the institution of the social, since 'the very institution of a new regime [. . .] presupposes the possibility that a previous social order is successfully displaced from its hegemonic position and thus de-instituted' (Glynos and Howarth 2007: 142).

Finally, the phantasmal is the domain in which the radical contingency of social reality can be concealed by a fantasy of perfect fulfilment.[3] This fantasy suggests a condition before the primordial loss, in which there are no threats to the identity of the subject. In other words, this fantasy is about a condition devoid of the Lacanian lack, which can be defined as the difference between 'what is' and 'what ought to be'. From the standpoint of the political subject, this is the condition where there are no contestations, differences or disagreements. In other words, this fantasy is about perfect consensus, devoid of differences and antagonism. While this fantasy denies the possibility of politics (for without opposition there cannot be a demand for change), it also shows the impossibility of total fixation of meaning; every layer of the structure is always contingent.

Political desires originate in the phantasmal. Chantal Mouffe (2000, 2005) argues that *desires* influence the production of collective identity thereby ensuring allegiance to political projects. Yannis Stavrakakis (2005: 73–74) notes that fantasy in the political is paradoxical as it is

> the imaginary promise of recapturing our lost/impossible enjoyment which provides the fantasy support for many of our political projects and choices. [. . .] On the one hand fantasy promises a harmonious resolution to the social antagonism, a covering of lack. Only in this way can it constitute itself as a desirable object of identification. On the other hand, this beatific dimension of fantasy [is supported with an opposite, which explains why things are imperfect]. There is an important by-product in this balancing-act: the exclusion/demonisation of a particular social group [that caused the lack].

This paradox is most explicit in phantasmal operations of ideology, utopia and myth, which either naturalize the radical contingency of the social or construct the lack as well as a way to cover it.[4] For instance, utopia constructs and describes a perfect society. Most utopian narrations tell of a society devoid of politics, that is devoid of differences, identity, disagreements or antagonisms. This tendency is apparent in the term utopia itself: when Thomas More used the term in the title of his book (now widely-known as *Utopia*), he was aware that while *utopia* meant 'a place that does not exist', its homophone *eutopia* suggested 'a perfect place'. More was utilizing the concept as allegory, suggesting the impossibility of such an ideal place to exist. This *perfect* society that does not (and cannot) exist, is different from the society in which/for which the author produces the utopian work: the differences between the utopia and the existing social order is a reproduction of the difference between 'what ought to be' and 'what is'. Hence, by highlighting these differences the utopian authors reveal what they regard as the impediment to reach the state of perfect fulfilment and identity. For instance, the impediment can be 'the heretics', 'the Jews', 'the colonial powers', 'the capitalist class', or 'the patriarchal institutions', whereas the perfect state can be defined by 'a united world under the rule of (the Christian) God', 'the society of purified race', 'the sovereign (native) state', 'socialist organization of production' or 'gender-neutral social order'.

Myths are more complex in the way they establish what is desirable:

Dvora Yanow (1992) argues that myths determine where communities stop asking questions. Without seeking rational explanations, they justify the *limits* of political change and thus maintain social structures. As Roland Barthes (1957 [1987]: 117) elegantly puts

> In myth [. . .] the signifier is already formed by the signs of the language. Myth has in fact a double function: it points out and it notifies, it makes us understand something and it imposes it on us. [T]he very principle of myth [is that] it transforms history into nature.

Barthes' understanding of myth as metaphor is taken up by Ernesto Laclau (1990: 63) when he explains that 'its concrete or literal content represents something different from itself: the very principle of a fully achieved literality. The fascination accompanying the [utopian vision stems] from this perception or intuition of a fullness that cannot be granted by the reality of the present'. Myths of origin typically provide societies with an imaginary which cannot be questioned, politicized and changed (without risking credibility, or position in society). Similarly, ideologies operate not as 'an illusion masking the real state of things but that of an (unconscious) fantasy structuring our social reality itself' (Žižek 1989: 33). Ideologies are successful to the extent that they can promise political subjects that *the lack* can be covered if they take a limited number of specific political steps. In sum, the fantasmatic element appeals to the desire of the single subject, by promising a re-articulation of the dislocated structure.

An important point here is the difference in the way the phantasmal functions, depending on the scope of the dislocation (or in Wæver's (2005) terms, depending on the depth of structural rupture): at times of partial, less severe dislocations, the *content* of the phantasmal is more important. At times of severe dislocations it will be more important to 'cover the lack' in whichever way possible. As noted in the previous chapters, Laclau recognizes this element in Hobbes' *Leviathan*, which has been possible only after the English Civil War, when *the content* of the order was much less important: the order of *any* Sovereign was better than radical disorder (Laclau 1996: 62, 2005a: 88). These two different categories of social transformation are important for the analysis of different types of social practices and political strategies.

> The hegemonic attempt to fill the gap in the dislocated structure by the construction of a myth raises the question of the relation between the function of the myth and its concrete content (Laclau, 1994: 9–10). The relation between *the filling* and *the filling function* seems to depend upon the size and scope of the dislocation of the structure. When structural dislocation goes deep down to the very bottom of the social, the need for order expands indefinitely. As a result

the filling function tends to become more important than the filling. (Torfing 1999: 151)

I will return to this critical difference when I discuss how hegemonic struggle is settled in each of these situations.

In exploring the three interlinked spheres of the social, the political and the phantasmal, the *logics* of each domain are indispensable for the discourse analyst. They not only help with the analysis of each domain, but also link the three domains to one another, explaining how each one of them is influenced by/influences the others. 'Social logics consist in rule-following, [whereas] political logics are related to the *institution* of the social' as well as its de-institution, contestation and defence (Laclau 2005a: 117). *Fantasmatic logics* concern the concealment of the radical contingency of the social, by suppression or containment of its political dimension: like an in-built immune system, they 'seek to maintain existing social structures by pre-emptively absorbing dislocations, preventing them from becoming [politicized and transformed]' (Glynos and Howarth 2007: 146). Political logics are tools to demonstrate how social practices are constituted and transformed, whereas fantasmatic logics reveal *why* certain political projects are supported as opposed to others, thus accounting for continuity and change.

The political and fantasmatic logics are studied in more detail in the following sections. What needs to be emphasized is the relationship between them: 'whereas political logics are used to explain the discursive *shifts* in the wake of a dislocatory moment, fantasmatic logics describe and account for the *vector* and *modality* of those discursive shifts, capturing the way in which the subject *deals* with the radical contingency of social relations as a subject of enjoyment' (ibid.). This is why discourse theory is particularly apt in the analysis of change within continuity.

3.2.3   Logics of Difference and Equivalence

When the existing system of meaning is unable to explain, represent, or otherwise domesticate new developments, the radical contingency of the social surfaces again. From the perspective of the political subject this is a break-down of the fantasmatic frame that hides the radical contingency. Inversely, the hegemonic discourse becomes 'dislocated' (Torfing 2005: 16) until or unless it finds a way to represent these events or demands. Consider the challenge posed by 'uncooperative communities' to the discourse of development cooperation. As soon as they have become numerous enough that the development institutions could not ignore them, participation has become a central point in the developmentalist discourse. This does not mean that their demands were met, but that development projects have become more inclusive to those community members with relatively unchallenging demands. Majid Rahnema (1992: 128) describes the dynamics of this process as follows:

> Planned macro-changes [. . .] are more the indirect result of millions of individual micro-changes, than of voluntarist programmes and strategies from above. In fact, they often represent a co-option of the unplanned micro-changes produced by others, elsewhere. When these reach a critical mass, and appear as a threat to the dominant knowledge/power centres at the top, they are co-opted and used by their professionals as an input for planned changes, aimed at turning the potential threat posed to the top into a possible asset for it.

When the challenge caused by micro-changes can no longer be contained, the hegemonic discourse seeks other ways of representing it. In discourse theoretical terms, this institutionalizing (or maintaining) force of the hegemonic discourse is the *logic of difference* and the contesting force of popular discourses is the *logic of equivalence*.

Simply put, the logic of equivalence is the strategy that aims to establish a discursive unity between separate elements, linking several social demands against an antagonistic 'other' (in most cases against the hegemonic discourse). It is an attempt to polarize the political space ('us' against 'them'). The logic of equivalence is typically the strategy of a resistance movement against the establishment. In contrast, the logic of difference tries to defy such polarization by trying to override antagonisms through assimilation, cooptation or concession. This is typically (although not necessarily or constantly) the strategy of the establishment (or the hegemonic discourse) towards antagonists.

Political logics explain the dynamics of political change underlying hegemony and antagonism. Summarizing how they operate step by step clarifies their use in discourse theory and introduces the main concepts of this analysis.

3.2.4   Chain of Equivalence

For Laclau, the basic unit of politics is a social demand, an articulation of an unfulfilled request or desire (originating from the Lacanian *lack*). When a group of people feel frustrated about a certain desire they have, their articulation of this frustration turns into a demand from the existing power structure, or eventually claims for a change in the political regime.[5] This can take place at all levels, from the national (for example the Zapatistas in Mexico) to the global/transnational (for example the alter-globalization movement). It is possible, particularly in times of dislocation, that several different demands start being articulated as equivalents (Laclau 2005b: 4):

> If, for instance, the group of people in that area who have been frustrated in their request for better transportation find that their neighbours are equally unsatisfied in their claims [for] security, water supply, housing, schooling, etc., some kind of solidarity will arise between them all: all will share the fact that their demands remain unsatisfied. That is, the demands share a negative dimension beyond their positive differential nature.

If all these groups start articulating their demands in a way associating with, for instance, the idea that the existing government does not fulfil its role, a *chain of equivalence* is formed among them, and a *dichotomic frontier* is formed between these groups and the government. This gives solidity and stability to the demands in question, but also restricts their autonomy, for they now have to 'operate within strategic parameters established for the chain as a whole' (Laclau 2005a: 129). The chain of equivalence homogenizes all these demands, as they are now articulated as equivalent, but simultaneously makes plurality possible. This balance (or tension) between the *subordination* and *autonomization* of the particular demands is 'inherent in the establishment of any political frontier', but it also has limits. If the demands forming the chain of equivalence are subordinated to the extent that their differences can no longer be articulated, the chain can no longer act 'as a *ground* for the democratic demands', holding them together (ibid.: 130). The particular dimension of each demand (for housing, schooling, and so forth), which I will call its particularism, must be maintained, so that the identities formed around these demands can act together. On the other hand, '*autonomisation* beyond a certain point [leads to] the collapse of the popular equivalential camp' (ibid.). If their differences are too strongly articulated the demands cease to be equivalent, and the chain of equivalence collapses.

3.2.5 Empty Signifier

As a chain of equivalence expands, one of these various demands takes on the role to represent the whole chain (in our example, this can be a demand, for example, for 'social justice'). It embodies the shared negation among all these demands; in other words it starts to represent what is equivalent among them. A signifier can 'step in' like this, only by reducing its own content to a minimum (Laclau 2005b: 7); hence, it no longer signifies a particular phenomenon (its *particularism*) but it can articulate different elements, to which it stands in a relation, and becomes the privileged nodal point that binds these other particular points into a discursive formation (Laclau 1996: 44). Metaphorically speaking, such a signifier empties itself (of its initial particularism) to be able to reflect the particularisms of all other demands in the equivalential chain. It acts like a mirror: whoever looks into the mirror sees the reflection of her own image; similarly, whichever group articulates the empty signifier sees the reflection of its own demand, and its own identity formed around that demand.

Once a signifier starts operating in this fashion, it is likely to attract more demands into the equivalential chain. In our example, as the term social justice starts signifying the whole of the popular movement against the government, more groups start articulating their demand in terms of or in relation to social justice: women's groups start articulating their demand for equal rights as a form of social justice and so do the environmentalists that demand higher standards for conservation – ecological justice. The contribution of all these groups to the popular camp means that the empty signifier is even further emptied of its particularism, and start representing a number of new things.

But to what extent can this expansion continue; and where are the borders of the political frontier? According to Laclau, the borders of the inside are determined by the outside: the equivalential chain can expand as long as the dichotomic frontier can be maintained. As all the demands in question are different from each other (they retain their particularisms), the *outside* that is excluded from the equivalential chain cannot simply be another difference. What lies on the other side of the dichotomic frontier *has to have* an antagonistic relationship to the inside, threatening the discursive equivalence. In our example, this *antagonistic other* would be the government, against which all demands for social justice are articulated.

Empty signifiers relate to the phantasmal in the sense that they signify the ambiguous and unarticulated fantasy of perfect fulfilment, or a-wholeness-yet-to-come. From this point of view, an empty signifier is the link between the political and the phantasmal: its deliverance would change 'what is' into 'what ought' and hence should be acted upon. As long as the empty signifier is able to insinuate this promise, the equivalential chain can function.

3.2.6 Hegemonic Struggle

The antagonistic other threatens the popular chain of equivalence by its own hegemonic project. The establishment and the existing hegemonic project constitute the main obstacle against the fulfilment of all the identities formed around several demands in the popular camp. Hence, the popular camp threatens the antagonistic other as well: it polarizes the social space between an 'us' and 'them'. As mentioned earlier, if the popular struggle is successful enough, that is to say if the challenge of the social justice movement threatens the stability of the government, the government needs to explain, represent, or in other ways domesticate it in order for the hegemonic discourse not to become dislocated. One way to do this is to try and integrate some demands of the social justice movement into its own paradigm. In our example, what the government might do, for instance, is to create a new equivalential chain, namely the 'communal infrastructure project', in short CIP. CIP rests on the premise that certain demands of the social justice movement (those that can be reconfigured as infrastructure related demands) are legitimate, while it renders others illegitimate. The women's demand for equality, the environmentalist's demand for conservation and so on are against the developmentalist/ conservative discourse which is the backbone of the hegemonic discourse of this fictional government. The logic of difference suggests that despite their differences some of the groups in the popular camp can articulate their demands and solve their problems within the existing system. By allowing for some of these groups to work together with the government, CIP can disrupt the equivalential chain of the social justice movement, and allow the hegemonic project to start representing some of these demands. A typical slogan would be: 'CIP: for developmental justice in line with *our* social values!'

In sum, if the equivalential chain of the popular camp is threatened or interrupted by that of the competing hegemonic project of the antagonistic other, this happens through the formation of an alternative equivalential chain, in which some of these demands are articulated in entirely different ways. A new regime of equivalences is constructed and the same demands exist in both of the projects, in different articulations (Laclau 2005a: 134–135). By doing this, the government operationalizes the logic of difference, articulating some of the demands in the popular camp in relation to its own hegemonic discourse. In this way, it not only attempts to co-opt certain elements in the equivalential chain, but also to reveal the possibility that despite all these different demands elements of the popular camp can operate within the bounds of the hegemonic discourse: it allows for surface change in order to keep the deeper layers intact.

The psychological dimension of this act can be illustrated by the mirror-empty signifier metaphor: the government tries to distort (or reposition) the mirror used by the popular camp, in such a way that 'the subject' that looks in the mirror can no longer see the reflection of its own identity formed around its own demand, but multiple potentialities of its identity, in relation to each rival hegemonic project. Because of this, the hegemonic struggle takes place *especially* around the empty signifier.

3.2.7 Floating Signifier

Laclau then considers the two possible results of the hegemonic struggle between the popular camp and the establishment. First, let us focus on the possibility that the logic of difference is relatively successful. He asks, what happens 'if the dichotomic frontier, without disappearing, is blurred as [the existing power structure itself becomes hegemonic], trying to interrupt the equivalential chain of the popular camp by an alternative equivalential chain, in which some of the popular demands are articulated to entirely different links?' (2005a: 131). In other words, what happens if the hegemonic discourse is successful and starts to articulate the empty signifier 'social justice' in relation to CIP (for example by building the infrastructure projects in question, such as the Justice Road, or administering the new water network through the 'Socially Just Distribution of Water Principles')?

> In that case, the *same* democratic [demand receives] the structural pressure of *rival* hegemonic projects. [I]ts meaning is indeterminate between alternative equivalential frontiers. I shall call signifiers whose meaning is 'suspended' in that way 'floating signifiers'. [. . .] The way in which the meaning of [the initially empty and at this moment floating signifier] is going to be fixed will depend on the result of a hegemonic struggle. (Laclau 2005a: 131–132)

What social justice signifies becomes blurred as it is articulated by both hegemonic projects. That it was already an empty signifier and therefore was representing several different identities allows for this second movement. Simultaneously, the existing power structure opens up to some of the demands from the popular camp (through the logic of difference). The more the empty signifier floats between two different meanings, the less it represents all the elements in the popular equivalential chain and the less stable the dichotomic becomes. Therefore, while the logics of equivalence and difference demonstrate *the dynamics* of the political, for Laclau (2005a: 153) 'the political consists in an undecidable game between "empty" and "floating"'. Inversely, what Gramsci called 'war of position' is for Laclau a continuous displacement of political frontiers (ibid.). The hegemonic struggle is never final. For instance, the popular struggle for social justice proceeds: a part of the 'popular' camp insists on its rightful 'position' by rejecting the new and limited definitions of social justice; and gets relatively marginalized. Another part integrates conservative/developmentalist values of the hegemonic discourse with the social justice discourse and starts working with the government. The hegemonic discourse is transformed by the struggle with the popular camp as well. Even when this transformation is not as radical as a revolution, moderate changes constantly take place (if CIP was a successful discourse it would be increasingly pushed towards more progressive lines by the remnants of the popular equivalential chain). The war of position is an ongoing struggle over who gets to dominate the way the world is conceived.

3.2.8 The Remainder and the Master Signifier

What happens, then, to the signifier in question, that was first the empty signifier and then the floating signifier? To answer this, we should first consider the other potential resolution of the hegemonic struggle: the success of the popular camp. In this scenario, the popular equivalential chain extends so much that the demand for social justice is supported by masses (that is a sufficiently wide collection of identities) to replace the existing hegemonic project with their own. Moreover, neither the CIP nor any other government policy is recognized as a way to restore social justice. Social justice then becomes the organizing principle that structures the whole system of meaning.

In more theoretical terms, for such a radical transformation of social structure to take place two conditions must be satisfied:

1. The popular equivalential chain must be able to extend. In other words, the empty signifier must be able to articulate the demands of (or be sufficiently appealing to) various groups (Laclau explores other options in 2005: 139–157).
2. The challenge posed by the popular camp against the establishment must leave it without the means of representing its demands.

If these conditions are satisfied, a new symbolic order would have to be established that can offer a solution to this crisis of signification. In such crises several concepts can be redefined, until 'some signifier fixes retroactively the meaning of the chain, sews the meaning[s] to [signifiers], halts the sliding of the meaning' (Žižek 1997: 101–102). In this sense, the *master signifier* retrospectively determines the meaning of other signifiers: after the Communist Revolution, the signifiers freedom, state, war and equality are all given their (communist) meaning, which are distinct from for instance their liberal-democratic meaning.

It is reasonable that the empty signifier (as in the example above, 'communism') operates as the master signifier, although hegemonic struggles among several groups within the equivalential chain might continue as well (for example the French Revolution). For this inquiry, revolution is of lesser concern, so we can return to the question about the signifier.

Laclau (2005a: 132) notes that 'empty' and 'floating' signifiers are structurally different from one another: the former 'concerns the construction of a popular identity once the presence of a stable frontier is taken for granted; [whereas the latter] tried conceptually to apprehend the logic of the displacements of that frontier'. While this is correct for analytical purposes, in practice they overlap. In fact, neither of the dimensions is imaginable in pure form. Thus, he concludes that '"floating" and "empty" signifiers should be conceived as partial dimensions – and so as analytically distinguishable – in any process of hegemonic construction of *a people*' (ibid.).

They are also partial dimensions from the perspective of the signifier, as structural linguistics informs us. However as I will employ the concepts described in the previous sections in the much more institutionalized context of international organizations with slower ideological shifts, I would like to pursue the life of the floating signifier further. In such a context, the undecided process of floating is extremely long even when the dislocation is deep. Global environmental governance is a demonstrative example: While the scope of the dislocation (that is the global ecological crisis as defined by eco-political movements) is great, and even when there is a consensus regarding the existence of the dislocation, it is difficult to suggest the formation of political identity strong enough at the global level. In international relations, the antagonistic other is diffused, or in constant transformation. It is diffused, because (unlike nation-level hegemonic struggles) at the global level there is no central authority but several establishments with distinct qualities. It is constantly changing, because in the globalization process both the international system and the state actors are in transformation.

In this context, the hegemonic struggle can define the meaning of the floating signifier in closer relation to either one of the hegemonic projects. Yet, the floating signifier can potentially continue floating and signifying radically opposing things for different political identities indefinitely. Or it may lose its importance in defining political identities all together. I will call such signifiers whose meaning have gone through these transformations *the remainder*, that is what remains once signification is disrupted: it has lost its particularism in becoming an empty signifier and its universal appeal was lost once the hegemonic struggle over its meaning was diffused. Its meaning is transformed as well as the hegemonic discourse. Often, it is qualified with an adjective: for example social democracy, participatory democracy, liberal democracy, popular democracy, authoritarian democracy and so on. The movement is far from being a forked vector or opposing definitions, as these are not options against one another. Democracy has become so universal that the particularism of each democracy needs to be expressed by a qualifying adjective. Democracy as such has become *a universal* on which everyone agrees, but it does not define identities; it has lost its desirability (in the sense Mouffe refers to), its fantasmatic function. In terms of social practice, it has sedimented in so many different ways that its minimum conditions have been reduced to elections and universal vote. As Chapter 6 explores, sustainability is also the remainder of the hegemonic struggle between developmentalist and eco-political discourses.

3.3   INSTITUTION/DE-INSTITUTION OF MEANING

3.3.1   Institutionalization as Decision-Making

Discourse theory is a powerful tool in the analysis of political change within continuity, particularly because it does not dismiss incremental changes as

- 'unreal' (as opposed to 'real' changes, as realist schools do);
- 'rhetorical change in the hegemonic discourse' (as opposed to 'structural' changes, as materialist schools do).

Laclau's conception that political change takes place between the institutionalizing logic of difference and the polarizing logic of equivalence entails the continuity of struggles over meaning infinitely. Glynos and Howarth (2007: 121–122) explain that in general the political dimension of a practice lies in aspects that '*generate, maintain, contain, or resolve* the public contestation of social norms'. Otherwise, when a new social norm is being institutionalized they are 'the aspects of a practice which seek to *"bed down" the new social structure* by providing incentives and disincentives which tempt subjects to more actively accept and identify with it' (ibid.). From this point of view, the hegemonic struggle and the social are no longer exclusive. On the contrary, it represents an incremental (or continuous) scale between the polarizing and institutionalizing forces that shapes the conception of institutions.

Arendt's (1970) suggestion that 'the most radical revolutionary will become a conservative the day after the revolution' also refers to the dynamic and contingent nature of the political subject. She refers to the institutionalization taking place at the end of all hegemonic struggles: if an existing social practice is successfully challenged, politicized and changed, those who initiate the change this time try to maintain and institutionalize this new meaning, and defend it against challenges. Hence, it is not a feature of a particular discourse to institutionalize or polarize the social space; every discourse has these elements as partial dimensions, which Laclau calls *heterogeneity*.

This *circular movement of meaning* (being challenged, politicized, changed followed by being maintained, institutionalized, defended) is repeated eternally, and generates politics. In time, all social practices get established, challenged, contested and re-institutionalized to some degree. Thus, Wæver's conceptualization of layered structures (or Foucauldian boxes) is critical in understanding how partial change of meaning takes place, in order to keep the deeper layers intact: not only does this apply to international relations, but is most acutely required for its analysis in a reflexive fashion. Analysing these layers with successive depth-levels can *specify* change within continuity: the extent to which one layer has changed in order to maintain the deeper layers. In a war of position, therefore, there can be moments of truce, which are temporary fixation of meaning. In this sense, what might be viewed as *cooptation* by one party and *logic of difference* by the other is in fact a point of temporary balance, if not unarticulated consensus between the hegemonic and the contesting discourses, resulting from negotiations and struggles.

It is on these premises that the earlier definition of institutions rest: from this point of view they cannot be understood as 'trans-historical and objective laws of historical development, or [. . .] unified subjects or agents endowed with intrinsic interests, [but as] discourses which, as a result of political and social practices, have become relatively practical and durable' (Howarth 1995: 132). In other words, institutions are *sedimented discourses*, '*partially fixed* systems of rules, norms, resources, practices and subjectivities that are linked together in particular ways' (Howarth 2009: 312, my emphasis). This should not be understood such that institutions are stable discourses that can condition agency, or that logic of institutions can be 'placed solely at the difference/syntagmatic plane' whereby they represent 'the social' in its sedimentation as opposed to the political (Hansen 2008). The act of institution is an act of selection and decision; if it becomes successful, the original contingency, contestation and decision are forgotten (Laclau 1990: 34). In this sense, I agree with Hansen that the logics of equivalence and difference are not simply equal to, or do not necessarily or solely belong to *the political* and *the social*. Rather, I argue that both of these logics exist within institutional practices, as institutionalization can also entail the sedimentation of conflict. The next section elaborates what this means for internationally negotiated institutions, such as sustainability partnerships.

3.3.2 Negotiations and Sedimentation of Conflict

Howarth's definition can be interpreted inversely, in line with Hajer's (1995: 46) conception of discourse institutionalization: successful discourses often solidify into an institution. However this inversion can be misleading when applied to internationally-negotiated formal institutions. International negotiations are platforms on which several discourses compete; negotiation presupposes plurality, differences of opinion and conflict, resulting from different constructions, interpretations and articulations of the actual. It is therefore problematic to interpret Hajer's idea of discourse institutionalization as a single successful discourse sedimenting into a single institution.

International institutions are formed with the consent or support of several country delegations, which in practice means that multiple discourses can be contained in the formation of a single institution; since the simple logic of an international negotiation subsumes this multiplicity. As a formal international institution is being negotiated, demands of several country delegations as well as bureaucrats from the UN and other agencies of global governance influence the end result. Their different *hegemonic projects* are molten into the agreed framework in a piecemeal fashion; hence, several hegemonic struggles settle into the logics of an institution as well.

These different subject positions nonetheless have a common point: International institutions are almost exclusively negotiated by the ruling elites. Such institutions do not emerge from the demands of societies in a bottom-up fashion. As Rahnema's quote highlights, they are at times top-down co-option strategies. Demands from competing hegemonic projects can be forced into a single organizational architecture *particularly because* there is a consensus among them that international relations take place in the negotiation platform. This is explicit, for instance, in the words of Tony Hill, the former head of UN's Non-Governmental Liaison Service (NGLS), when he mentions the transformation of NGOs involved with the UN:

> the majority of civil society participants act as a 'loyal opposition' to the UN (i.e. do not put into question its existence, principles and objectives), [although] the opening of the UN to national NGOs has also allowed the participation of very conservative national [NGOs that seek to] curtail UN agreements in areas such as women's reproductive rights, firearms control, and pre-emptive military action, and who even advocate the virtual abolition of the UN in some cases.

Hill is describing a homogenization, a reduction in the differences among subject positions that takes place after the negotiation process. The sedimentation of conflicting or inconsistent discourses into an institution is also a process of reduction from multiple potentialities to a singular actualization. This actualization is not final, but less contingent: a partial fixation ensured by the negotiated text. Once an institution is formed the hegemonic struggles continue but in a more contained way, within the institution itself.

Certain contestations are settled by the marginalization and co-option of some of the discourses at work. Inversely, after discourse institutionalization, the institution starts a life of its own. The hegemonic struggles continue within its structure. If the negotiation stage was about the struggles over the organizational architecture, in this second stage struggles continue over different manifestations of the same architecture. These different manifestations can be policies and programmes the institution operationalizes, national implementations of international agreements, sectoral implementations of national regulations, or specific partnerships within the partnerships regime.

We should, then, qualify the initial definition that institutions are sedimented discourses: often, an institution is the sedimentation of several discourses and, arguably, certain conflicts and contestations among these discourses, and several particularisms belonging to plural discourses may also solidify in the logics of the institution. Because they are heavily negotiated constructs the dynamics of formal (particularly international) institutions are even slower, steadier and more bureaucratic. The frontiers and contestations are blurred, and hence difficult to trace for the discourse analyst. This disadvantage is to some extent alleviated by the numerous documents these settings produce, particularly in the process of founding new institutions.

To explain the process of discourse institutionalization in discourse theoretical terms, we must turn to Laclau's depiction of empty signifiers. In a chain of equivalence several demands have a commonality: their resistance against the oppressor. An empty signifier is basically what comes to represent this common aspect of resistance. Laclau (2005a: 130) depicts this situation with a graph, in which T stands for an oppressive regime and D for demand (Figure 3.1). The equivalential chain rests on a common aspect among all the demands: that they are against the oppressive regime. The empty signifier represents this common element. But there is one more common aspect among these demands: that they also retain their particularisms. So for the purposes of this study, Laclau's graph could be adapted such that the top half of the circle represents the commonality among these different demands (or articulations, identities, groups and so on), whereas the lower half represents their particularism (the icons in grey). As it becomes the empty signifier D_1 loses its particularism, while the other

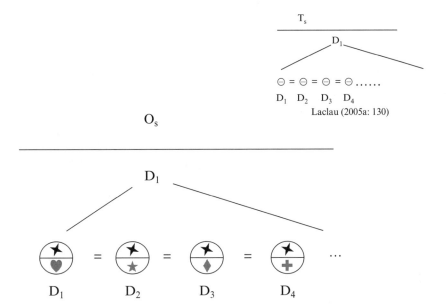

Figure 3.1   Adaptation of Laclau's depiction of empty signifiers

demands retain theirs: otherwise the chain of equivalence no longer serves to bring different identities together.

The presence of particularisms plays a critical role in the formation of international institutions. They are articulated by various groups as the correct policy decision to achieve the consensual goal, which is the empty signifier that represents the demand for change. The resulting decision (institution, regime, or agreement) comprises various particularisms, which may contradict each other. In Figure 3.2 these are represented by the heart and star icons. Naturally, some other (diamond and cross icons) particularisms are declined. In Wæver's terms they may come from different Foucauldian boxes; and levels below the surface might clash. Managing these conflicts is critical for the new institution. This is one reason for implementation deficits: conflicts may prove impossible to reconcile on the ground, or actions may cancel out one another.

To illustrate: it took painstaking negotiations to agree on the Kyoto Protocol, which does not even aim to provide a long-term and complete solution to climate change, but only to create a process. The initial hegemonic struggle took place between supporters and opponents of having an international treaty on climate change. Later, the details of the protocol

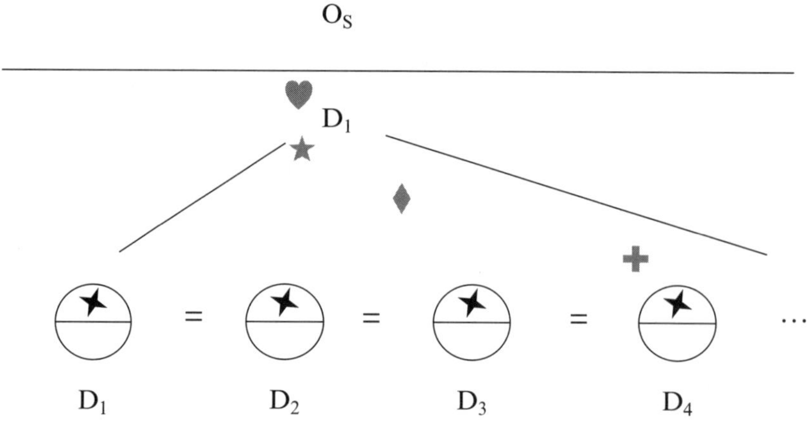

$$O_S$$

Figure 3.2   Competing particularisms in international negotiations

gained importance: if reducing carbon emissions was the demand representing all other demands, *how* to achieve this was the platform for particularisms to be articulated. For some, building nuclear power plants; for others, using renewable energy could bring the change. Others identified carbon reduction with reducing logging in existing forests, or creating carbon markets. Still others disagreed with the need for more electricity production altogether and focused on energy efficiency and even a radical transformation of the global economic system. Several of these ideas with rather different and conflicting conceptions of the problem, the solution, and what is desirable were incorporated into the negotiated text of Kyoto Protocol. Some, such as nuclear energy, or a strict regulation of furthering fossil fuel consumption were not. In sum, the negotiations have been processes in which particularisms of different demands fought for recognition in the final institutional framework. The resulting protocol was full of contradictory terms, embedded in the institutions it has generated.

From this point of view, it is a necessary conclusion that once an agreement is reached regarding the definition of a policy institution, homogenization takes place. On the one hand, this definition is only a partial fixation of meaning. On the other hand, a reduction in the differences among subject positions is inevitable for the following reasons. Laclau (1990: 34) understands the *act of institution* as an act of selection and decision, which can only be successful if it is forgotten. Accordingly, acts of institution often ensure that the institution is regarded more or less legitimate by most of the parties involved, and those parties that fundamentally disagree with the definition are excluded from the negotiation platform. As Hill's quote reminds us about the UN, for instance, the NGOs that have been *allowed in* are the groups that do not challenge the existence, principles and objectives of the UN system.

Hence, the scene after discourse institutionalization is less diverse, although this does not suggest that the contestations cease to exist. As the new institution comes to life, various conflicts (and at times hegemonic struggles) manifest themselves in its operations, or in its different branches or examples.

Partnerships for sustainable development were heavily negotiated outcomes constructed through a number of PrepComs and the WSSD. Studying these negotiations would help trace which of the particularisms linked with certain discourses have sedimented, or were left out. The negotiations examined in the next chapter were the first step towards fixing the meaning of 'sustainability partnership' from among various meanings it could have acquired. Thereby, it was a contestation ground for various particularisms.

NOTES

1. The difference between nature and Nature is the status it is given in the register of sciences. As Arturo Escobar (1999: 1) argues, we might be witnessing 'the final decline of the modern ideology of naturalism, that is, the belief in the existence of pristine Nature outside of history and human context'. This ideology takes nature (which is in fact always co-constructed by culture and society) as an essential principle, an independent domain with a more immediate representation of truth. Thus, anti-essential works often refer to this category with a capitalized Nature, whereas lower case nature refers to the idea of nature 'constructed by meaning-giving and discursive processes, so that what we perceive as natural is also cultural and social; said differently, nature is simultaneously real, collective, and discursive – fact, power, and discourse – and needs to be naturalized, sociologized, and deconstructed accordingly' (ibid.).

2. The most authoritative theorizing in this regard is Foucault's (1977: 27) idea of power/knowledge: 'Knowledge linked to power, not only assumes the authority of "the truth" but has the power to make itself true. All knowledge, once applied in the real world, has effects, and in that sense at least, "becomes true". Knowledge, once used to regulate the conduct of others, entails constraint, regulation and the disciplining of practice. Thus, there is no power relation without the correlative constitution of a field of knowledge, nor any knowledge that does not presuppose and constitute at the same time, power relations'.

3. This is related to Jacques Lacan's notion of *jouissance* (enjoyment). *Jouissance* is not synonymous with pleasure (although, it could mean 'unconscious pleasure'), but rather relates to the Freudian concept of primordial loss (the realization of the subject that (m) other is a distinct identity) and the libidinal urge to escape this loss. The phantasmal derives 'from a Lacanian ontology of enjoyment, insofar as fantasy is understood as the frame which structures the subject's enjoyment. [The subject subscribes to a social or political practice if] it can tap into the subject's existing mode of enjoyment and thus fantasmatic frame' (Glynos and Howarth 2007: 107).

4. David Howarth (2009: 321–322) refers to the epistemological aspect of this process by asking 'how then to capture the exercise of power that works to prevent subjects from translating dislocatory experiences into demands and challenges without recourse to a notion of ideology as false consciousness? How are we to think about the organization and shaping of subjective desire without simplistic notions of manipulation and ideological deception, which rely primarily on epistemological criteria of demarcating truth and falsity?' Howarth's answer lies in the Lacanian conception of fantasy, which explicates the enjoyment obtained from identification with certain signifiers and the exclusion of others. Critically, 'fantasy is not just an illusion or a form of fake consciousness that comes between a subject and social reality. Instead it *structures* a subject's "lived reality" by concealing the radical contingency of social relations, and by naturalizing the various relations of domination within which a subject is enmeshed'.
5. The ambiguity in the term is duly noted by Laclau (2005a: 73): 'The notion of demand is ambiguous in English, it can mean a request, but it can also mean a claim (as in "demanding an explanation"). This ambiguity [. . .] is useful for our purposes, because it is in the transition from request to claim that we are going to find one of the features of populism'.

4. Partnerships as sedimented discourses: the emergence of Type-II outcomes[1]

BOX 4.1   PARTNERSHIPS AS THEY COULD HAVE BEEN (REJECTED PARTICULARISMS)

During negotiations, various principles were proposed to guide CSD partnerships, but were turned down. A fictional conglomeration is presented below.
Partnerships are voluntary initiatives among state and non-state actors that aim to achieve the MDGs, through projects in line with 'the sustainability criteria' established at the WSSD. To ensure their compatibility with the sustainability criteria and assess their contribution to the MDGs in time, they are screened, monitored and overseen by, and report to the CSD.
The work of partnerships cannot conflict with international agreements, and must aim to:

1. help reach MDGs, through concrete and tangible projects with direct, measurable aims;
2. go beyond the commitments of the states – not replacing the efforts of national governments to implement internationally binding agreements;
3. make sustainability understandable to the general public;
4. mainstream implementation of international treaties at regional and global levels;
5. enhance the participation and access of influenced communities to the decision-making processes in the implementation of MDGs and international treaties.

The partnership watch (five groups that cover the five critical issue areas of water, energy, health, agriculture and biodiversity operating under the CSD) determines whether a partnership meets these standards both in terms of their aims (during screening) and in terms of their achievements (during monitoring). Synergies between Type-I and Type-II outcomes are monitored by an external system while the CSD remains responsible to oversee the geographical and thematic diversity of partnerships.
Partnerships must aim to find intersection points between international agreements and local needs (defined by influenced communities). Accordingly, partnerships can only register if governments of the donor and recipient parties have ratified the treaties relevant to their work.

Partnerships cannot be funded by governments or UN agencies, so that official development assistance (ODA) cannot be repackaged as additional funding. However countries party to North Atlantic Treaty Organization can direct military expenditures to sustainability partnerships. Existing multilateral cooperation projects cannot be registered as CSD partnerships.

Partnerships are guided by the specific criteria on transparency, accountability, non-intimidation, non-coercion (whereby the influenced communities have the right to decline), empowerment of the historically disempowered, equal access, precautionary approach, ecosystems approach, corporate accountability (in line with COCA, the newly negotiated binding Convention on Corporate Accountability), a code of conduct among partners (binding within the country of implementation), and commitment to all existing UN conventions.

4.1   INTRODUCTION

The list above consists of various elements that 'could have' comprised the framework for the UN partnerships regime. In fact, all of the items listed above were proposed and discussed in the last PrepCom Meeting before the WSSD. These suggestions were ultimately turned down and sustainability partnerships were defined as 'voluntary multi-stakeholder initiatives which contribute to the implementation of inter-governmental commitments in Agenda 21, the Programme for the Further Implementation of Agenda 21 and the Johannesburg Plan of Implementation'.[2] Without a set of screening, monitoring or reporting criteria, or a central body overseeing the overlaps and deficiencies in their work, partnerships have become an official part of United Nation's environmental governance at the WSSD, despite opposition from several civil society groups and some country delegations.

Nevertheless, the conglomeration of various official and unofficial requests presented in Box 4.1 is as important for our understanding of the partnerships regime as the official definition of partnerships, for several reasons. For instance, when cited on its own, the official definition appears to be an obvious defeat of the environmentalist NGOs and a victory for business lobbies. But various national delegations and civil society groups were involved in the negotiations of partnerships, because they could have influenced the end result. The list in Box 4.1 reveals the reasons of various groups to discuss the concept, and why they found it potentially useful for sustainability governance. Secondly, Box 4.1 shows which options were eliminated during the negotiations. If sustainability partnerships are to be reformed or improved, some of these options can be critical to correct the existing regime. Thirdly, it reveals the limitations of the partnerships regime: The point is not that partnerships are or are not functioning as well as expected but that they are functioning as can be expected considering the type of partnerships approved at WSSD.

This chapter focuses on the emergence of the partnerships regime during its negotiation.[3] It pays specific attention to discourse institutionalization and sedimentation of conflict via negotiations. First it embeds the negotiations to the three important changes that took place in environmental governance between the Rio Earth Summit and the WSSD: the implementation deficit in global environmental governance, the increasing tendency towards private governance mechanisms and the prioritization of the developmental pillar of sustainable development. Then it reveals different subject positions during the initial negotiation of partnerships as Type-II outcomes, relying on witness accounts. Finally it compares the rules set by the Bali Guidelines to the actual partnerships regime.

4.2   BACKDROP: THREE SHIFTS FROM RIO TO JOHANNESBURG

The official definition of sustainability partnerships points to a particular formation that emerged out of the political conjuncture of the WSSD. The *voluntary* nature of partnerships and *non-state* actor participation indicate a significant trend of the time: instead of binding regulations, private governance mechanisms were (and are) increasingly preferred in global environmental governance. On the one hand, *multi-stakeholder* initiatives often suggest a more democratic participation; on the other, the role of partnerships is strictly defined as *implementation*. This ambivalence reflects the tension between the participation and implementation foci of the UNCSD and the WSSD processes, respectively. Finally, the *sustainable development* focus and the condition of *intergovernmental agreement* indicate another change: the minimum consensus, which only existed on very basic and vital MDGs, has dominated the WSSD agenda, while environmental conservation has become secondary.

There are three levels to which the emergence of sustainability partnerships can be contextualized: negotiations over Type-II outcomes, the WSSD in general and global governance at large. All these contexts have been important in the resulting definition and formation of Type-II outcomes. As Najam and Cleveland (2004: 544) observed, 'Type-II agreements were a reflection of the massive change in landscape that had occurred over the previous 10 years; [but also] they were a reflection of the WSSD organizer's desperation and desire to get something memorable out of the summit'. Unlike UNCED, the WSSD fell short of creating binding agreements. Moreover, the proposed time plan to achieve the Johannesburg Plan of Implementation (JPOI), the main document produced by the conference, was declined. Type-II outcomes were the only concrete result of the summit, even according to the chairs of partnerships negotiations, who insisted that partnerships should not substitute international agreements (Kara and Quarless 2002). In sum, the atmosphere at and the expectations from the WSSD were very different than its predecessor United Nations Conference on Environment and Development (UNCED). The official definition of partnerships points towards the transformations in global environmental governance that took place between the two summits. To contextualize the emergence of partnerships as official governance mechanisms within the UN, it is necessary to look into these prevailing trends and transformations. These shifts also serve as platforms for the discourses analyzed in the later chapters.

4.2.1   The Shift from Regulation to Implementation

The Rio Earth Summit is remembered by the international agreements it produced. The first one, *Convention on Biological Diversity* entered into force in 1993. The convention also produced the Cartagena Protocol on biosafety, adopted in 2000. Nonetheless, by 2002 concerns were being already voiced, particularly about the global *implementation* of these treaties (Cooney 2001). The second one, *UN Framework Convention on Climate Change* entered into force in March 1994. It set no mandatory limits to greenhouse gas emissions, but it paved the way to the agreement on the Kyoto Protocol, which set preliminary mandatory limits. The Kyoto Protocol was opened for signature in 1997, but had not entered into force until February 2005. By the time of the Johannesburg Summit, only one of its two conditional clauses was satisfied (the '55 countries clause'). Its entry into force was not regarded proximate, particularly because the United States and Australia have failed to ratify the Protocol, making the '55 per cent clause' difficult to fulfil.

In other words, the binding agreements signed in Rio were not being implemented as foreseen. In IR literature, similar problems were already being studied as 'governance deficits' (Haas 2004), and this problem was called the 'implementation deficit' (Held and Koenig-Archibugi 2004). Explaining this atmosphere, a Southern country representative reflected:

> [Critics of partnerships] refer to binding agreements in Rio, [. . .] but how binding are they? Not very. I am concerned about the fact that when people talk about agreements, they assume that [governments] have agreed to take some actions. I think you can't justify that looking at history. What happens if [governments] don't do [as they promised]? Nothing. What's binding about it?

Nothing. There are targets and timetables; what happens if they are not met? In most places, nothing.[4]

The focus of global environmental governance in the context of WSSD was therefore no longer the production of binding agreements but rather ensuring their implementation. This focus both made partnerships possible and transformed their definition. In the run-up to the WSSD, partnerships were increasingly mentioned as a potential means to address the implementation deficit, and arguably this has facilitated their legitimation. The documents produced during UNCED conceptualized partnerships as a means to address the democratic deficit, that is to ensure participation and increase the democratic quality of environmental governance. By the end of the WSSD, the function of partnerships was restricted to implementation of inter-governmental commitments. In other words, the discursive shift from regulation to implementation is manifest in the formation of partnerships, as their participatory function was replaced with an implementation function. The tension between participatory and implementation functions of partnerships are examined in Chapter 7, which analyzes the discourse of participatory democracy.

4.2.2   The Shift from Inter-Governmental to Private Governance

Throughout the 1990s many voluntary and market-based mechanisms have been adopted in environmental governance, some of which not only included non-state actors into the decision-making process but also were initiated by them (for example Clapp 1998; Cashore 2002). Although the study of non-state actor influence is not novel in IR discipline (Biermann and Dingwerth 2004), the intensity and directness of NGO and corporate involvement has increased since the end of the Cold War. While private involvement and influence span from interstate negotiations, to hybrid public–private partnerships and fully private initiatives (Pattberg 2005), there has been a distinctive shift towards the latter, as reflected by the title of Benjamin Cashore's 2002 article, 'Legitimacy and the Privatization of Environmental Governance: How Non-State Market-Driven (NSMD) Governance Systems Gain Rule-Making Authority'. Cashore argued that if new private governance mechanisms ultimately challenge the existing state-centred authority and public policy-making processes, they would reshape power relations in global environmental governance.

The UN frameworks and documents adapted to this change with initiatives such as the Global Compact, which is both voluntary and corporate, or the invention of carbon markets as a mechanism to tackle global climate change. This adaptation was partially due to the liberal policies and frameworks chosen and initiated by Secretary-General Kofi Annan, who has promoted voluntary, business-oriented policies and practices throughout the UN system, in line with the zeitgeist. Its application to the UN's environmental discourse is manifest in the MDGs, but perhaps more clearly established in *The Environment Millennium*, a UN publication on environmental governance issued at the beginning of 2000. Here, Annan (2000a) conceptualized four priorities to reverse the worrying trends in environmental issues: *public education* to explain sustainability to citizens; *mainstreaming* the environment into economic policy; sound *scientific information* for technological breakthroughs; and *enforcement of environmental agreements* by governments. This last point, he explained, could be achieved if governments 'cut the subsidies that sustain environmentally harmful activities each and every year [or] devise more environment friendly incentives for markets to respond to' (ibid.). In other words, governmental regulation was no longer the obvious policy instrument to resort to, in global environmental issues.

Another reason for this transformation was the influence of economic liberalization on environmental discourses. The WSSD was the first environmental summit after the formation of the World Trade Organization (WTO) in 1995. The trade–environment conflicts resolved by the WTO have almost exclusively prioritized free trade over environmental protection. Government regulation for environmental conservation has been discouraged (if not punished) by the global trade and financial systems. In combination with the implementation deficit mentioned above, this background made global regulation an unlikely expectation, before the summit.

This was also a time of increased corporate involvement in global governance, including the UN system, resulting in the labelling of the summit as Earthsummit.biz (Bruno and Karliner 2002). Partnerships, according to a UN official, were originally designed so as to make it possible for businesses to take responsibility, to get the spotlight, and to channel further funds to MDG projects.[5] The documents resulting from WSSD, especially JPOI, were regarded as documents that legitimize neo-liberal globalization as endorsed by global trade agreements and the WTO; and that partnerships fit impeccably to this framework (Bernstein 2005: 159).

The tendency towards market-driven, voluntary and business-oriented environmental policies is examined in Chapter 5. The last shift in the global political background that was critical for sustainability partnerships was the prioritization of developmental goals over environmental ones, which is the focus of the following subsection.

BOX 4.2   THE MDG ON ENVIRONMENT[6]

Goal 7: Ensure environmental sustainability
Target 7A: Integrate the principles of sustainable development into country policies and programmes; reverse loss of environmental resources.
Target 7B: Reduce biodiversity loss, achieving, by 2010, a significant reduction in the rate of loss.
Target 7C: Halve, by 2015, the proportion of the population without sustainable access to safe drinking water and basic sanitation.
Target 7D: By 2020, to have achieved a significant improvement in the lives of at least 100 million slum dwellers.

4.2.3   The Shift in Focus to Developmental Goals

Between 1992 and 2002, arguably the most significant UN document produced on the issues of environment and development was the Millennium Declaration. The MDGs emerged out of each chapter of this document, and were designed with very concrete aims and deadlines. The only exception was the MDG on environmental sustainability, which was neither concrete nor tangible but, most importantly, was hardly addressing the most important issues of global *environmental* sustainability (with the exception of the target on biodiversity loss, which ambiguously aimed at a 'significant reduction').

The MDG on 'environmental' sustainability had four targets, two of which were in fact about development, one about institutional mainstreaming and only one about conservation (Box 4.2). This single and rather vague MDG excluded most environmental concerns, focusing on the only relatively successful global policy process, biodiversity conservation. The other seven MDGs were at best indirectly relevant to environmental protection or governance. Although only months ago in March 2002, Monterrey Consensus on Financing for Development addressed these issues, MDGs have also become a focal concern of the WSSD process. In fact, they formed the backbone of the draft plan of implementation.

Although in UNCED the official discourse was already embedded in the concept of sustainable development, whereby the governance of environment *and* development were to be tackled together, its unofficial name, the 'Earth Summit', reflected the main concern of the summit quite clearly. WSSD, however, has been much more concerned with the developmental aims of sustainable development. Until the Bali PrepCom prominent environmentalists demanded to unofficially rename WSSD an Earth Summit and redirect it towards a more environmental focus (Shiva 2001).

Furthermore, it could be argued that as UN officials actively invited corporate funding, issues supported by the private sector were more easily agreed upon (Bruno and Karliner 2002). Being more tangible and in line with the business agenda, developmental aims had the advantage of corporate support. After all, partnerships have been a national level policy tool for service supervision by the private sector instead of the public sector. The global level application of this principle would be more service provision, particularly at the infrastructure and other conventional forms, in line with developmental goals of almost every nation with a development plan. Thus, both WSSD and the resulting sustainability partnerships have prioritized the developmental aspect of sustainable development over its environmental dimension.

This trend continued, as only about 25 per cent of the partnerships supported by UNFIP focused on environmental issues by the end of 2004 (UNFIP 2005 in Andonova 2005). The prioritization of the developmental dimension of sustainable development is examined in Chapter 6, which aims to put the sustainable development discourse into a historical perspective and analyze the developmentalist and environmentalist discourses of sustainability.

4.3   THE NEGOTIATIONS: DEFINING PARTNERSHIPS

4.3.1   UN DESA's Failed Initial Vision

Although the concept of partnership was in the UN jargon since 1992, to consider them as Type-II outcomes for the WSSD was first mentioned in the Second Preparatory Committee meeting, that took place in New York, between 28 January and 8 February 2002. Several respondents that observed the process reported that they have become aware of the increasing significance of partnerships for the summit around this time. In fact, in PrepCom-1, partnerships were already mentioned in the final decisions: it was envisioned that the first week of the summit would consist of a plenary on organizational matters 'followed by a series of partnership events involving NGOs and other major groups accredited to the Summit' (IISD 2001). Only afterwards would the heads of states participate in the negotiation process. Once the negotiations started, only 'a short multi-stakeholder event involving the highest level of representation from major groups and governments' would be organized to symbolically 'adopt final documents' (ibid.).

But it was in PrepCom-2 that partnerships were named as Type-II outcomes of the summit, and 'the US expressed appreciation for the non-binding Type-II outcomes and called for "space" at WSSD to allow for related dialogues' (IISD 2002). Although the term was coined by Nittin Desai,[7] the concept had been developed earlier by DESA, for the following reasons:[8]

> We were speaking about the activities we wanted to see in the WSSD: to show what communities [other than the governments] were doing [and give NGOs] the opportunity of not only a wider [but also] a tangible expression of their involvement. Secondly, after 10 years, we were evaluating [the post-Rio process only on the basis of] what the governments have done [which would not] give a true reflection of the world's commitment to sustainable development. [We wanted to] formally acknowledge the contribution of the international NGO community. [Finally], we had donor fatigue: every responsibility was being put at the feet of the governments. There was a strong push that it should be shared.

To make a full evaluation of sustainable development since UNCED, to include civil society into decision-making and negotiations, and to officially acknowledge (and thereby encourage) non-governmental efforts for sustainable development, DESA suggested the organization of a high-level, 'partnership event' to the organizing committee. According to some accounts another important reason was to attract new funding for MDG-focused projects by creating an important media opportunity for non-governmental donors (that is business and industry). Others argued that this was intended to be a process to reduce the governmental and non-governmental separation in the UN – at least in some processes, if not immediately in decision-making.[9] The process DESA suggested, running parallel to the WSSD, would aim to synchronize the governmental and non-governmental efforts, and was largely supported at PrepCom-2, by donors, the South, as well as NGOs:

> They came up with this rather cute separation of Type-I and Type-II outcomes: negotiated and voluntary outcomes. That came from the bureau and was supported by the community, [particularly] the donors. It showed that there was a support for sustainable development efforts in the developing countries as well. It gave [NGOs] the recognition that they didn't have before and legitimized their participation as partners in a process as important as this.[10]

Another respondent[11] from the WSSD organizing committee gave an alternative account of how partnerships entered the WSSD agenda. She noted that the term partnership originated in the context of major groups[12] and 'was already in the language' to describe non-state cooperation.

> In the context of Johannesburg, [we were] a small team trying to design the process, [and] trying to figure out how to move beyond decisions made during negotiations, how to do more implementation, how to move towards these communities that are clearly making the greatest impact on implementation. And that's where it came out: 'partnership cases and commitments' was the first [term] we used. We wanted different sets of actors to come together, find a problem, define one language to call that problem, put in some money and tell the whole world community 'in five years, we're going to achieve this together'. That's what we wanted.

This is a more efficiency-oriented, implementation-focused reason for partnerships. Nevertheless, the two accounts are similar regarding how the concept was transformed later, during negotiations. The intended format of *the UN partnerships regime* was very different than the end result. First and foremost, the expectations from both Type-I and Type-II outcomes of the summit were transformed:

> This was [DESA]'s concept of what would be the outcome of Johannesburg: [A Type-I] commitment among the governments to go forward within that inter-governmental framework, and the Type-II outcome was to be the expressed, demonstrable commitment of the donors and the wider community to help developing countries by a range of partnership initiatives, which would express the broader participatory approach to development support that the international community as a whole was also committing itself to.
> So, one was to be state-to-state, intergovernmental agreement and the second was to be the developed countries with the NGO community and the science community and UN system and all of these actors with the developing countries, so you get the whole kitchen sink. And there would be a number of high profile projects: Partnerships. In fact there was [supposed to be] a special session where they would announce these partnerships and this was really where the [big corporations] were clustering in, all of them wanted to be involved in a partnership. [. . .] Everybody wanted their names in the bright lights. *Time* magazine devoted a whole issue on the WSSD. This is major for PR [public relations], you can't pay for that.[13]

The bright lights were already a part of DESA's plan to attract corporate funding for development projects. The commitment of donors and the international community to implementation of MDGs would assure developing countries, so that intergovernmental agreements could go further on new and more challenging issues. However partnerships did not end up adding to the Type-I outcome, as the governments failed to agree on any issue at the WSSD.

Secondly, the necessity for Type-II outcomes of the summit was reduced to their implementation function:

> [In the run up to the WSSD] we were talking about outcomes. An outcome need not be implementation, but it has been narrowly defined as implementation. Partnership was intended to be more of a coordinated and collective approach to provide development support. The question is how you define that development support. Unfortunately, because we were dealing with very specific concerns, we ended up attaching the guideline to an entity which became a project or programme.[14]

In sum, the initial conceptualization of Type-II outcomes was somewhat different than the decisions made at the PrepComs about their organization at the WSSD, the negotiation of Bali Guidelines, and the summit results.

4.3.2   PrepCom-3: Raising Suspicions

During PrepCom-3, the US and the major group for business and industry explicitly supported this vaguely defined process, which raised suspicions from both NGOs and developing countries. The first lines were drawn as a response to the US support:

> The US was a bit stand up-ish on this partnership idea, which was unusual. Then we had a meeting with the US delegation at PrepCom-2, [and explained] how we would be able to do things that would go *beyond intergovernmentally made decisions*. We must have done such a good job that they became champions of partnerships, which can backfire in [the UN] because there are well set perceptions about governments and their decisions. When the US overly supports something, everybody starts wondering why. [. . .] The minute the US government started talking close to the partnerships, the other parties suspicions expanded all of a sudden. In fact we had to go and tell them quietly not to do it anymore. Some of these are anecdotal, funny things but all had an impact on how the partnerships got shaped up and emerged.[15]

According to another respondent, the US support has opened the space for other countries to avoid binding decisions:

> Another thing that kills any initiative [to be] seen as an opportunity to opt out of responsibility. The strongest moment in which the US policy pushed these partnerships, the developing countries [perceived them as such]. [The United States was] the most visible advocate of these partnerships. The concern of the developing countries was that the States would not agree to [any binding agreements]. And it was seen as opting out of responsibilities on both sides.[16]

In less diplomatic words, the US support for partnerships at PrepCom-3 has signalled to the developing countries that the States would either not agree to new multilateral environmental agreements (MEAs) or fail to ratify them, as it is often the case. Hence, they re-focused their strategies to avoid potential loss that could result from this new governance mechanism, both in terms of ODA and autonomy in environmental decision-making. According to a Southern country delegate,

> [When] the secretariat introduced Type-I and Type-II [outcomes], the developing countries had the biggest concern, because they felt that this is going to bypass binding obligations of states and channel money outside of governments: Instead of money flowing bilaterally or multilaterally, the [donors] could now pick a project and bypass the government. If you look at the US partnership in the Congo Basin, the Forest Partnership, [the money] bypasses all the governments, goes straight to WWF. This is against what has been done for years in funding conservation. There never was [this way of funding] US-based NGOs [or] consultancies.[17]

More suspicion was built when the business support to partnerships has become evident:

> Business was absolutely supportive. [. . .] There is a certain amount of self-interest in non-state actors. Here was an opportunity for particularly large business actors. There is a tremendous cache attached to the UN's acknowledgement. At that time [a developing country] was knocking heads with a big oil multinational. G77 was concerned that [this could] whitewash them: You give these companies the UN stamp, a green stamp of approval, of CSR. The multinationals have done [much environmental damage], and now they were absolved of these crimes by virtue of partnerships. Developing countries felt very strongly about this.[18]

All respondents from within the organizing committee, ECOSOC and DESA agree that the concerns of the South were being 'very forcefully expressed, [draining] all the enthusiasm from partnerships' (ibid.). The resistance was building specifically on two issues (ibid.):

> When we came up with this idea [of partnerships], paranoid thoughts immediately emerged: One was of course the G77, mirrored by southern NGOs that the secretariat was taking the responsibility from liable parties and loading it off – on to major groups. [We actually] meant all parties [would] be equally responsible for their partnership. Some others (especially NGOs) thought we were [relieving] the CSD from making heart-breaking decisions, as [delegations] could later say 'we have a partnership on this we don't need to legislate'. But that wasn't our point [either]. You have a partnership but there are still decisions to make about new emerging issues.

Similarly, European Union (EU) delegations and environmental NGOs were worried that partnerships could be an instrument to repudiate international environmental agreements. Another concern of the NGOs was the increasing involvement of multinational corporations in the UN, and the green/blue-washing of invasive corporate activities. Finally, a further and largely unforeseen concern also surfaced during the PrepCom-3 and 4, once again frustrating the organizing committee's initial formulation of partnerships:

> We came up with the partnerships with a slightly different vision: Partnerships redefine everybody's status in the process. [As a] partner in a publicly announced partnership with specific goals, you're accountable, and and you go beyond being an NGO, a member state, an intergovernmental secretariat etc. You're almost (and almost is very important word) *almost* at an equal level with your partners. If you take that premise to intergovernmental level, the decisions would be taken in a multi-stakeholder basis, and that would have changed the governing structure of the CSD and that of the UN positively. That was our iterative thinking. It may be naive, but [by the time of WSSD] there was a lot of pressure on the secretariat to come up with ideas, and we [learned at the CSD] over the ten years that when people work together on a common goal the outcome is better, it is more sustainable, there is more ownership of it. So clearly the same level of engagement and participation should be brought into the next level of CSD.[19]

As the concept has been reformulated in several different ways before a specific definition of partnerships was made, delegations from the South have started to perceive this as a threat to their sovereignty. G77 delegations (among them China, Indonesia and Malaysia were specifically mentioned), have become increasingly weary of the possibility that developmental projects within their national borders would be (not only financed by donor governments or corporations but also) organized through international or national NGOs of donors' choice. As a result, some delegations raised questions on non-state actor participation, and China went even as far as authorizing a list of acceptable NGOs. This issue will be addressed in Chapter 7.

In order to address these issues, it was decided that the Bali Guidelines were going to be discussed in the PrepCom-4. One of the respondents from the organizing committee of the WSSD reflected that they failed to alleviate these worries before PrepCom-4:

> This was our job during the preparation process. Perhaps we weren't persuasive enough, or we didn't explain it enough or maybe the suspicion was too much for us to handle, because we were also [understaffed]. It was a basic [human resources] issue.

As a result, the first discussions regarding the nature of partnerships within the UN system started only a few months before the summit, in PrepCom-3. These informal discussions aimed to 'clarify questions with regard to the scope and modalities of potential partnerships' (UNCSD 2002a), but in fact they provided a sketch of the concerns and worries: Type-II outcomes were not intended to substitute intergovernmental commitments and MEAs; they would be of a voluntary, self-organizing nature; their registration would be based on simple and flexible parameters although their genuine contribution to the WSSD outcomes should be screened; their alignment with all dimensions of sustainable development should be monitored; they should be participatory with a sense of equality among partners.

4.3.3   PrepCom-4: The Negotiation of Bali Guidelines

The framework that was negotiated at PrepCom-4 was meant to address these various concerns so as to make partnerships an agreeable outcome to all parties involved. However the negotiation process was long and cumbersome. According to Diane Quarless,[20] the co-chair of partnerships discussions at PrepCom-4, one of the reasons for this frustration has been the alienation of business from the process:

> Corporations [had] an interest in CSR, therefore the process had to be selective. So the idea was first to make them sign the CSR code-of-conduct through registration. That, I think, drained the enthusiasm of the private sector. These [concerns] leading up to the Bali Guidelines killed the initiative. Bali was critical: the enthusiasm that has been built evaporated.

Another reason was that the concerns of the developing countries prolonged the process and resulted in a loss of momentum. Jan Pronk[21] argued that the idea of an inclusive process within the UN was frustrated because the guidelines were particularly discouraging new and big initiatives to be effectively created in the short term. Quarless agreed that the negotiations took too long: 'It all changed at Bali. That's where [the initiative] was killed. Partnerships could only be announced at Johannesburg because we took so long to agree on [. . .] the Guidelines, on the basis of which you form a partnership'.[22]

The resulting document, titled *Bali Guiding Principles* (the Bali Guidelines) is the only framework that guides the formation of partnerships and their registration with the UNCSD (2002b). While respondents from partnerships often thought they were ambiguous, UN representatives and experts focusing on governance regarded them as a failure, for several reasons. A part of these reasons was the way in which the issues above were addressed. Another part concerned the content of the guidelines: what they invoked and what they left out. Finally, the significance of the guidelines was greatly affected by legal status of the document itself.

4.3.3.1 Concerns
Although they reflected the concerns of several parties, the guidelines did not effectively address these problems. For instance, one of the guidelines stressed that Type-II outcomes should not substitute commitments of governments. Yet, in a document for guiding partnerships it is difficult to ensure that governments would not bail out of their commitments. Another guideline clarified and restricted their objectives as a contribution to the implementation of intergovernmental decisions, implying that newly emerging issues on the environmental agenda would not be tackled through partnerships. According to research that was conducted five years later, Neil Gunningham (2007) suggested that partnerships are most effective and influential in these issue areas. But without an institutional body to initiate or invite partnerships on these new issues, and with the condition that partnerships could only address issues with intergovernmental consensus this was not possible in practice.

Negotiations also concentrated on the inclusion of business actors into the decision-making process. Two criteria were proposed: a code of conduct to be signed by all corporate actors involved, and a strict commitment to CSR. Both of these proposals were ultimately turned down. Regarding the involvement of NGOs, three steps were taken. Some delegations agreed to Type-II outcomes only if they had the chance to approve the list of all NGOs from their country that could be partners. According to a respondent from the organizing committee, although partnerships were 'not sufficiently significant to raise havoc', if any government wished to nullify a registration, they could, on the basis that the only partnerships that were actually negotiated and agreed upon were those registered during the WSSD. Finally, conceptualizing partnerships as implementation mechanisms as opposed to decision-making mechanisms (or means to ensure participation of non-state actors) remedied this problem to a large extent. In sum, the participatory function of partnerships was ruled out.

4.3.3.2 Framing of partnerships: ideals and contradictions
Regarding their content, the guidelines were successful at framing an ideal type for partnerships. However they also restricted their potential to reach these ideals. For example, it was highlighted that partnerships should address the economic, social and environmental dimensions of sustainable development in their design and implementation, even though they were mere implementation mechanisms that could not go beyond

inter-governmental decisions. This has been one of the reasons for partnerships to list a number of aims and functions in their registry, although
they did not have the means to fulfil all of those promises. In most cases,
CSD partnerships only elusively relate to the environmental aspect of
poverty reduction, or vice versa.

While addressing the three pillars of sustainable development, partnerships should fit into the 'sustainable development strategies and poverty
reduction strategies of the countries, regions and communities where their
implementation takes place' (UNCSD 2002b). This statement assumed
that the strategies of the countries of implementation were in place and
accurate. Partnerships were not to make significant political changes, or
move beyond the existing frames of reference.

Although it was stated in the guidelines that partnerships should be
multi-stakeholder initiatives among partners with equal say in the design
and workings of the project, they would 'preferably involve a range of significant actors in a given area of work' (ibid.). In other words, partnerships
were restricted to reassert the existing power imbalances. This is specifically
important for the local communities on the recipient side. Introducing a new
technology, governance scheme or way of living to a community comprises
hegemonic relationships, which can be further exacerbated. Another guideline that contradicts the empowerment of the recipient communities suggests that 'while the active involvement of local communities in the design
and implementation of partnerships is strongly encouraged (bottom-up
approach), partnerships should be international in their impact' (ibid.).

While the guidelines suggested that all partners should be involved
in the design of the partnerships they also advised that 'as partnerships
evolve, there should be an opportunity for additional partners to join on
an equal basis'. Finally, partnerships should be transparent and accountable, but they would be 'self-reporting'. This leads to questions regarding
what was left out in the formation of partnerships.

4.3.3.3   Lack of monitoring and enforcement

Another set of problems regarding the content of the guidelines can be
identified, which result from what was absent: partnerships should be
voluntary, self-organizing, transparent and accountable and that they
should be multi-stakeholder initiatives with equality among partners.
Partnerships should identify funding and resources, have tangible goals
and clear timeframes to reach them. However they did not suggest any
screening or monitoring mechanisms to ensure these qualities.

According to Quarless,

There were lengthy discussions within the bureau as to how we were going to monitor partnerships. [In the two-year CSD cycle] there was supposed to be one year where we would do nothing more than reviewing them, [which] has not happened. [Eventually], we got the lowest common denominator, which has broken my heart, really. Because they said, 'we do not want DESA to take a leadership role in conceptualizing partnerships'.

Neither DESA nor the CSD was given authority over the reviewing and monitoring of the partnerships. CSD's authority was limited to screening and selection at a very minimal level. Despite all the contradictions above, the Bali Guidelines could have significantly different effects had there been such mechanisms in place and an overseeing central body. These could ensure a more balanced focus on different issue areas, as well as geographical distribution, and actor participation. Furthermore, had they been binding rules, even with limited authority the CSD could partially maintain such qualities. The ideal partnership sketched in the guidelines may be practically impossible for every partnership to achieve, yet could still be reflected in the partnerships regime. Unfortunately, as non-binding principles, the guidelines merely reflected the disagreement among parties involved without taking any precautions against the actualization of their worries.

In sum, the guidelines consisted of conflicting suggestions regarding the role, function and nature of partnerships. While warning about potential negative effects, they failed to address and avoid them. While framing partnerships in an ideal form they simultaneously restricted partnerships to evolve towards such an ideal. Most importantly they remained non-binding principles with no monitoring mechanism, to which registered partnerships had to pay no attention. The next section compares the existing partnership initiatives to the ideal type defined by the guidelines.

4.4   THE ACTUALIZATION: SUSTAINABILITY PARTNERSHIPS

As the UN official quoted above states, CSD partnerships have not become significant enough for explicit articulations of conflict *after* their negotiation. Nonetheless, many respondents have expressed their frustration with the negotiation process. Furthermore, even supporters of the partnership concept expressed dissatisfaction with the existing partnerships regime and with the current sustainable development agenda. This section examines the contradictions and ambiguities in the partnerships regime that surfaced *after the negotiations*. Once the actualization begins, conflicts that are sediments in the logics of the institution can no longer be traced in the official declarations. As the partnerships regime actualized, it started conflicting with the Bali Guidelines.

Examining all the partnerships registered with the CSD could reveal whether the non-binding nature of the Bali Guidelines and voluntary nature of partnerships have resulted in large discrepancies between the ideal type and the actual partnerships regime. The GSPD as well as the CSD's own data are used to demonstrate these general trends, even though some of these indicators are proxies. Some of the guidelines are too ambiguous for such comparison, such as the guideline that advises an integrated approach to sustainable development (between environmental *versus* economic and local *versus* global concerns). These can be better understood in the light of the discourses studied later in the book.

4.4.1   Objective of Partnerships

The Bali Guidelines (UNCSD 2002b) describe the objective of partnerships as 'to contribute to and reinforce the implementation of the outcomes of the intergovernmental negotiations of the WSSD [. . .] Agenda 21 and the MDGs'. Among the many issue areas CSD partnerships work on, knowledge production appears to be the most popular, followed by resource-oriented partnerships focusing on issues such as water, energy, and oceans, coastal zones, lakes, rivers and river basins (Figure 4.1).

Although this categorization profiles CSD partnerships, it also hides several details. For instance, technologies incompatible with earlier UN decisions have been introduced to UN platforms through partnerships. This allowed many of their practices in the poor countries to be legitimized under the guise of technology transfer, development aid or humanitarian aims. While other such technologies have been studied elsewhere (Mert and Dellas 2012; Mert 2013; Deibel and Mert 2014), the most intriguing example of this has been nuclear energy.

At the CSD-15 meeting that was held in New York in May 2007 some of the CSD partnerships had their stands at the Partnerships Fair. Until 2007, the CSD did not have any nuclear energy partnerships in its portfolio, however CSD-15 was specifically about energy in the context of sustainable development and the Partnerships Team's call for new registries attracted the nuclear lobby. The last two partnerships registered to the CSD before the meeting also participated in this fair: Generation IV International Forum and World Nuclear University (WNU), both promoting different aspects of nuclear energy. Generation IV refers to the latest nuclear plants and advocates their security advantages compared to earlier technologies. The WNU focuses on educating nuclear engineers while simultaneously 'correcting the misunderstandings [of the public] regarding nuclear energy'.[23] To this

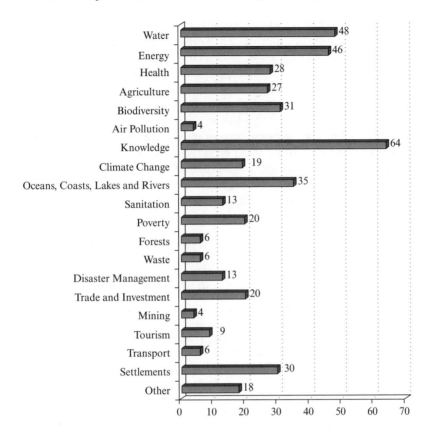

Source: GSPD.

Figure 4.1   Issue areas of CSD partnerships

end, the WNU organized a high profile side event at the CSD, titled *The Contribution of Nuclear Energy to Sustainable Development*, advocating the use of nuclear energy for the cause of sustainable development. While two speakers focused their presentations on the ways in which nuclear energy could be publicized, the opening speech of Susan Eisenhower was distinctly political. She claimed that under the pressure of climate change nuclear energy was under review again, since

> it has been and will continue to be the largest source of emission-free energy. Nuclear energy is the only source of energy that can provide consistent and substantial levels of energy while reducing [correction:] while *producing* emission-free.[24]

Eisenhower's correction was important, as the nuclear power plants were not reducing emissions, and neither were they producing 'emission-free' electricity, since nuclear power plants emit other greenhouse gases than carbon. Eisenhower was introducing nuclear technologies as a sustainable, environmentally friendly source of energy at the UN Headquarters on the basis of three points:

1. That nuclear energy production is safe, especially compared to other security and environment concerns: 'You have to live near a nuclear power plant for over 2000 years to get the same amount of radiation that you get at a standard medical X-ray' (ibid).
2. In addition to solving climate change nuclear energy production would also be the solution to proliferation problems:

> I know we're talking about sustainable development but everybody has to be deeply concerned about those developing nations and the poten-tial of their access to nuclear technologies that may, as we discuss in Washington and elsewhere, lead to proliferation concerns. Ironically, I am a security expert who feels very strongly that we [cannot] address proliferation problems without nuclear energy. 20% of the [US] nuclear energy comes from Soviet era warheads blended for reactor use. [. . .] We have a perfect storm, a perfect opportunity to make excess nuclear mate-rials appropriate for reactor use thus solving some of the deep concerns we have about their misuse (ibid.).

3. Her vision was inspired by her grandfather President Dwight Eisenhower's Atoms for Peace Program, which suggested peaceful use of nuclear technologies through the establishment of the International Atomic Energy Agency (IAEA) and sharing nuclear technologies with developing countries. Some of these countries later refused to sign the Nuclear Non-Proliferation Treaty, which appeared to be the cause of Eisenhower's concerns.

In other words, the health and environmental effects of nuclear energy production were put aside and proliferation resulting from the dual use of uranium enrichment was reversed (into uranium enrichment as a solution to proliferation). Finally, the origins of nuclear technologies based in the Atoms for Peace Program were regarded yet again as an ideal. In Laclau's thought, this would be a succinct example of an attempt at 'forgetting' the original contingency, contestation and decision made by the act of institution.

In the context of the WNU, this vision of 'peaceful and sustainable use of nuclear technologies' was supported by John Ritch (Director General of World Nuclear Association), James Lovelock (Author of *Gaia Theory*),

Hans Blix (IAEA Director General-Emeritus), Mohamed El-baradei (Director General of IAEA), Sir David King (Chief Science Advisor to the UK Government) and representatives of nuclear industry. At the inaugural ceremony of the WNU, Blix was pointing out to the security threats of climate change, proposing a transition from Atoms for Peace to Atoms for Sustainable Development; while El-baradei was suggesting the necessity of nuclear power for development.[25] Lovelock, too, emphasized that climate change made nuclear energy indispensable, and that 'it is a foolish fantasy to think that we could [produce sufficient renewable energy] soon enough to avoid risking a greenhouse catastrophe'.[26] Finally, Geoffrey Ballard, the CEO of General Hydrogen, was linking all concerns into one, in a way framing the reasoning behind *the nuclear renaissance*: as economic progress increased per capita energy consumption, and since all other forms of social progress was dependent on this,

> for society to continue its progress in medicine, social responsibility, science, education and quality of life, we must assure that there is an ever increasing supply of energy per capita. With human populations still on the rise, progress will not be sustained if we attempt to further reduce, or even stabilize, our energy production by reducing the emissions of the current energy source mix. We must increase our supply of energy, not reduce it. (Ibid.)

It is important to note how the discourse around clean energy production is increasingly being subdued to concerns over climate change, while the circular reasoning results in the suggestion that more energy production can solve all social problems. Both the WNU and Generation IV International Forum regard climate change and sustainable energy production as their primary goals and argue that nuclear energy production is sustainable on the basis that it is free of carbon emissions. WNU states its mission as 'increasing use of nuclear power as the one proven technology able to produce clean energy on a large, global scale' and its contribution to *Agenda 21* as the protection of the atmosphere, protection of the quality and supply of freshwater resources, transfer of environmentally sound technology, and contribution to science for sustainable development (UNCSD Partnerships Database 2007). Neither of the partnerships addresses nuclear waste, the main problem of nuclear energy production.

While the Framework Convention on Climate Change and the Kyoto Protocol do not recognize nuclear energy as a suitable and sustainable way of mitigation, lack of screening and monitoring of CSD partnerships allows for a controversial technology to gain recognition in the UN. Furthermore, other issues on the CSD agenda, such as changing unsustainable consumption and production patterns, end up being subjugated to doubtful techno-fixes to remedy climate change. Finally, the main implication of this discursive shift is that focusing merely on reducing carbon emissions sets aside the common cause of environmental problems, unsustainable lifestyles (O'Hara 2007).

To summarize, the main principle of the Bali Guidelines that determines the objectives of partnerships has been circumvented through various rhetorical strategies, and partnerships have become a platform on which controversial technologies could be represented as sustainable solutions. These projects were funded by major corporations, whose financial contribution to other partnerships has been very limited once the negotiations ended.

4.4.2   Complementing Type-I Outcomes and Implementation

During their negotiation, one of the concerns that was most explicitly voiced was that partnerships could impede multilateral agreements. While the first guideline framed their objectives, the second and the third guidelines refined it: partnerships should link with globally agreed outcomes through implementation, rather than substitution. Moreover, the outcomes of partnerships should be tangible and specific.

However neither the WSSD nor the international processes that followed produced binding agreements on sustainability. Does this suggest that non-binding mechanisms work better? Do partnerships even aim at implementation? According to a survey held by the Organisation for Economic Co-operation and Development (OECD 2006: 24) on the UN's environmental partnerships, only 28 per cent of responding partnerships considered themselves as providing direct benefits. On closer examination, the report concluded that only four of the 32 partnerships they researched had direct environmental benefits, while the rest facilitated impact further down the line. The report also notes that the main beneficiaries of their work were partners themselves. Among CSD partnerships, more than half reported their primary goals in rather vague terms such as 'strengthening means of implementation', 'building institutional frameworks', and 'supplying information for decision-making' (Biermann et al. 2007: 247).

A useful proxy for implementation-oriented functions would be the goals of partnerships. Functions related to implementation in the GSPD are institutional capacity building (29 per cent), technical implementation (17 per cent) and technology transfer (15 per cent). Only 43 partnerships (13 per cent) aim for these goals. Most of the output produced by partnerships is research and publication of policy or campaign documents, organizing and participating in conferences. Only 12 per cent of CSD partnerships have on-the-ground implementation projects.

4.4.3   Voluntary Nature and Multi-Stakeholder Approach

According to the Bali Guidelines (UNCSD 2002b) partnerships are 'of voluntary, "self-organizing" nature; [. . .] should have a multi-stakeholder approach and preferably involve a range of significant actors in a given area of work. As partnerships evolve, there should be an opportunity for additional partners to join on an equal basis'. While participation in partnerships is likely to be voluntary, to be 'self-organizing' is a vague term, as CSD partnerships require a lead partner that initiates and organizes the partnership and registers it with the CSD. Studying the lead actors can reveal whether partnerships are driven by powerful actors (GSPD 2008): 81 per cent of CSD partnerships have only one lead partner. State actors (24 per cent), intergovernmental (12.5 per cent) and UN (17 per cent) organizations often lead the partnerships, whereas NGOs (8 per cent), business actors (3 per cent) and local governments (5 per cent) are not dominant. Although this does not definitively suggest a top-down decision-making model in each partnership, it reveals a trend. Only 11 per cent of CSD partnerships have a hierarchical mode of operation, whereas 19 per cent have a network-type, diffused organizational model. Most partnerships have mixed organizational models with layered decision-making systems. While the participatory success of partnerships is discussed in Chapter 7, it should be noted that 37 per cent of partnerships have closed membership, and 56 per cent restrict future partners.

4.4.4   Follow-Up and Monitoring

The Bali Guidelines (UNCSD 2002b) required each partnership to 'be developed and implemented in an open and transparent manner [so that] outcomes [would be] shared among all partners, [all] equally accountable'. Not only should they 'specify arrangements to monitor and review their performance against the objectives and targets they set and report in regular intervals ("self-reporting")' through publicly accessible reports but they should also keep CSD 'informed about their activities and progress in achieving their targets'.

In 2004, Hale and Mauzerall examined 250 CSD partnerships and found that 69 per cent had a reporting system. However activity reports do not necessarily include monitoring. Less than half of this sample had a monitoring mechanism in place. The more recent OECD survey (2006) found that while 81 per cent of their sample planned an evaluation, only 56 per cent were going to evaluate 'their contribution to the Millennium Development Goals'. None of these partnerships on environmental protection had monitoring mechanism in place. GSPD data on partnerships registered until 2009 suggests that only 46 per cent of partnerships have any activity reporting system at all. Only 11 per cent of CSD partnerships stated that they would report to the UNCSD. The rest suggested that reporting would take place through restricted internal websites, or project reports.

4.4.5 Funding Arrangements

Whether the registration process requires detailed information on existing and future funds is ambiguous. The guideline suggests that 'available and/or expected sources of funding should be identified. At least the initial funding should be assured at the time of the Summit' (UNCSD 2002b). Nonetheless, many partnerships (48 per cent) made no financial information public; 28 per cent explicitly stated that they are in need of further funding, while 24 per cent stated they were not (GSPD 2008). This data appears in conflict with the information in the Secretary-General's Report on Partnerships (UNCSD 2008: 11), which suggests that 87 per cent of the CSD partnerships provided funding information. This may be because these partnerships provide data through unofficial channels, or possibly because many entries were not updated after the WSSD and simply registered zero (according to this report over 140 partnerships had no funding).

This guideline relates to the expectation at the time of the WSSD regarding corporate funding for sustainable development projects. Partnerships would be a means to commit further corporate funding to sustainability projects. Hale and Mauzerall's (2004: 235) study showed that partnerships registered at the WSSD committed less than USD250 million in resources. In the following two years, the total funding has increased four-fold to USD1.02 billion, mostly because of the reclassification of already existing intergovernmental programs of the UN and the World Bank as CSD partnerships (ibid.). The following two years have once again provided little additional resources, a mere USD230 million (Biermann et al. 2007: 246).

Intergovernmental and state funding is the main financial resource for partnerships to this day. Despite their initial support of partnerships during the negotiations, business actors have not initiated many partnerships (as lead partners) or provided funding for them (only 2 per cent of all partnerships received private funding). Their participation as partners has also been sporadic (Figure 4.2). Clearly, business involvement is limited to issue areas with large global markets, such as water and energy partnerships. Other popular issues for partnership projects, such as knowledge production and sharing or oceans, lakes and rivers where profits would be marginal, business actors do not get involved.

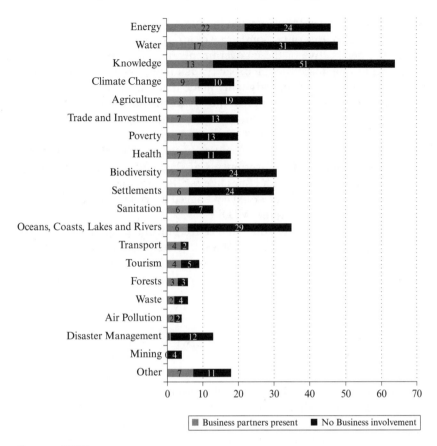

Source: GSPD.

Figure 4.2   Business involvement in partnerships by category

4.4.6   New or Value Added Partnerships

In order to encourage further private spending on sustainability, the guidelines required partnerships to be new, 'i.e. developed within the framework of the WSSD process', or to have 'a significant added value' (UNCSD 2002b). Despite the worries that only existing partnerships would register and no new projects would be launched, only 31 already existing partnerships were registered at the WSSD. Most of the 250 partnerships registered during the summit were in fact new partnerships. To some extent this was due to the initiatives of the Indonesian and South African governments, which hosted the last PrepCom and the summit and were eager for results. They were also the only Southern countries that were lead partners. From the perspective of these governments, partnerships have an added value regarding institutional capacity building. Their experience with Johannesburg partnerships arguably made them more prone to building more partnerships. For instance, at the twentieth anniversary of the World Economic Forum (WEF) on East Asia, the Indonesian Vice-Minister of Trade suggested and launched a partnership with 14 food companies and the WEF's New Vision for Agriculture Initiative. He reflected that this model was preferable for governments as they could 'talk more openly, more frankly even, on tough issues like tariffs, subsidies, biofuels – those tough issues that sometimes would get bogged down by intergovernmental negotiations like [those at] the WTO'.[27]

However the reclassification of intergovernmental programmes as CSD partnerships took place after the WSSD, which explains the dominance of UN-led partnerships. These efforts to raise the profile of CSD partnerships proved unsuccessful and the number of partnerships registered after 2004 fell sharply.

4.5   CONCLUSIONS: SEDIMENTATION OF CONFLICT

This chapter examined the political dimension of partnerships, by focusing on the process that resulted in partnerships as official outcomes of the WSSD. It captured the sedimentation of conflict during international negotiations, including several alternative ideas about partnerships that were sidelined or unsuccessfully implemented. Discourse theory has the distinct advantage that elements of different demands and competing hegemonic projects can be identified even when they act together to establish an institution.

In a chain of equivalence, the empty signifier represents the common aspect (against the existing hegemonic order). In Chapter 3, I have argued that during the negotiation of international institutions, not only this common aspect but also the particularisms of the demands play a critical role. How does this framework apply to the account provided above? According to some respondents, the initial references to partnerships in the Rio documents were in fact a challenge to the status quo in global environmental governance. For the major groups, partnerships represented participation in decision-making at all levels.

DESA's early conceptualization of partnerships too had a subversive edge: for the organizers of the WSSD, the partnerships regime was a means to include corporations into the accountability mechanisms in environmental governance, which would reduce the stress (and hence increase the chances) of treaty negotiations. For the DESA staff, it was a way to monitor business activities regarding sustainable development, and exert power by endorsing certain CSR conducts as opposed to others. DESA's conception of partnerships was also an attempt to change the existing rules of sustainability politics, which often fails to address local problems of small and/or poor countries. The demands of many groups were articulated in this conception: corporations would sign a code of conduct and a commitment to CSR. In return, they would receive recognition and credibility as well as international support. States would focus on issues they could agree on, and sign binding treaties.

However this conception did not have the status of an empty signifier, representing many demands in a bottom-up fashion and bringing different groups together against the hegemonic order. Before a chain of equivalence was formed, partnerships have already been accepted and supported by the existing hegemonic project. The business lobby, some NGOs, and governments of rich and powerful countries have redefined the concept and fixed its meaning such that with mere surface changes, the existing procedures favouring neo-liberal globalization and the dominance of the rich countries could continue and be furthered.

It was not only the dominant neo-liberal ideology that defined partnerships. At the negotiations, hegemonic struggles took place between supporters and opponents of partnerships, but more critically, among the supporters of different conceptions of partnerships. Different particularisms can be categorized according to their success during the *act of institution*: during the first three PrepComs, several suggestions were made as to how to understand, define, form and monitor partnerships. The list at the beginning of this chapter (Box 4.1) points to those particularisms that have not 'made it' to the final document, the Bali Guidelines. I will call these the *rejected particularisms*.

At the end of PrepCom-3, it became clear that some of these suggestions were going to be discarded. Concerns about potential repercussions of endorsing Type-II outcomes were voiced. Actors involved in the negotiations have articulated these concerns according to their various subject positions, based on their ideologies and perceived interests. This second group of demands have found their way to the Bali Guidelines, in the form of warnings. These can be called *sedimented particularisms*. Two features of this group are critical: their effects were limited as the guidelines never gained a strict legal status; and their sedimentation did not assume harmony or consistency. They were included in the guidelines whether there was a conflict between them or not. Many conflicts were present in the description and framing of partnerships in this document (for example that partnerships could not substitute intergovernmental treaties, that they should address all dimensions of sustainable development, that they should be transparent and accountable but also only self-reporting). Conflicts were also available in the organization of the partnerships regime (for example the elimination of their participatory function, the alienation of less powerful major groups, the limitation of their scope to intergovernmental outcomes).

The last set of particularisms defined and described partnerships in both official texts and non-official ways: I will call these *dominant particularisms*. For instance, the voluntary nature of partnerships was mentioned in the Bali Guidelines, while the practice of partnership formation also supported this principle. As a result, parties strongly supporting the Type-II outcomes had no obligation to form any partnerships once the endorsement was secured. This is very different than the principle on accountability, which was not supported by the practice of self-reporting, or the principle of complementarity that in practice failed as the WSSD achieved no international treaties.

In sum, the Bali Guidelines were the result of various contestations over the meaning of partnerships. Conflicting interests and interpretations have left residues in the formation of the partnerships regime. Demands of several country delegations as well as bureaucrats from the UN and other agencies of global governance influenced the end result. Their different hegemonic projects are present in the agreed framework in a piecemeal fashion; hence, several hegemonic struggles settled into the logics of the institution.

As discussed in Chapter 3, reaching an agreement on the definition of an institution results in homogenization; a reduction in the differences among subject positions. Despite the sedimentation of conflicting discourses into the Bali Guidelines, partnerships have nevertheless been defined in a particular way. The guidelines were a partial fixation for the term 'sustainability partnerships'. After discourse institutionalization, diversity decreases: opponents of partnerships no longer involved themselves in the partnership negotiations, such as the trade unions.

However this does not suggest that contestations ceased to exist. As the partnerships regime started a life of its own, different hegemonic projects asserted themselves as different manifestations of the same architecture – in the form of actual partnerships, or the lack thereof. For instance, despite their support for the concept during the negotiation process, the business and industry did not initiate major projects under the CSD. Several institutions and technologies, previously unable to secure UN recognition in their issue areas, have found a way into the UN system and have been 'blue washed'. Certain actor constellations, issue areas and organizational models were favoured whereas others were absent. Some issues were covered extensively by partnerships, while others were overlooked.

We can see that there are two stages in the life of an international institution with fundamentally different dynamics. The first stage, wherein habitual social practices begin to form, can be called *discourse institutionalization*. Sometimes, as Hajer (1995) suggests, a successful discourse solidifies into an institution. When there are international negotiations involved, institutions often contain *sediments of a number of available discourses*, taken up by various parties. In a mosaic-like structure these sediments solidify into the logics and practices of the institution. At times the whole contains too many pieces from conflicting backgrounds. The success of such an organization depends on the extent to which a consistent discourse can be brought out of this assortment of demands, in a short time. This is a different stage in the life of an institution, and it is what politicians refer to when they talk about *momentum*. As Jan Pronk argued, the CSD partnerships regime failed as the momentum was lost in the few months after the WSSD. The idea that institutions are sedimented discourses could therefore be supplemented with this more dynamic view, and with the recognition that they have different cycles of formation. While the WSSD resulted in a weak partnerships regime, individual partnerships still have considerable impact and political influence at several levels of governance. Moreover, the influence of specific CSD partnerships can be considerable on their respective issue areas, as has been demonstrated by the examples of controversial technologies.

The introductory chapter noted that any myth is 'to some extent reality' if sufficient number of people with sufficient temporal, financial and human resources believe and act upon it. With their negotiation at the WSSD, partnerships have acquired such endorsement at the global and transnational levels. In the next few chapters, the mediating discourses that are the components that shape the 'reality' of partnerships are studied in greater detail.

NOTES

1. This chapter draws on an earlier article: Mert, A. (2009), 'Partnerships for Sustainable Development as Discursive Practice: Shifts in Discourses of Environment and Democracy', *Forest Policy and Economics*, 11 (5–6): 326–39.
2. The UNCSD website: http://www.un.org/esa/sustdev/partnerships, accessed: 10-4-2007.
3. Henceforth the term 'sustainability partnerships' refers to the totality of partnerships

registered with the UNCSD, whereas 'partnership initiatives' refer to individual partnerships.
4. Interview with Southern country delegate to the WSSD process; Denpasar, 2006; New York, 2007.
5. Interview with UN DESA representative; New York, 2007.
6. The UN website on MDGs: http://www.un.org/millenniumgoals/environ, accessed: 10-12-2010.
7. Interview with UN DESA officer responsible for Major Groups; New York, 2008.
8. Interview with UN DESA representative; New York, 2007.
9. Interview with Northern country delegate to the WSSD process; Denpasar, 2006; and interview with Jan Pronk; The Hague, 2008.
10. Interview with UN DESA representative; New York, 2007.
11. Interview with UNEP representative, and organising committee member of UN environmental summits; New York, 2008.
12. The major groups of civil society, as defined by *Agenda 21*, are women, children and youth, indigenous people, NGOs, local authorities, workers and trade unions, business and industry, scientific and technological communities, and farmers.
13. Interview with UN DESA representative; New York, 2007.
14. Interview with UN DESA representative; New York, 2007.
15. Interview with UNEP representative, and organising committee member of UN environmental summits; New York, 2008.
16. Interview with UN DESA representative; New York, 2007.
17. Interview with Southern country delegate to the WSSD process; Denpasar, 2006.
18. Interview with UN DESA representative; New York, 2007.
19. Interview with UNEP representative, and organising committee member of the UN's environmental summits; New York, 2008.
20. Interview; New York, 2007.
21. Interview; The Hague, 2008.
22. Interview; New York, 2007.
23. Transcribed from the presentations made in the Side Event to the CSD-15, 1-5-2007.
24. Transcribed from the presentations made in the Side Event to the CSD-15, 1-5-2007.
25. The WNU website: http://www.world-nuclear-university.org/about.aspx?id=15904, accessed: 16-11-2009.
26. Ibid.
27. The World Economic Forum website: http://www.weforum.org/news/leaders-commit-partnership-sustainable-agriculture-and-food-security-east-asia?fo=1, accessed: 3-3-2012.

PART II

Analyzing the mediating discourses

5. Partnerships and the discourse of privatization[1]

5.1 INTRODUCTION

Since 2006 Dow Chemical sponsors the Blue Planet Run to 'bring safe drinking water to 1.2 billion people' (UNOP 2010). Coca Cola Foundation and Procter & Gamble promote the provision of a water disinfectant and 'behavior change techniques directed towards improved hygiene' in water-deprived poor countries (UNCSD Partnerships Database 2004). Royal Dutch Shell is involved in the Clean Air Initiative to enhance air quality and reduce emissions (CAI-Asia 2010). Monsanto contributes to the mitigation of 'the threat posed by invasive species' (UNCSD Partnerships Database 2008). These are only a few examples of corporate involvement in partnership initiatives launched to tackle environmental and socio-economic problems relevant to (if not caused by) their core business activities. All these initiatives are registered with the UN as means to achieve the MDGs.

Globalization and the increasing power of transnational corporations comprise a critical background for analysing partnerships. This chapter focuses on the relation between *partnership* and narratives underlying globalization. To do this, the business context, out of which the business meaning of partnerships emerged, is linked with the later developments in global capital markets and the perceptions of modern corporation. These perceptions and narratives are intrinsically linked with the way the concept is employed in governance of environment and development today. My aim is to re-construct debates and symbolic contexts that are related to 'partnerships as private governance mechanisms'. These reflect certain transitions in the global order and point to possible structural limitations in the legitimacy and effectiveness of private governance institutions.

One of the historically relevant debates is the introduction of *limited liability* to the commercial law of nineteenth-century England. Issues of contracts, managerial control, ownership, risk and free circulation of capital emerge within the context of this debate. The resulting separation of the capital from the capitalist (what Karl Marx labels 'the socialization of capital') is critical in the historical formation of types of business ownership with limited liability, in the form of *limited liability partnerships* as well as the *modern corporation*. But more significantly, this process is the starting point of the increasing legitimizing, economic, and discursive power of capital markets. The principle of limited liability underlies the dual origin of the modern forms of business ownership (both the partnership and the corporation) and the ever-freer and global-yet-still-expanding capital markets. Later on, these processes remained conceptually as fused as when they were conceived; a connection that was concealed especially by the intensifying rhetorical separation of politics and the markets. The links between these two contexts can be revealed by tracing them back in time, towards their origins and historical intersection points.

Similar to the rhetorical separation of capital and the markets, concepts of *private* and *public*, too, are often pitted against each other. Claire Cutler (2002: 34) recognizes that the separation of public and private spheres is not natural, organic, inevitable or inherently meaningful. The democratic, formalistic and legalistic associations of authority with the state and the public sphere obscure the trend towards more private, ad hoc, discretionary practices of business actors (ibid.: 24). This trend, sometimes called 'the liberal art of separation' (Walzer 1984) serves to conceal increasingly more spheres of social life from public scrutiny.

At this point, it is necessary to explicate and relate the analytical category (*private* governance) and the political process (*privatization* of governance). To begin with, I would like to set down definitions of the words *private* and *privatization* in three separate (albeit related) domains. This would allow for a thorough examination of these terms, their development and nuances. The word *private* has a long history (approximately dating back to the late fourteenth century); it derives from *privare* (Lat.), meaning 'to deprive, release, or separate (to oneself)'.[2] Its connotation of 'not open to the public' dates back to 1398. The phrase *private enterprise* is first recorded in 1844, but it took several decades before the first verb form, *to privatize*, and the conjugated form *privatization* were recorded, in the mid-twentieth century. From these details it can be noted that the meaning of the word changed, from signifying a relation with the sphere of the non-communal, to that of the economical.

In its contemporary usage, *to privatize* means: 'to make private; especially to change (as a business or industry) from public to private *control or ownership*' (MWC 1996, my emphasis). This definition represents the traditional usage of the word: transfer of control and ownership of industrial production and/or service sectors from public to private control. More comprehensive and commonplace descriptions can be found in digital non-peer reviewed sources. For instance, Wikipedia refers to additional meanings of *privatization*:

1. transfer of any government *function* to the private sector including governmental functions like revenue collection and law enforcement;
2. nongovernmental interaction involving the buyout of all shares of a public corporation or holding company's stock by a single entity, privatizing a publicly traded stock.

It appears that the concept of *privatization* in fact derived from a public/private divide, although what was meant by public (and therefore private) seems to have changed in time. In contemporary definitions the word gains economic and political connotations relating to ownership, control, public and private sectors, governmental functions and, in a more particular form, a buyout of stocks. It is indeed a word of political and economic spheres.

The public/private divide explicit in these definitions point towards the use of the term in IR literature, as well. In this context, *private* governance and *privatization* of governance are two separate but related concepts. The former refers to a realm of social practice characterized by rules and norms initiated solely or mainly by non-state actors, often taken as a given realm of enquiry, much in the same way natural science understands its empirical objects as natural phenomena. However the involvement of non-state actors does not sufficiently define private governance, as it is ensured and normalized through various processes, spanning from 'more traditional interstate negotiations, [. . .] to hybrid public–private partnerships and fully private co-operations' (Pattberg 2005). Nonetheless, 'governance without government' (Rosenau and Czempiel 1992) has been increasingly institutionalized in global politics in the last few decades. Some scholars attribute this change to the end of ideological clash (Keck and Sikkink 1998), others to democratization (Glasbergen 2002), or to the increasing complexity of governance issues (Biermann and Dingwerth 2004). Another vein of IR scholars recognizes the direction of this institutionalization, and labels it 'privatization of governance' (Sassen 1996; Cutler et al. 1999; Hall and Biersteker 2002). They reveal the neo-liberal connotations of this transformation by focusing on the features of this political process, such as:

- deregulation in some levels and areas of governance;
- an emphasis on voluntary schemes of non-/self-regulation;
- deployment of market-based approaches;
- change in the nature of non-state actor involvement (towards actual rule-making).

On this basis, privatization of governance can be redefined as *a process through which non-state actors are increasingly included in the political decision-making – either by state actors willingly relinquishing some of their functions, or by unwillingly being abided by private authority – and in which regulatory approaches based on state-coercion are replaced by market-based and voluntary mechanisms.*

The next section opens up a fantasmatic space wherein concepts such as contracts, liability, risk, loss and payback relate to one another. Section 5.3 focuses on the business meaning of partnerships, whereas Section 5.4 links these meanings to the narratives of globalization.

5.2   FANTASMATIC LOGICS: DEBT, CONTRACT AND A POUND OF FLESH

SHYLOCK: Say this:
'Fair sir, you spit on me on Wednesday last,
You spurn'd me such a day; another time
You call'd me dog; and for these courtesies
I'll lend you thus much moneys'?

ANTONIO: [. . .] If thou wilt lend this money, lend it not
As to thy friends – for when did friendship take
A breed for barren metal of his friend?
But lend it rather to thine enemy,
Who if he break thou mayst with better face
Exact the penalty.

SHYLOCK: Why, look you, how you storm!
I would be friends with you, and have your love,
Forget the shames that you have stain'd me with,
Supply your present wants, and take no doit
Of usance for my moneys, and you'll not hear me.
This is kind I offer.

BASSANIO: This were kindness.

SHYLOCK: This kindness will I show.
Go with me to a notary, seal me there
Your single bond, and, in a merry sport,
If you repay me not on such a day,
In such a place, such sum or sums as are
Express'd in the condition, let the forfeit
Be nominated for an equal pound
Of your fair flesh, to be cut off and taken
In what part of your body pleaseth me.
[. . .]
ANTONIO: Yes, Shylock, I will seal unto this bond.
(Shakespeare 1596 [1987]: 76–78)

The late nineteenth- and early twentieth-century implications of *The Merchant of Venice* are traditionally discussed around issues of educational reform, women's politics, and the 'Jewish question' (Rozmovits 1998: 3). At its time, these themes, converging in the plot, indeed tied the meanings in the play to questions being debated in the world outside it. In the late Victorian era, the play was regarded as a reference point that 'set the standard for commercial conduct' since all characters were 'brought into relation with the getting, or keeping, or spending, or losing of wealth, [and were tried by their] attitude towards wealth' (ibid.: 115). Others suggest that *The Merchant* has a timeless, universal appeal as an eloquent piece, 'pitting tit-for-tat contractualism against unconditional love' (Ajzenstat 1997: 269). In fact, the nature of the contract, the contingency of the criteria of a just contract, and liabilities of investors and creditors when their venture failed were all pieces of the economic question *The Merchant* portrayed.

The play centres on a contract between Shylock, a Jewish money-lender, and Antonio, a Christian merchant, signed on Shylock's demand and Antonio's free will: Shylock will receive no usury from the money he lends, but demands the collateral of 'a pound of flesh' from Antonio's body if the loan is not repaid by the due date. The climax of the play takes place in front of the court as Antonio fails to pay his debt on time and is brought to court by Shylock demanding the pound of flesh (Antonio's heart) on the basis of *pacta sunt servanda*. Shylock's conflict with the virtuous capitalist, personified in Antonio, turns their contract into a symbolic intersection point of debates on justice, interpretation and enforcement of contracts, and the political nature of law and economics. In understanding the formation of legal concepts concerning business ownership in general and business partnerships in particular, three issues of *The Merchant* are critical: questions regarding fairness of contracts, the risks and liabilities that are bestowed upon the creditor and the borrower, settlement of disputes in cases of failure to pay back the debt. The famous court scene embodies three characters and their dilemmas, important for their time and relevant as a symbolic representation of these questions.

5.2.1 Shylock's Revenge

As the case is taken to the court, Shylock is proposed three times the amount he has lent, to redeem Antonio. He refuses the money because it is late and demands the contract to be carried out. Shylock embodies the conflict of Jews at the time: although the proposal is in fact a win–win solution to the conflict, his insistence reveals that his motives in lending the money were not financial. As Margaret Atwood's (2008: 158) analysis of the play suggests, 'he thus violates the code of business practice – make a profit, whatever else – as well as the Mosaic code of the redemption of pawned objects, and opts for vengeance instead'. Despite being the creditor he is not the ideal economic man fulfilling the imperatives of liberalism. From the point of view of the society depicted in the play (and of England at the time), he is an outsider with radical predispositions, which dispose him of the ability to pursue his rational interests.

As the quote above shows, Shylock does not hide his intentions for revenge: he is angered by the behaviour of Antonio towards himself and lending him money is his way of taking his chances to teach him a lesson. The court scene is critical: 'At precisely that moment when he must succeed, Shylock falls prey to that violence that money was invented to replace' (Buchnan 2001: 90). Moreover it represents how failure to pay the debts can result in 'unjust' or 'irrational' exercise of contract law, especially when the intentions of the creditor and borrower are divergent or hostile. In Section 5.4, CSD partnerships are evaluated on the basis of the intentions of partners involved and the potential results of their divergent interests.

5.2.2   The Duke's Dilemma

The divergent interests of the parties to a contract put the governing body into the decision-making position. Shylock confronts the Duke of Venice, who presides over the trial, with the fact that his decision about this contract stands for the trustworthiness of every contract, and the very order he represents. Just as slaves are property of much of the population in the city of Venice, he has 'bought' the pound of flesh: if his demand is denied, 'there is no force in the decrees of Venice' (Shakespeare 1596 [1987]: 55). The court scene closes with the arguments of the young doctor of law, Balthasar, who makes the case that Shylock is not entitled to kill Antonio. Despite saving Antonio's life, it is playfully suggestive that Balthasar is an impostor.

This point is critical from the point of view of political authority: as the Duke's position is built on upholding the law, he cannot help Antonio. In an instant, Shakespeare reveals the co-dependence of commercial conduct and political authority. Dispute settlement, law enforcement and ensuring compliance are functions of the state critical to the establishment of a legitimate and accepted system of rule. These functions have also made the historical development of 'the market as we know it' possible. Section 5.4 focuses on the co-dependence of markets and state regulation.

5.2.3   Antonio's Heart

Antonio's seeming benevolence is balanced by his overbearing behaviour towards Shylock. As they sign the contract, he insists that Shylock lends the money to him as if Antonio is his enemy. In the court, too, Antonio agrees with Shylock when he insists on exacting the penalty, although it would kill him. He signed the bond and hence regarded himself liable. It was the other characters in the play that reflected on the injustice of the contract.

The question explored by the play is clearly whether or not those liabilities granted by contracts must be limited in some fashion. Early modern political debates over contracts and liability of this kind have been critical in the evolution of business ownership models, particularly of partnerships and corporations. In what follows, liability and its gradual limitation in the last three centuries represent a piece of the puzzle regarding how a business concept evolved into an environmental governance mechanism.

5.3   PARTNERSHIPS AND CORPORATIONS IN GOVERNANCE

5.3.1   Partnership as Corporate Vocabulary: Contracts and Resemblances

At the CSD, there is consensus among the representatives of NGOs and UN employees that *partnership* is a 'corporate vocabulary'. This has been emphasized most clearly by trade union and business representatives: while the former claimed that 'a corporatist world is being born out of [partnerships]',[3] the latter used a normalizing tone: 'Partnerships is part of the way business operates; when you cannot do something alone you take a partner, and do it together'.[4]

'Partnership' has three related meanings, only one being immediately related to business activities (MWC Dictionary 1996):

1. the state of being a partner: participation
2. (a) a legal relation existing between two or more persons contractually associated as joint principals in a business (b) the persons joined together in a partnership
3. a relationship resembling a legal partnership and usually involving close cooperation between parties having specified and joint rights and responsibilities.

In most dictionary definitions, legal contracts appear as a condition to partnerships. The resemblance in the last definition is more likely to apply to non-business partnerships; non-contractual relationships that 'involve close cooperation between parties' make the word partnership so ubiquitous. In the UN context, this resemblance allows for the use of 'partnerships' for *Type-II outcomes*. Yet, 95 per cent of CSD partnerships indicate no protocol or contract, or even a non-binding memorandum of understanding among partners or between the partnership and the UN (Mert 2012). This raises questions about how and where the ' joint rights and responsibilities' are specified, what is meant by them among partners of significantly divergent interests, and who is liable in case of failure.

The first question, how and where are the so-called *joint* rights and responsibilities that are being specified, is difficult to answer in terms of single partnerships, due to their diversity. At an aggregate level, the goal of CSD partnerships is defined by the Bali Guidelines, which fail to answer questions of liability and compliance. This vagueness is also present in the *partnerships for development* of the Global Compact, defined as 'voluntary and collaborative relationships between various parties, both State and non-State, in which all participants agree to work together to achieve a common purpose or undertake a specific task and to share risks, responsibilities, resources, competencies and benefits' (UN Global Compact 2003). Despite the emphasis on cooperation, these definitions do not suggest any joint rights and responsibilities, or ensure liability and compliance. Nevertheless, there appears to be a convergence in both initiatives to facilitate business interests: the Compact is 'first and foremost concerned with exhibiting and building the social legitimacy of business and markets'.[5] For CSD, General Assembly Resolution *Towards Global Partnerships* (UN 2001a, my emphasis) fervently encourages the private sector to cooperate with the UN:

> Stressing that efforts to meet the challenges of globalization could benefit from enhanced cooperation between the United Nations and all relevant partners, *in particular the private sector* [. . .]
> [The General Assembly notes] numerous valuable examples of cooperation between the United Nations and all relevant partners, *in particular the private sector* [. . .]
> Stresses also the need for international cooperation to *strengthen the participation of enterprises* [. . .]
> Invites the Secretary-General to continue to seek the views of relevant partners, *in particular the private sector, on how to enhance their cooperation with the [UN].*

This cooperative tone is questioned by parties less inclined to collaborate with the private sector, and concerns about legitimacy, accountability and transparency were 'very forcefully expressed' at the PrepCom Meetings. Quarless observed that disagreements were not only expressed by developing countries but also by major groups.[6] This was one of the hegemonic struggles that took place during the institutionalization of the partnerships regime, as Carol Bellamy, Executive Director of UNICEF (1999) suggested:

> It is dangerous to assume that the goals of the private sector are somehow synonymous with those of the United Nations, because they most emphatically are not. Business and industry are driven by the profit motive – as they should and must be, both for their shareholders and their employees. The work of the UN, on the other hand, is driven by a set of ethical principles that sustain its mission [. . .]. In coming together with the private sector, the UN must carefully, and constantly, appraise the relationship.

Similarly, Ann Zammit's (2003: *xx*) report on UN–business partnerships suggests that 'while at one level there can be easy agreement on immediate goals or outputs, this does not necessarily entail an identity of ultimate interests'; hence, partnerships should also be assessed in terms of their indirect, 'possibly unintended outcomes that have development implications'.

A business representative agreed on the divergence of main goals:

> [The private sector] cannot solve poverty. They are not really responsible for solving poverty, and they can't do it alone, but they can really contribute to this [through] a partnership. That's why there has been an increase in [the number of] partnerships: because of this realization that actually these issues are business issues.[7]

In addition to the lack of an official document that specifies joint rights and responsibilities, there is also a general agreement that business and UN interests are different. Moreover, there is a lack of consensus with regard to the definition of partnerships. A trade union representative directly challenged the business take on partnerships:

> [Partnerships] are substituting privatized activity, here in the heart of the UN. Business and industry these days call everything they do a partnership. Anytime you hear that rhetoric, you should become suspicious. When you agree to supply certain services to me for a certain amount of money, you are not my partner!

The third question is: who bears the risk if a partnership or the partnerships *regime* fails? Empirical studies suggest that such failure is probable: partnerships are unlikely to fill the so-called 'implementation deficit' in sustainable development because they lack the human and material resources; they are unable to create additional funding; they focus on building institutional frameworks rather than projects with direct impact; and contrary to the MDGs, they tend not to be implemented in 'the least developed' countries (Biermann et al. 2007). Most CSD partnerships do not evaluate their contribution to the realization of MDGs (OECD 2006). Furthermore, lack of binding contracts results in institutions with less direct goals and less stringent modes of operation, that do not fill implementation deficits, but rather voluntary, preferential gaps, as predicted by Kenny Bruno (2002) of CorpWatch at the end of the WSSD:

> With the world's most powerful governments fully behind the corporate glo-balisation agenda, it was agreed even before the Summit that there would be no new mandatory agreements. Rather the focus was to be on implementation of old agreements, mainly through partnerships with the private sector. In other words, those aspects of sustainability that are convenient for the private sector would be implemented.

While it is likely that the partnership regime will fail to solve environmental problems, its failure will be difficult to assess and no party will bear the responsibility. In sum, partnerships for sustainable development only *resemble* contract-based business partnerships, despite inheriting their positive connotations. Yet, the symbolic order from out of which partnerships emerged has several implications on the questions of risk and liability in global environmental governance.

5.3.2   Ownership, Partnership and Liability

In management studies and commercial law, *partnership* appears as a type of business ownership, among three others: sole proprietorship, corporation and cooperative. Each type indicates distinct advantages in forming, operating and dissolving businesses. The most discernible separation is whether the firm has a separate legal person. In a proprietorship and in some types of partnerships, the business entity has no separate legal existence from its owner/s, whereas in corporations, limited liability partnerships and co-ops it does. Therefore the business entity can (legally) operate like a real person, while having no relationship with the biological persons who own the business.

This separation has two implications. Firstly, the control owners have over the management of the enterprise differs on this basis. Generally, if the business has no separate legal existence, the management is done by the owner/s (*sole proprietorship* and *general* or *liability partnerships*). If the enterprise is a legal person, there is usually a board and a professional management team, such as corporations, where owners are shareholders with no managerial role and limited decision-making power. *Limited liability partnerships* are managed directly by partners, and co-ops by all members.

Secondly, the firm's separate legal person protects the owner/s from risk with limiting the liabilities. While *unlimited liability* refers to owner/s being personally responsible for all the debt that may result from the venture (all the property of the owner/s could be liquidated to pay the debts), *limited liability* means that each owner's responsibility is limited to the amount she invested in that particular business (owner/s can only lose their initial investment unless there is fraud or illegal activity). Limited liability, therefore, reduces the risk for the investor and hence presumably increases the likelihood of investment.

In different types of business ownership liabilities differ. For partnerships, liability conditions are the determining factor in their categorization and regulation. In a *general partnership* each partner is personally liable for any debts of the company; in a *limited liability partnership*, all partners have limited liability; in a *limited partnership* the silent partners have limited and managing partners have unlimited liability.

In sum, the most critical similarity between corporations and partnerships are in the distribution of risk and liability. In both cases, owners are protected from the possible failure of their ventures. This comparison is critical to understanding sustainability partnerships because the similarities between business partnerships and corporations structure the actualisation of sustainability partnerships. Their resemblance to the modern corporation results from a shared historical origin. Using the same business background, the next section focuses on different perceptions of the corporation, and how the change in perception relates to corporate involvement in global governance.

5.3.3   Corporations and Partnerships: An Intertwined History

The neo-classical theory of the firm is based on the definition of a company as the nexus of contracts, wherein the enterprise is considered a legal person whose relationship with its employees, its creditors and debtors, and the larger community is determined by various contracts. It emphasizes that the sole objective of the firm is profit-maximization, and the role of professional managers is to secure benefits on behalf of shareholders. This perception of the firm is regarded as 'the shareholder view' and has been a dominant understanding in modern capitalist societies until the 1960s. By this time, the neo-classical theory of the firm was questioned by alternative theories of firm motivation. Profit was still important, but only as a means to achieve other objectives. It was argued that: (1) the dispersal of share ownership in large corporations gives their managers some freedom in pursuing non-profit goals; and (2) the personal values of senior managers, the pressures of interest groups and the dynamic position of the corporation in the market (determined by its resources and opportunities) influence the corporate objectives (Lowes and Dobbins 1978: 70). As a result of these pressures there emerged a new and alternative view on the role of corporations in modern societies: 'the stakeholder view of the corporation' emphasized the responsibility of a firm towards its employees, customers and the larger community. As the stakeholder view became hegemonic, CSR programmes, developmental and environmental projects, and partnerships with local/national governments settled in the agendas and operations of corporations.

In the 1980s, the stakeholder view became increasingly popular, with the tenacious privatization policies of the Thatcher and Reagan administrations. The New Right ideology promoted the ideas of New Public Management and 'public-choice' schools, based on the assumptions that the private sector provides a more efficient mechanism in producing public goods and services, and in order to downsize the public sector should retreat from these areas. This was a turning point for the debates on the powers of the corporation. Firms were given governmental approval and were invited to provide for all the stakeholders and the society. These institutions, through which corporations would provide public services, would be labelled *partnerships*.

Building partnerships with the private sector, governments could ensure the provision of public services without undertaking them. From the perspective of the private sector, partnerships were a means to expand to sectors that they were previously barred from, such as public utilities. These sectors were critical in highly urbanized, modern societies. The governments' decision that companies would provide these services more efficiently meant that companies were in service of the community. As a result, corporations enjoyed a number of public relations benefits from building partnerships with national governments and local communities.

In international politics, the influence of transnational corporations as economic and political agents became evident in the late 1980s. For the so-called 'developing' countries, their role was critical not only because of the foreign direct investment they could bring, but also due to the social, economic and environmental effects of their operations. This was a time when globalization became the prevailing background for developmental and environmental policies; embedding these issues in liberal markets dovetailed the neoliberal shifts in the global economy. The demand to moderate the impacts of financial globalization and to place liberalism in a broader set of values (environmental concerns, human rights, labour rights, and so on) resulted in 'the compromise of liberal environmentalism' (Bernstein 2001).

In the beginning of this process, the notion of 'sustainable development' was conceptualized, seemingly reconciling economic growth and environmental protection. Bernstein (2000) notes that UNCED institutionalized these norms at the global level and legitimized the evolution of governance discourses towards liberal environmentalism. The Rio Declaration on Environment and Development (UN 1992a) regarded an open international economic system as a requirement for 'economic growth and sustainable development in all countries'. The assumption that free trade, economic development and environmental protection are compatible was reinforced at the WSSD: the Johannesburg Declaration and the JPOI performed a 'legitimating function for major trade agreements, including the WTO', and *sustainability partnerships*, which fit perfectly to this framework, were endorsed as the Type-II outcomes of the Summit (Bernstein 2005: 159). Once more, 'partnerships' were going to provide, what governments failed to do, and more efficiently.

The Global Compact and the CSD partnerships are manifestations of the neoliberal paradigm within the UN system. Types and functions of hybrid and private governance mechanisms have been steadily increasing outside of the UN system as well. For instance, rather than assuming a watchdog role, increasing numbers of standardization mechanisms began to involve the private sector, such as the Forest Stewardship Council, World Commission on Dams, and Marine Stewardship Council. Another example is the progressive transformation of science policy networks into multi-stakeholder science–industry policy centres, most visible with the expansion of the CGIAR programme in the 1990s. While the business interests have always influenced politics in many ways, there is an increasing trend towards direct involvement of corporations in the governance of their *core business activities*.

In sum, the rise of the corporation as a powerful institutional model in modern society and the invention of partnership as a governance institution were intertwined processes. But what did this mean for a study of partnerships? How was the semiotic network around the partnership concept transformed? And how did it reflect the transformation of ownership rights in legal and economic terms? These are the subject of the next section.

5.3.4 Stakeholders, Shareholders and Ownership Rights

Business partnerships and corporations differ in terms of ownership and control. Unlike limited liability partnerships, shareholders of a corporation are numerous and dispersed, while managers operate the day-to-day business, which is termed in business law as 'the divorce of ownership from control' (Berle and Means 1932). Inversely, with this separation of shareholders from managers in corporations, rights of ownership are unbundled.

In management theory, shareholders are generally regarded as having the *ownership* of a corporation. Some argue (cf. Blair 1995) that this is a misconception owing to a 'legal and social convention'; throughout most of history, private property was in the form of physical property. Hence, rights of possession and control are customarily packed together with the right to receive benefits (through the use of the asset) and the responsibility for bearing the risk (incurring from its misuse). However, in corporations these rights and responsibilities are unpacked and distributed to several participants in the enterprise. Scholars of this view (Berle and Means 1932; Dodd 1932) note that a shareholder does not effectively undertake all the responsibilities that ownership of real, physical property normally implies, and is reduced to a 'recipient of the wages of his capital' (Berle and Means 1932: 2). Therefore, she should not be entitled to rights normally associated with ownership (ibid.: 355–356):

> The owners of passive property, by surrendering control and responsibility over the active property, have surrendered the right that the corporation should be operated in their sole interests – they have released the community from the obligation to protect them to the full extent implied in the doctrine of strict property rights. [. . .] They have placed the community in a position to demand that the modern corporation serve not alone the owners or the control but all society.

It is, therefore, argued that in addition to the shareholders, a larger body of stakeholders are influenced such as the managers, workers, creditors, whose interests need to be considered in the operations of a corporation. This is one of the ideational origins of the CSR paradigm.

The conceptualization of the 'corporation as a social institution' was in direct contrast with the shareholder view of the firm (as the 'nexus of contracts'). This was most famously advocated by the Chicago School, and claimed that the relationship between the owners and all other stakeholders were already organized by contracts. Accordingly, the rights of creditors, employees and others should be dealt with under contractual and common law and firms should solely pursue the interest of the shareholders (Allen 1992: 10).

Opponents of the shareholder view argued, however, that all other stakeholders 'are not compensated by means of "complete" contracts (that specify exactly what is to happen in all circumstances)' (Blair 1995: 230). Moreover, there was the problem of residual risks and claims: shareholders of a corporation are investors that provide the common shares similar to the stockholders in early joint-stock companies that gathered the capital necessary for expeditions in exchange for securities (stocks) on future profits. Similarly, corporations raise their initial capital from shareholders (through equity funds) and creditors. In return, shareholders have claims on a proportionate share of the net profits, after all debts, credits and other obligations (for example employee wages) have been paid. Shareholders are said to take a *residual risk* and therefore to have a *residual claim* because payments to shareholders are paid last, so they risk not making any profit. For neo-classical economics this is another reason for corporations to pursue the best interests of their shareholders, and not a larger stakeholder group. However, the principle of limited liability for shareholders is in direct contradiction with this assumption that shareholders are the only residual risk claimants and therefore residual risk bearers (ibid.: 225–234): Not only does limited liability shift some of the residual risk to the creditors (for example bankruptcy), but also to workers (for example lay-offs) or the rest of the society (for example failed infrastructure projects).

The proponents of the stakeholder view noted that the political legitimacy of corporate power was hardly challenged after the Great Depression, due to its 'brilliant performance' in generating wealth during and after the Second World War (WWII). They were cautious, however, because this has made the discussion of corporate power even more pressing (Votaw 1965: 87):

> Corporations are the possessors of substantial amounts of power, and properly so. Without it they could not perform the tasks society demands from them. In a free society, however, we cannot leave the subject there. Power, in either private or public hands, raises difficult questions: How much power? In whose hands? Power for what purposes? To whom are the wielders of power responsible? What assurances are there that the power will be used fairly and justly? Is there machinery by which the power and the method of its exercise can be made responsive to the needs of society?

By the late 1960s, the legitimacy questions faded further into the background as business leaders embraced the stakeholder view, and assumed more responsibilities (Blair 1995). Proponents of the stakeholder view suggested that the influence corporations were gaining was legitimate, but should be discussed publicly so as to ensure its accountability (for example Votaw 1965). The Chicago School's response was probably best reflected in Milton Friedman's (1970: 33) article, 'The Social Responsibility of Business is to Increase its Profits', in which he wrote 'businessmen who talk this way are unwitting puppets of the intellectual forces that have been undermining the basis of a free society these past decades'. Social freedoms were being threatened by the expectation that the private firms should serve public interests, whereas 'the tendency to allow and even to impel the corporations to use their resources for [ends other than profit] confer upon them undesirable and socially dangerous powers' (Hayek 1985: 100). In sum, both parties were concerned about the accountability dimension of this trend.

Today, the debate on whether the corporation should be perceived as *the social institution around which the society is organized* is even more critical. As corporations assumed more and more leverage in the public domain, their inclusion into governance has been increasingly institutionalized and normalized. Ironically, today, the liberal understanding of the Chicago School reappears in development economics as the only way to restrict the corporation and embed it back into the legal frameworks of societies. It is beyond the scope of this study to conclude such an extensive debate, but there are important points for analysing the privatization of governance.

Firstly, corporations do not operate in a social vacuum and assume many social responsibilities, even when their actions are geared towards profit-maximization. This is demonstrated every time they employ or lay off large amounts of workers, succeed or fail to accomplish projects, enter or leave markets, destroy or conserve ecosystems with their activities. Assuming corporations can act only on behalf of their shareholders without affecting the public sphere is assuming that authority solely belongs to public actors. Such an assumption would make the study of the increasing societal acceptance and political legitimation of private authority impossible (Cutler 2002). Secondly, the fundamental assumptions of liberal economics (for example that firms operate under conditions of complete market transparency and information; that prices and property rights are determined for all products; that contracts are complete) often do not hold, neither for macro-economic policy nor for corporate organization (Stiglitz 2003). Under conditions of uncertainty, the ultimate motive of the firm is no longer restricted to profit, but also involves its *stability* and *survival* (Fligstein 2001).

Pursuit of survival can be seen as a logical consequence of corporations being given a perpetual existence *together with* limited liability: limiting liability in early joint-stock companies was restricted with the time of the expedition or undertaking, whereas the modern corporation is a legal person with perpetual life. Hence, the long-term survival strategies of corporations can no longer be regarded as against the benefit of their shareholders if better working conditions or self-imposed environmental standards are perceived as significant for the survival of the firm. Perpetual existence also brings the firm the *pursuit of stability*. Corporate self-regulation of social/environmental externalities and business demands for internationally standardized regulation must be viewed in this light.

To conclude, an entity with perpetual life and rights similar to (or even more expansive than) those of the individuals or communities is an exception in economic history. If anything, having a non-biological, non-ethical and immortal individuality, the modern corporation resembles the deities of Ancient Greece, who interacted with the mortals but had a separate and supreme order. But before a new 'Olympian' order of market economy was established, that is, before perpetual existence was granted to corporate legal persons, it was necessary for the capital to depart the mortal body of the capitalist. This has taken place with the introduction of limited liability to commercial law, which is the focus of the next section.

5.4   LIMITED LIABILITY AND GLOBAL CAPITAL MARKETS

To link the modern corporation with the Olympian order of market economy requires us to go back in time, and establish the context in which limited liability became a part of commercial law. This section starts with a summary of this experience in nineteenth-century England, a microcosm of the great transformations in the capitalist world. Debates surrounding limited liability are relevant for this study for three reasons. Firstly, commercial law was the contestation area between the so-called landed aristocracy and the increasingly wealthy merchants that formed the financial and commercial bourgeoisie. It was in the centre of political economy debates, as well as in Karl Marx's analysis of the socialization of capital. This attention was not purely symbolic; the changes in partnership and liability laws transformed the architecture of commercial and financial governance in advanced-capitalist societies, particularly those heavily engaged in sea trade and thus were compelled to invent commercial techniques to limit liabilities in order to raise capital for expeditions (for example the Netherlands and Italy).

Secondly, the inclusion of non-state actors is the first premise of my definition of privatization of governance, which instigates debates regarding sovereignty, authority and legitimacy in international relations. These debates are particularly concerned with corporate involvement in governance, an incident which has been traced back to the changes taking place in nineteenth-century England by historians periodically (Formoy 1923; Cooke 1950; Ferrarini 2002).

Finally, limited liability is still a critical principle in the regulation as well as the analytical categorization of business partnerships. The application of the term in international environmental and developmental matters points to a change in global governance towards limitation of legal responsibilities, which I regard as the second condition of privatization: a shift towards non-binding, market-based, voluntary governance mechanisms. Looking into the history and business definitions of partnerships can therefore help us associate certain difficulties in the application of the business rationale in international relations, and help us explain some of the structural limitations on their effectiveness and legitimacy.

5.4.1 'Socialization of Capital' in Victorian England

In England, the introduction of limited liability to commercial law took place in the context of changes in the law of partnership, and was a highly controversial parliamentary issue from 1818 to 1856. There were a number of problems in the legislation, such as difficulties in suing and being sued, settlement of disputes, and that any person taking an interest in the profits became liable as a partner.[8] However, the Parliamentary debate soon focused on the aptness of limiting the liability of investors (Saville 1956: 418).

According to Rob Bryer (1997: 38) two opposing camps emerged 'between two competing world-views, [based on] two competing systems of political economy', which he calls *the modernisers* versus *the great capitalists*:

> [The modernisers] anticipated Marx's critique and development of the political economy of Adam Smith. [. . .] For Marx capital becomes 'social' by being pooled in and across joint-stock companies run by 'mere managers', and the 'capital owner, . . . a mere money capitalist', who demands that all capital earns the risk adjusted general rate of profit; an 'equal return for equal capital'. [Their opponents] embraced Adam Smith's vision of a world of individual capitalists: a world still dominated by landowners [. . .] and a few large capitalists, but with a mass of smaller individual capitalists whose direct interest and involvement in trade, agriculture, or manufacture, and unrestricted competition, ensured Britain was the best of all possible capitalist worlds.

There was no clear division between economic classes; both discourse coalitions attracted individuals from all sections. At first, *the modernisers* demanded limiting liability for the protection of the working class from investment losses (Saville 1956: 418–423). Simply put, when a firm formed a partnership with another firm trading at a different place, and the latter went bankrupt for its separate ventures, to hold the remaining firm liable for the debts of the other was unjust, because only larger capital could bear such a burden. This argument already understood the firm as an individual, but the emphasis was on increasing the possibilities for the working class to invest. *The great capitalists* opposed this: it was not necessary to encourage investment; limiting liabilities would increase fraud, cause risky and speculative investments; and workers would be better off investing in public funds.

It was John Stuart Mill, who recognized the potential contradiction in the principle although he favoured limited liability to enhance cooperative production:

> The great value of a limitation of responsibility as relates to the working classes would be not so much to facilitate the investment of their savings, not so much to enable the poor to lend to those who are rich, as to enable the rich to lend to those who are poor.[9]

As he had foreseen, once the coalition supporting limited liability included more capitalists, the emphasis shifted from the benefits of small ventures for working class investors to systemic issues such as freedom of contract, right of association and equal competition. Eventually, the discussion expanded into 'a general analysis of the workings of industry and commerce, the psychology of business men and the relationship of the business world with society and government; [. . .] and the issue was placed squarely in the context of the arguments for *laissez faire*, a question of free trade against monopoly' (ibid.: 422–430).

The issue was discussed for a decade with several contestations in Parliament and resulted in changes in mercantile laws. The duration of the controversy indicates the power of traditional methods of commerce and industry as well as customary modes of thought. However, in the free-trade backdrop of the 1850s the earlier view on unlimited liability, that the law had to 'protect the public from the ruin with which they were threatened' (Robertson in Saville 1956: 431), could not be supported. It soon was replaced by the view that it prohibited individuals from 'the unrestrained and unfettered exercise of their own talents and industry' and hence it was against the interest of the community (Bramwell in Bryer 1997: 48).

In the end, limited liability was included in the law of partnership, with the 1855 Amendment to the Joint-Stock Companies Act of 1844. The application of *laissez faire* principles expanded from business and commerce to money, which now had its own market, free circulation and rights of association separate from its possessor. Thus, 'the equality of capital' (or in Marx's terms 'equal return for equal capital') and 'the divorce of ownership from control' were legally established. These principles swiftly materialized in early twentieth-century England, particularly with the resulting growth of the joint stock companies (Hannah 2007).

These developments set one of the milestones of the transformation from commercial capitalism to industrial capitalism, and led to Marx's analysis of the *socialization of capital*. In *Capital*, Marx (1867 [1991]: 567–568, my emphasis) links this transformation with the shift in the perceived role of companies:

> A social concentration of means of production and labour-power, [which] now receives the form of social capital (capital of directly associated individuals) in contrast to private capital, and its enterprises appear *as social enterprises as opposed to private ones*. This is the abolition of capital as private property within the confines of the capitalist mode of production itself [. . .] This result of capitalist production in its highest development is a necessary point of transition towards the transformation of capital back into the property of the producers, though no longer as the private property of individual producers, but rather as their property as associated producers, as directly social property.

This observation resonates that of a banker from Manchester, opposing limited liability: 'It seems to me that we deal, and ought to deal, with men as individuals not with *an abstraction called capital*, which we are thus called upon to recognize as *possessing a separate and independent existence*'.[10] The responsibility of debts resulting from an investment no longer belonged to the investor's real person; separate investments by the same investor had independent lives, debts and consequences. As a result, 'capital the abstraction' was taking command of production, by freeing itself from its possessor. For Marx, this was how capital could free itself 'from the idiosyncrasies of its owner and conform to the law of social capital, [since] from the point of view of social capital, an "equal return for equal capital" was of a higher moral order than the responsibility of individual capitalists for their debts' (in Bryer 1997: 49). From the point of view of the capitalist, his two functions (supplying capital and organizing production) were separated as this new order of capitalism matured (Rosdolsky 1977). What Marx termed the separation of the provider of capital (the money capitalist) from the organiser of production (the industrial capitalist), was the divorce of ownership and control.

Steven Toms (2007: 6) understands *socialization of capital* as an historical continuum: its application to ownership begins with the invention of partnerships in business law, expands with the promotion of capital mobility through capital markets, and peaks with the breakdown of restrictions on the transfer of globally accumulating capital. This process continues as regulations on capital mobility are further reduced, and by the institutionalization of these rules through global financial organizations securing free trade (especially in capital markets). For instance, whenever national economic interests obstruct capital mobilization and transfer, the WTO ensures that national legislation is overruled by a new, global set of rules. As Lipschutz and Fogel (2002: 119) point out 'from the perspective of global capital, it is preferable to deal with single sets of rules that apply to all countries', therefore what we observe is not only national legislations being brought in line with this global set of rules, but also an increasing standardization of global trade rules. The next section examines this 'higher order', how it institutionalized into capital markets and the organizations of the Washington Consensus.

5.4.2 Myths of Globalization: Self-Regulating Markets and Forces of Nature

After capital became an abstraction separate from the capitalist, socialization of capital began to further capital mobility. The logical end result of this process was the organizing of fragmented national economic policies into a somewhat uniform rule-system. The second half of the twentieth-century is marked by the increasing accumulation of financial power in the corporation (the actor) and by the creation of capital markets and global governance institutions such as the International Monetary Fund (IMF), the World Bank and the WTO (the architecture). Hardt and Negri (2004: 107) argue that the rules prescribed in the name of regulatory harmonization and market cohesion are codes of conduct among business actors. The more influence corporations exert on the normative processes regulating globalization, the more capital operates in a conventional but weak form of 'global governance without government': 'The resulting regime of global law is [. . .] not an external constraint that regulates capital but rather an internal expression of agreement among capitalists. This is really a kind of capitalist utopia'.

With the empowerment of global governance institutions, financial interactions are increasingly regulated at the global level. As capital can flow from one territory to the other effortlessly regardless of social repercussions, 'the fact of being global gives [corporate] actors power over individual governments' (Sassen 1996: 41). While the domestic financial policies promote deregulation, increasingly uniform and expansive regulation defines global financial governance. Socialization of capital continues with what may be called 'selective regulation' (Lipschutz and Fogel 2002).

Two crucial discursive elements accommodate the way socialization of capital and financial globalization affect and transform statehood and the international system: *the narrative of inevitability* (of globalization) and *the myth of the self-regulating markets*. The former ensures compliance to global financial rules by reducing fragmentation among national *economic* policies. The latter maintains fragmentation in *social and environmental* legislations.

From a neo-liberal perspective, selective regulation in the economic realm ensures certainty and stability, and reduces transaction costs for international economic actors. More importantly, it eliminates politics from polarized issue areas by shifting regulatory authority from the domestic to the global sphere, where contestation is limited (ibid.). The liberal appreciation of such de-politicization is problematic as this does not indicate consensus, but rather shows how difficult it is for local and national actors to influence global policies. Regulation at the *global* level causes a fundamental de-politicization of the market economy, through narratives of inevitability and inalterability of economic globalization. To illustrate: These narratives were operationalized, when Tony Blair (2005) declared resisting, discussing (therefore politicizing) globalization redundant by equating it to a 'force of nature':

> I hear people say we have to stop and debate globalization. You might as well debate whether autumn should follow summer [. . .] In the era of rapid globalization, there is no mystery about what works – an open, liberal economy, prepared constantly to change to remain competitive.

Blair 'warned' his audience against the temptation to use the governmental action against 'the onslaught of globalization', such as regulation, subsidy, or tariffs. Unless its opportunities were 'ruthlessly exploited', globalization would have catastrophic consequences. Such narratives of inevitability discursively restrict public debates on alternative models of globalization and related policy options.

Cameron and Palan (2004) note that the narrative of the market economy has consequences for the practice of statehood since it externalizes globalization, and makes it an irresistible force that states can only adapt to. Openness and competitiveness institutionalize in the structure of the contemporary world system as the states are 'disciplined (and in fact self-disciplining) by outside pressures should they fail to realize the logic of transition' from national statehood to competitive market statehood (ibid.: 123). The external disciplining forces are the *hyper-mobile capital* and the *institutions of global governance*. The former can always flow to other markets in line with standardized global regulations. The latter ensure compliance of states by restricting policy options and creating enforcement mechanisms. For example, the WTO 'regulate[s] the behaviour of states engaging in trade' rather than trade *per se* (ibid.: 124).

This perceived inevitability was disputed by Kofi Annan (2000b). In explaining his attempts 'to bring business in', he agreed that globalization required adaptation, but it could be altered:

> It has been said that arguing against globalization is like *arguing against the laws of gravity*. But that does not mean we should accept a law that allows only heavyweights to survive. On the contrary, we must make globalization an engine that lifts people out of hardship and misery, not a force that holds them down.

To reverse the 'laws of gravity' and introduce social and environmental limits to the negative effects of globalization was also demanded by alternative globalization movements in Seattle, Doha and Porto Alegre. But selective regulation also characterizes globalization in terms of different regulatory areas (Lipschutz and Fogel 2002). While uniformity is institutionalized in global *financial* regulation, in spheres of *global environmental* or *social regulation* it is regarded as inefficient, as it would introduce politics into issues that should be addressed by efficient markets. The theme of inevitability in globalization discourses rests on this assumption of 'the invisible hand', the myth of self-regulating markets.

A system that is able to regulate itself indeed resembles a force of nature; this is what *homeostasis* refers to in systems theory. Such self-regulating systems do not require intervention, as this can disrupt the 'natural processes'. However, the markets are not natural systems and their survival-as-usual need not be the utmost goal maintained by the international system. Furthermore, the very possibility and meaning of self-regulation is problematic as described by Rousseau (1762 [1968]: 68):

> It is not good for him who makes the laws to execute them. [. . .] Nothing is more dangerous than the influence of private interests in public affairs, and the abuse of the laws by the government is a less evil than the corruption of the legislator, which is the inevitable sequel to a particular standpoint. In such a case, the State being altered in substance, all reformation becomes impossible. A people that would never misuse governmental powers would never misuse independence; a people that would always govern well would not need to be governed.

This scepticism about corporate self-regulation should not suggest that fragmentation of social/environmental legislations is dictated by corporate agendas. There is considerable divergence in corporate, sectoral, regional and national interests regarding social/environmental legislations. This divergence of interests not only makes it unlikely to reach international consensus, but also creates clear advantages (for both corporate and state actors) for pursuing market-based, self-regulatory schemes: different corporations can opt for different national legislations whereas states can

exert some degree of control on their economic policies, by creating regulatory environments that promote certain sectors. More importantly, the
so-called 'developing' countries resist global standards on environment as
they are likely to be dictated by industrialized countries.

Karl Polanyi (1944: 3) regarded self-regulating markets as a 'stark
utopia', because the evolution of markets and regulation were intertwined,
and markets needed rules in order to function. Moreover, the social order
would inevitably be disrupted by a self-regulating market. The famous
'double movement' he conceptualized, demonstrates how *the paradox* of
the self-regulating market is resolved in practice: dislocations caused by
free markets are almost always counterbalanced by actions of various
classes in society, as well as the state. These cushioning acts keep the speed
of *laissez faire* forces under control and allow for social adjustment. This
is still the case, as different social groups (now transnationally) try to
limit the disruption of the socio-ecological fabric by demanding 'global
regulation of social/environmental externalities' (Lipschutz and Fogel
2002: 136).

However, as Rousseau (1762) has foreseen in the quote above, the
state, altered in substance, no longer assumes this responsibility. On the
contrary, as Blair's speech highlights, capital is invited, and further promoted while social values are adjusted to the new order. Governments
act as mediators when IMF prescriptions must be accepted by or forced
upon the society, as has been the case in Argentina and Turkey in the
early 2000s. Protests of dislocated peoples against large-scale development projects (often supported by a development bank) reveal how this
new role of the state is played out in countries that prioritize industrialization (such as India, Laos, Brazil and Israel). In this context, the corporation represents the medium between hypermobile capital and the public
sphere. Its image, as the primary if not the only *social institution* capable
of embracing *and* benefiting from the new global order, further consolidates the stakeholder view of the firm. Moreover, the diffused global
order of the corporations (that is capital markets) challenges the order
among states. This does not suggest governance *without* government,
but a redefinition of the role of state actors, the only accountable representatives of people in international relations. If governments no longer
perceive their role as 'counterbalancing the disruptive effects of the global
market economy (i.e. market failures) on the society', but as 'to facilitate
the market' in establishing and consolidating its order, how could it be
argued that state sovereignty is withering away? The next section focuses
on this question.

5.4.3   Turning the Tables Around: Markets Correct State Failures

In the earlier narratives of liberal capitalism the invisible hand of the market was expected to take care of inefficiencies and externalities within a certain capitalist system. The neo-liberal narratives of global free trade and open markets rely on the notion of competitive statehood facilitating these processes. Thus, market failures take place at the global level and not only do they become more difficult to detect, but also more difficult for (most) actors to intervene. Simultaneously, statehood as such is being transformed as national legislations are subjugated to global regimes. With the increasing influence of the WTO on trade policies, the IMF on monetary policies and the World Bank on developmental policies, it is often states that are regulated by the institutions of the 'market order'. The architecture of global governance consolidates the dominant narratives of neo-liberal globalization into concrete structural programmes, international agreements and governance mechanisms.

To take part in this new order, state actors reinvent their functions, but the state is hardly withering away. While questioning the self-regulating capabilities of the market, Hardt and Negri (2004: 107) also note that 'the private authority that emerges in this realm of business contracts can exist only with the backing of political authorities. [. . .] Behind every utopia of capitalist self-government there is a strong supporting political authority'.

Faced with increasingly stringent global regulations, governments may even *benefit from* the blurring boundaries between public and private, and from the obfuscation that national economic policies are dictated by global financial markets.

One way states exercise such power is the production of *new forms of legality*, which are in line with the order of global capital markets. These *new* forms of legality are not the not-so-recent Bretton Woods institutions (which seamlessly merge with an international legal system), but private governance institutions of the last two decades, such as partnerships, private standardization and self-regulation institutions, or carbon markets. These new mechanisms maintain (and even symbolize) the fragmentation of global social/environmental policies: Type-II partnerships, initially designed to complement international agreements (the Type-I outcomes), reveal how governments failed to reach an agreement on *any* environmental issue discussed at the WSSD. Carbon markets represent not only a minimal and ineffectual consensus among governments, but more importantly, their agreement that climate and energy policies remain within their jurisdiction. When state actors perceive a private standardization mechanism as harmful to their interests, they endorse other similar 'private' mechanisms – the competition that the Malaysian

Timber Certification Council posed to the Forest Stewardship Council's standards by more relaxed private regulation is an example. Mostly, the fragmentation maintained by these arrangements is agreeable to both state and corporate actors.

With their emphasis on market-based approaches and voluntary/private origins, new forms of legality transform the social/environmental sphere towards compatibility with the logic of the market. The effectiveness and sustainability of these approaches remain ambiguous, since they are not regulated or monitored. Yet, in the regulatory vacuum of globalization, private governance mechanisms fill a certain gap resulting from the fragmented interests of political actors. Thus, privatization of governance represents the consolidation of partial, fragmented, and preferential solutions to social/environmental problems originating from the very process of globalization.

Global private governance mechanisms appear to function as remedies to the 'inevitable' consequences of globalization, where one can observe, this time, not market failures but *state failures*. Governance deficits simply refer to these state failures as creating an internationally uniform set of rules that arches over fragmented national policies. Such an image is put forth by the partnerships concept that the United Nations develop, as mechanisms to implement what states failed to implement, or in the creation of environmental or labour standards by corporate actors as mechanisms to regulate where states fail to regulate. However, even when international legislation is in place, states are not able to implement these decisions. Even if these agreements are viewed as a response to social demands for remedying the disruptive consequences of self-regulating markets, states fail in their implementation, as their authority to regulate and enforce is curbed by the rules of the rival 'market' order.

5.5   CONCLUSIONS: NEW FORMS OF LEGALITY

The aim of this chapter was to open up certain obscured debates related to partnerships in the context of globalization, by critically approaching privatization of governance. Partnerships may be only one form of private governance institutions, but they are both widespread and important as they are historically, socially and economically linked with privatization and its endorsement by the UN in achieving sustainable development since 2002. Analysing the historical background of the concept first in business law and then in relation to globalization reveals several important points about global governance in general and environmental governance in particular. Specifically, the application of the term partnerships to hybrid mechanisms of environmental governance points to a change towards the limitation of legal liabilities. Not only are failures difficult to detect due to the voluntary, unmonitored nature of these arrangements, but in case of failure the responsibility is so diffused that no party can be held accountable.

In this process, liabilities of the partners involved are limited in three ways. Firstly, *corporate partners* involved in partnerships providing social and environmental goods or services gain public credibility. This may reduce public scrutiny. More critically, their liability regarding the side-effects of their core business activities are limited to the stringency of national environmental regulations or the standardization mechanisms of their choice. Secondly, *state partners* involved in partnerships do not assume monitoring functions. States consider their regulatory function limited by the 'requirements' of global capital. Finally, the UN's role in CSD partnerships also signifies the vacuum in global governance in general, summarized by governance gaps: accountability and monitoring mechanisms to oversee the activities of partnerships and the systematic effect of the partnerships regime are absent.

Some of these problems can be remedied, at least to some degree, if the CSD partnerships are obliged to sign two types of contracts. The first type of contract would be signed between the UNCSD and the partnership, with standard clauses regarding the monitoring of partnerships' activities and give some authority to the CSD partnerships team. The second type of contract would be signed among partners. These could vary on the basis of the nature of the project, but clearly state the role of each partner and establish accountability measures in cases of failure. This step would remedy some of the ambiguities in the partnerships regime, as well as providing better information for the decision-makers and the CSD regarding its systematic effects. However, it would not resolve the problems resulting from lack of political commitment; and the problem of partnerships with controversial approaches to sustainability would also remain unaffected.

Another conclusion to be drawn from the analysis is that the new forms of legality result from certain transformations at the global level. As the narratives of globalization and markets consolidate homogenization in financial governance the state resumes new functions, and invents ways of internalizing globalization and resisting it at once. By inventing new forms of legality the state system copes with the market order, while the continued fragmentation of social/environmental governance allows for state actors to maintain some degree of control over their economies. In contrast, the corporation becomes both a legitimate stakeholder in global politics and the medium between hypermobile capital and the public sphere. Hence, its social influence is consolidated.

While this is the case for the actors, privatization of governance also represents a change in understanding. As market failures are not corrected by the states and regarded as inevitable, they are transformed into *state failures* in social/environmental spheres. Governance deficits simply refer to these failures in creating a uniform set of global rules over fragmented national policies. Implementation deficits highlight how states are unable to implement, even when international environmental legislation is in place. Addressing governance deficits through private governance mechanisms presumes that global financial markets correct state failures. Sustainability partnerships, for instance, are mechanisms to implement what states failed to implement, (self-)regulate where states fail to regulate.

In this context, private governance institutions keep legislative discourses in social/environmental issue areas analogous to those of financial governance, operating within the same frames of reference. The question, then, is not so much whether the corporations and markets possess authority over social and environmental issues, but whether these demands should be made from them. Should *social and environmental* regulation fall in within the purview of markets or politics? In the final analysis, the answer will determine the legitimacy of privatization of environmental governance and its emerging institutions.

NOTES

1. This chapter draws on an earlier article: Mert, A. (2012), 'The Privatisation of Environmental Governance: On myths, forces of nature and other inevitabilities', *Environmental Values*, 21(4): 475–498.
2. All subsequent references to etymological roots are from Ernest Klein's (1971) *A Comprehensive Etymological Dictionary of the English Language*, Amsterdam: Elsevier.
3. Interview with trade union representative to CSD; New York, 2007.
4. Interview with business and industry representative to CSD; New York, 2007.
5. Global Compact website: http://unglobalcompact.org/AboutTheGC. Accessed: 2-5-2009.
6. Interview; New York, 2007.
7. Interview with business and industry representative to CSD; New York, 2007.
8. *First Report of Select Committee on Joint Stock Companies*, Parliamentary Papers, 1844, VII (in Saville 1956: 418).
9. *Select Committee on the Law of Partnership of 1851* Q.9 (in Saville 1956: 418–423).
10. *Evidence to the Mercantile Laws Commission*, 1854: 109 (in Bryer 1997: 37).

6. Partnerships and the discourse of sustainable development

6.1 INTRODUCTION

The most paradigmatic of all discourses that shape sustainability partnerships is that of sustainable development itself. It is their *raison d'être*, as well as the logical space in which CSD partnerships, in all their variety, appear as a single type of institution. It is not only into partnerships that the discourse of sustainable development has sedimented, but several other types of institutions as well: the UN's environment and development programmes in particular, but most UN system institutions use the term in their mission statements; international summits are held in the name of sustainable development; governments construct sustainable development programmes; corporations write sustainable development reports and establish their own global 'council' on the matter, and NGOs make sure that they merge it with their various aims and demands. Wherever one looks, one can find it is constantly reified.

Such omnipresence makes it difficult to analyze social phenomena, as it inhibits the construction of a uniform reality; what Arturo Escobar (1995: 5), following Michel Foucault, calls 'colonization of reality'. To critically analyze such hegemonic discourses, Ivan Illich's concept of 'radical monopoly' is useful. He observes that certain ('manipulative') institutions not only limit other modes of thought, but also make alternative institutions, technologies and lifestyles impossible. This chapter analyzes the colonization of reality by the sustainable development paradigm. The next section traces its ideological roots (developmentalism and environmentalism) in Western myths. Sections 6.3 and 6.4 examine the historical formation of these two ideologies separately, followed by a study of their merger, sustainable development. Conclusions address how sustainable development is appropriated by partnerships, and how sustainability partnerships have become radical monopolies.

6.2 FANTASMATIC LOGICS: MYTHS OF HUBRIS AND NEMESIS

Munck and O'Hearn (1999: 2) argue that development is a specifically Western myth that in many cultures and languages has no equivalent. While 'the West has demystified the myths and narratives of [other cultures], it has failed to deconstruct its own myths', and instead universalized them and made them 'the manifest destiny of all peoples' (ibid.: 21). Discourses of modernization and development have become central to social imaginaries across the globe and have been appropriated by non-western cultures as well. Nevertheless, the myth of development was indeed a product of Western history, and belonged to the Western psyche in particular.

In the centre of this Western imaginary is the idea of infinity; a point emphasized most famously by two philosophers from different ends of the political spectrum: Oswald Spengler and Cornelius Castoriadis. Castoriadis (1975 [1987]) reflects that the social imaginary of development, growth and infinity has replaced the notion of 'God' (the social imaginary of earlier times), and relates this change to its political and economic repercussions:

> Since there are no limits to the march of knowledge, there are no more limits to the march of our 'power' (and our 'wealth'); [. . .] limitations, when they present themselves, have a negative value and must be transcended. Certainly, whatever is infinite is inexhaustible, so that we will perhaps never achieve 'absolute' knowledge and 'absolute power'; but we ceaselessly draw nearer to them.

Spengler's (1919 [2011]) insight, in his *The Decline of the West*, was that the *prime symbol* (that represents social imaginary) of the modern Western civilization was *infinite space* while its counterpart in antiquity was a finite *point* in space (or the material and individual body). Michael Pretes (1997) observes this difference in arts (representations of the body *versus* an ethereal and infinite God), sciences (Euclidean geometry *versus* irrational numbers), architecture (a façade *versus* a skyscraper) as well as narratives (mythology *versus* history). Accordingly, the notion of development in Greek antiquity was a constrained growth relating to the inner logic of the being (its *telos*) unlike the modern Western variant, which understood development as infinite and linear growth.

Luigi Zoja (1993 [1995]: 7), in *Growth and Guilt: Psychology and the Limits of Development*, studies this change in the social imaginary by means of history and mythology, and notes that 'the myth of growth found its genesis in the disruption of the principles of moderation that originally flourished in ancient Greece' but the Western psyche still continues to 'nourish the taboos and fears of punishment that in the past were associated with arrogance and excessive fortune' and lives in fear of catastrophe. Zoja sees the myth of unlimited growth equivalent to the developmentalism observed in the contemporary (particularly Western) societies.[1] Accordingly, he sees *growth* as a metaphor that is increasingly prevalent in modernized societies that signifies *life itself*, and endless growth as an 'ingenuous metaphor for immortality' (ibid.: 12).

The Greeks acknowledged, feared and avoided the infinite, as their social imaginary was based on limits and a myth of moderation (Maor 1987: 4; Pretes 1997: 1422), which has equivalents in Taoist, Confucian, Buddhist and Hindu myths as well. This myth is based on *hýbris* and *némesis*, two central concepts of ancient Greek social and political organization (Zoja 1993 [1995]: 38–39). *Hubris* (presumption toward the gods) was the gravest of sins, committed by the transgression of the limits of one's conditions. A just man would not attempt to reproduce the qualities of gods,[2] which would be subtracting the quality from the god who represented it. If he did, he would invoke nemesis (divine wrath). The word *némesis* derives from *nemes*, indicating a just indignation, or a retributive justice, often provoked by the person whom it strikes. Zoja argues that the circularity between *hýbris* and *némesis* would function as distributive justice, which the Greek would experience as an unconscious drive unlike the modern rational notion of justice (ibid.: 53). When a hero infringed the sphere of gods, that is transgressed the borders of *humanness*, limits would be forced upon him by gods, as has been the case with the famous stories of Icarus, Prometheus or Phaeton. Icarus's story demonstrates the centrality of these concepts: when inventor Daedalus tries to escape from captivity by constructing two pairs of wings for himself and his son Icarus, he advises his son not to fly too high or too low, so that the wax holding the feathers together would neither melt nor get wet. When Icarus, excited by the flight, starts flying towards the heavens, he falls and dies. Deadalus's hubris is not respecting the laws of nature (or thinking natural limits can be overcome by technology), which brings divine wrath on his family.

The myths of limits and moderation demarcate the borders of human might, but they also have a 'natural' aspect. While the concept of *nemesis* represents 'divine vengeance visited upon mortals who infringe on those prerogatives the gods enviously guard for themselves', *Nemesis* the goddess represented, '*nature's* response to hubris: to the individual's presumption in seeking the attributes of a god' (Illich 1975: 34–35). As such, *nemesis* was about restoring the natural order. In the case of Icarus, for instance, there was no deity exacting the punishment; he simply fell as his wings no longer supported his weight. Even when there is divine involvement (such as the myth of Prometheus), the punishment is often a reminder of the cycles of nature and life.

The idea of 'divine limits' and the golden rule of 'maintaining the proper mean' were central to Greek thought, symbolized in the tale of Icarus by altitude, or by the principles governing the ideal city-state in Plato's *The Republic* (ca. 380 BC [2006]). Unlimited growth would be equivalent to theft from gods, as anything infinite was their prerogative. This principle of moderation was only dismissed after monotheism has rationalized the myth that the universality of Christianity and the Roman state would assume a global model on the basis of a coherent 'civilization of growth' (Zoja 1995: 105–114, my emphasis): accordingly, the goddess Nemesis embodied the ethics of limits and therefore stood at

> the line of demarcation that separates two Western concepts of history: to the one side we have the Christian and modern concepts that attribute history with tasks of rebirth, growth and improvement; to the other stands the Greek concept – closer to the typically Oriental attitude [. . .] – that sees the finest realization of history as a return to the confines of proper limits and thus as a restoration of a natural order that has come to be disturbed. *Various modern ideologies that attempt to restore morality to collective events by curbing the excesses of capitalism, of imperialism and of aggressive abuse of the environment can be understood as a re-evaluation of such a scheme*; and in terms of the psychogenesis of symbols that represent a return of the repressed goddess Nemesis.

In this sense, growth-focused developmentalism and limits-focused environmentalism reflect the central myth of Western cultures. Environmentalist movements, often accused of 'scaremongering', have a psycho-mythical relation to *némesis*. This is not to argue that developmentalism causes environmentalism, but rather that the mythical elements noted above can help us intuitively understand how the environmentalist critique belongs to same fantasmatic space with developmentalism. As Pretes (1997: 1424) notes, the practice of the Western social imaginary of infinite space consisted of 'controlling and taming of nature (deemed separate from humanity) for the benefit of the society [as well as] bringing all other societies into the Western worldview'. By doing so, he relates the environmentalist critique of development with the problems resulting from the social imaginary of infinite space and the myth of growth. He also implies a connection between colonialism and developmentalism, which is explored in the following section.

6.3 DEVELOPMENTALISM IN HISTORICAL PERSPECTIVE

This section analyzes the discourse of development starting with some deeper historical layers that structures contemporary international relations. Narrations around colonization, decolonization and developmentalism represent a historical continuity; many ideas remained intact whereas semantic constellations around development changed. Each section below highlights how the rhetoric was transformed significantly so that the residuals of earlier discourses are carefully concealed, while the direction of these discourses remained remarkably similar to the earlier ones.

This section also aims to reveal the political logics wherein colonialism, developmentalism and sustainable development have dealt with discursive challenges. This is not to suggest that anti-colonial and eco-political demands simply *caused* the change in the earlier hegemonic discourses, but reveals their presence and political influence.

6.3.1 Development in Colonialist Discourses

Max Havelaar, the polemical nineteenth-century novel by Multatuli (1860 [1987]), gives the Western account of the colonial developmentalist psyche in its full complexity. Multatuli's semi-autobiographical story entails the most progressive stance of its time, with its perturbing account of the ill-treatment and oppression inflicted upon the native peoples of today's Indonesia by the Dutch colonial administration. This exposé of the conditions of the native peoples under colonial rule created a big stir-up in Dutch society when it was first published, and led to welfare reforms in the Dutch Indies.

The protagonist Max Havelaar, after whom the global fair trade movement was named, is intensely concerned about the human condition. He finds himself in a position to help the Javanese people oppressed by their native prince as much as the colonial coffee trade. There is famine, migration and extreme poverty when Havelaar is appointed to the office of Assistant Resident of Lebak (in Java). When he arrives at Bantan-Kidul, he gives an inaugural speech to the native princes, capturing the essence of well-meaning developmentalism in the colonial era (Multatuli 1860 [1987]: 115–124). He starts with explaining his joy for being appointed to a poor region:

> I know that there is much that is good in Bantan-Kidul! But not only because of this was my heart rejoiced. [. . .] I perceived that your people are poor, and

> for this I was glad in my inmost soul. For I know that Allah loves the poor, and that He gives riches to those whom he will try. But *to the poor He sends the one who speaks His word*, that may lift up their heads in the midst of their *misery*.

Havelaar's sincerity is proven throughout the novel; he helps the natives, even when it might bring his downfall. He refuses his appointment to another district when his position and possibly life is in danger. He does these since he perceives himself as 'the one that speaks God's word', and that he is sent to help those in misery, almost like a prophet. The colonial rationale (coffee trade) for the impoverishment is absent in his speech, but he regards the Chiefs of Lebak as the responsible party (see below). Havelaar starts his analysis of poverty in Lebak by listing what he perceives as its symptoms:

> Is not the husbandman poor? Does not your paddy often ripen to feed those who did not plant it? [. . .] Is not the number of your children small? [. . .] Is it not bitter for you, to [. . .] see the mountains that bear no water on their flanks? Or the plains where never a buffalo drew the plough? Yes, yes. . . I say unto you that your soul and mine are sad because of these things. And for that very reason are we grateful to Allah that He has given us the power to labour here. [. . .] we have acres for many, though the dwellers in it are few. And it is not the rain which is lacking, for the tops of the mountains suck the clouds from heaven to earth. And it is not everywhere that rocks refuse room to the root, for in many places the soil is soft and fertile, and cries out for the grain, which she wishes to return to us in the bending ear.

He observes that there is no war in the land, nor sickness, drought, or floods. He claims that it is Allah's will that the place flourishes. But this is not the case. His perception of poverty and the indications of misery have several provocative aspects. Firstly, he recognizes that the land given by god is rich and fertile, therefore famines, immigration and lack of a healthy and abundant labour force are not normal. Secondly, this abnormality can be corrected, as it is not 'natural'. Thirdly, the labour of correcting this abnormality is a blessing and a responsibility for the colonial administrator. This is consistent with his understanding that 'the paddy that ripens to feed those who did not plant it' as an indication of poverty before it is a matter of injustice. In other words, poverty is a *function* of injustice or as we will see below, that of bad administration. Hence, it should be corrected. Redistribution, and the transformation of the Javanese social institutions, is therefore not only a matter of establishing order and ensuring justice, but also the condition that will allow for god's will (the labour of flourishing the land and increasing the yield) to be realized. Throughout the speech Havelaar makes it explicit that such an intervention is his god-given duty:

Our land is poor because we have made so many mistakes. [. . .] Chiefs of Lebak! We *all* wish to do our duty! But should there happen to be amongst us those who neglect their duty for gain [. . .] who shall punish them? [. . .] Listen to me, and I will tell you how justice would then be done.

In this exhilarating speech, reflecting his good intentions and idealism, Havelaar claims to be the one to know how justice will be done, and to deliver it. It is also his job to envisage the development of the region in the following fashion: 'If everyone is left in enjoyment of the fruit of his labours, there is no doubt that [. . .] the population will increase both in numbers and in possessions and culture, for these things generally go hand in hand.' If labour yields to individual possession, the region would develop economically and culturally.

Max Havelaar is such an important narration not only because of its literary value or social impact, but also because:

- Its *setting* is critical: it takes place at a time and place in which colonialism has already transformed the way the pre-colonial Javanese society has operated. The native princes in question oppress the people of Lebak owing to the combined effect of traditional values (such as largesse) and the tributes they pay to the Dutch government. When princes have responsibility towards the Dutch colonial administration rather than their community, problems of a (possibly already imperfect and unfair, but presumably previously functioning) social system is amplified.
- It is not an account of the evils of colonialism as such, nonetheless it is very realistic: it is a tragedy in which not only the idealistic colonial administrator finds no support in the Dutch colonial system, but also the parallel narration, the famous love story of a Javanese couple Adinda and Saïjah, ends up in their destruction. Multatuli sees the possibility of the local population to break this vicious circle of poverty and oppression as virtually non-existent.
- It openly talks about injustice and poverty caused by colonization and views 'the white man' as being in a position to do something about it. It is in the administrator's power and is his god-given duty to end misery, by ensuring 'development'. Hence, the inaugural speech Havelaar delivers sketches the colonial logic based on the ethic of 'the white man's burden' and equates it to the development of colonized lands.

This is not to say that the colonized societies were not being violently transformed. The idealistic profile of Max Havelaar is interesting because he is an outlier, and most of colonial rule was far from being so deeply concerned with the well-being of the colonized. As it depicts the best of colonial intentions, limitations become all the more obvious. Havelaar's interest in the well-being of the people of Lebak brings his own doom, showing how the identity of the colonized cannot be signified by the colonialist discourse. In fact, such humane considerations were so exceptional that Edward Said observes that Marx was one of the rare thinkers 'still able to sense some fellow feeling' with the suffering of the colonized, although he ultimately had to return to 'his protective Orientalized Orient' (1978 [1995]: 153–154). Here, Said refers to the underlying Romantic/messianic narrative wherein the white colonizers are depicted as missionaries helping out those in misery. This 'Orientalized Orient'[3] did not allow for a discussion of its people as individuals or communities with distinct identities: 'As human material the Orient is less important than as an element in a Romantic redemptive project'; the Orient was made up of 'artificial entities, [. . .] races, mentalities, nations, and the like' and hence it provided the grounds on which its population had to be treated in other ways than their Western counterparts (ibid.). He rightly observes that Marx (1853) gives up the humane consideration when he writes on the British rule in India:

> [S]ickening as it must be to human feeling to witness those myriads of industrious patriarchal and inoffensive social organizations disorganized and dissolved into their units, [. . .] and their individual members losing at the same time their ancient form of civilization, and their hereditary means of subsistence, we must not forget that these idyllic village-communities, inoffensive though they may appear, had always been the solid foundation of Oriental despotism, that they restrained the human mind within the smallest possible compass, making it the unresisting tool of superstition, enslaving it beneath traditional rules, depriving it of all grandeur and historical energies.

For Marx (1853), England had 'a double mission' in India; one destructive, as it annihilated the old Asiatic society, and the other regenerating, as it established the material basis of Western society in Asia. He saw historical materialism manifest in the process of colonization: England was causing a social revolution, the means of which need not be justified as she was only an 'unconscious tool of history in bringing about that revolution', without which Asia would not be able to 'fulfill its destiny' (ibid.). Marx's and Max Havelaar's narratives are similar in representing production as an ideal as well as the end goal of development; the native rule as oppressive; and in delinking the role of colonizers from that of the native oppressors. For this reason, Said notes that Marx was falling back on the Orientalized Orient and reproducing the same category of representation. This representation (justified whether by historical materialism or by Judeo-Christian conceit of god-given duty) created its mirror image on the side of the colonized, as the burden that the colonial rule leaves behind: a transformation that cannot be reversed, even after (or particularly because of) decolonization. This linear reading of history was depicted by Arundhati Roy (of the anti-/alter-globalization movement) in her prize winning novel *The God of Small Things* (1997: 52–53), when the once Oxford student Chako tells his cousins that

> though he hated to admit it, they were all Anglophiles. [. . .] Pointed in the wrong direction, trapped outside their own history, and unable to retrace their steps because their footprints had been swept away. [. . .] history was like an old house at night. With all the lamps lit. And ancestors whispering inside. 'To understand history', Chacko said, 'we have to go inside and listen to what they're saying. And look at the books and the pictures on the wall. And smell the smells. [. . .] But we can't go in [. . .] because we've been locked out. And when we look in through the windows, all we see are shadows. And when we try and listen, all we hear is a whispering. And we cannot understand the whispering, because our minds have been invaded by a war. A war that we have won and lost. The very worst of war. A war that captures dreams and re-dreams them. A war that has made us adore our conquerors and despise ourselves.'

Disdain of traditional ways of living and adoration of the Western ways colonized the reality of the native elite in the colonized lands, which later on became the governors of decolonized 'independent' countries (cf. Fannon 1961 [1967]). What matters most about Chacko's narration is the closing down of the way back: history becoming a house the colonized feel they are locked out of, even after decolonization. The psychological implication of this on the political subject is not an independent self-creation as suggested by the Enlightenment myths of national self-determination; on the contrary, it results in replicating similar systems of rule, of oppression and of depression in the aftermath of decolonization. Understanding colonization as a narrative of 'bringing civilization to the uncivilized' is the mirror image of the romantic albeit impossible longing for what was before colonization (nativism) as the colonized are locked out of their own history. Hence, Chako continues:

> We're prisoners of War. [. . .] Our dreams have been doctored. We belong to nowhere. We sail unanchored on troubled seas. We may never be allowed ashore. Our sorrows will never be sad enough. Our joys never happy enough. Our dreams never big enough. Our lives never important enough. To matter. (Roy 1997: 53)

In *Culture and Imperialism*, Said (1994: 27–28) observes how the dreams of the colonized have been doctored and re-dreamt, when he observes

*Table 6.1   The legitimation of 'ontological absence' of the colonized and
the responsibility language used in international treaties in the
nineteenth and twentieth centuries*

Year	Document	Agreement included
1884–1885	The General Act of the Berlin (Congo) Conference	'to educate the natives and to teach them to understand and appreciate the benefits of civilization'.
1892	The General Act for the Repression of Slave Trade (The Brussels Act, Article 2)	'to increase their welfare; to raise them to civilization and bring about the extinction of barbarous customs'.
1919	League of Nations Covenant (Article 22)	to assume tutelage for the well-being and development of 'peoples not yet able to stand by themselves under the strenuous conditions of the modern world'.
1945	United Nations Charter (Article 73)	to 'promote constructive measures of development' and assume guardianship of 'peoples who have not yet attained a full measure of self-government'.

that 'imperialism has monopolised the entire system of representation' and therefore, even after the colonizers physically depart, they retain the colonies as markets and as 'locales on the ideological map over which they continued to rule morally and intellectually'. From the perspective of the colonizers, this was a furtherance of their mission based on the idea of bringing civilization to the uncivilized, who are unable to invent and/or appreciate it (see Table 6.1 for the continuing ontological absence of the colonized as the political subject). In parallel fashion, decolonization was often led by the elite, formed and produced by the same colonial power. In effect, they 'tended to replace the colonial force with a new class-based and ultimately exploitative one, which replicates the old colonial structures in new terms' (ibid.: 269).

Decolonization is not a reconciliatory process. In the West, it failed to create a public space for an account of what the colonial rule undermined. Contemporary Western discourses on colonization still exclude what was terminated (of the traditional ways of living and being) from the space of representation mainly by reifying how 'the colonized world was in some ways ontologically speaking lost to begin with' (ibid.: 28). This is manifest in the Western perceptions of the Orient, in which the authoritarian and/ or corrupt regimes, inequalities, poverty, violence and oppression in the former colonies were brought in as evidence to this ontological inferiority. Later, the same narratives were employed to legitimize development projects, or even military occupation. Neither is decolonization a reconciliatory process for the former colonies that experience their independence through nationality, nationalism and nativism. As Said observes (ibid.: 277), these are increasingly restrictive processes that result in increasingly authoritarian rules. The circle is thus closed as more oppressive regimes justify further Western interventionism. For Said, to break this circle would require recognizing the interdependence of the histories of the colonizers and the colonized.

Most importantly, the independence myths that romanticize the pre-colonial native disregard the contingency of the social. In other words, decolonization did not produce a return to pre-colonial systems of rule. This could not have been the case, either: firstly because of the ontological absence of the colonized as political subjects for extended periods of time, secondly because the elites leading decolonization were incapable of capturing the inequalities, injustices and the antagonisms of native systems, and finally because the native systems (and peoples) too would have changed in time – hence, systems from the times before colonization would be impossible to directly re-establish. Thus, decolonization replicates the mirror images of *burdened white man* and the *locked-out native*. In Roy's narration, the history has been 'locked' by colonization and the key cannot be retrieved as post-colonial societies cannot address their modern problems with pre-colonial, native rules. This practical observation also implies that symbolically, a myth of origin must be 'perfect' and signify fantasmatic wholeness.

With the post-WWII decolonization process, the Western supposition of 'civilizing' the colonies could no longer be maintained. In the Atlantic Charter, the United States determined one of the terms of its engagement in the WWII as 'the rights of all peoples to choose the form of government under which they live' should be respected; after the war the US pursued this clause to make sure several empires gave up their colonies. Paradoxically, while *Max Havelaar* ended up in the compulsory curriculum in the new Indonesian Republic (with a change in the story of Adinda and Saïjah into a heroic happy ending), Havelaar's colonial developmentalism was no longer a feasible discourse. White man's burden was lifted. The new United Nations Charter (UN 1945) employed a new vocabulary: to 'promote constructive measures of development' and assume guardianship of 'peoples who have not yet attained a full measure of self-government' (Table 6.1). Thus colonialism and developmentalism were discursively unlinked.

Throughout the Cold War, both the Soviet Union and the United States went through rapid industrial development and economic growth (see below). Both superpowers ensured that countries under their hegemony (and sympathetic movements in the countries under the other's sphere of influence) were supported ideologically and financially. Their strategies were rather similar although the rhetoric each employed reflected their ideological positions. In this sense, developmentalism (as intervention) was a particularly American concept, as opposed to the notion of 'internationalist class formation' that the Soviet Union employed to justify these interventions. Although the military side of these struggles and aid is by no means minor, in order to remain focused on the history of developmentalism, the following section studies the new semantic constellation, in which development was placed. For this, it juxtaposes a non-fictional and far better known inaugural speech to Max Havelaar's: Harry Truman's *Four Point Speech* (1949), which he made after the first post-war elections in the US.

6.3.2   Developmentalism as the New International Paradigm

An entry point to the study of the new semantic network in which development was a central node is Harry Truman's inaugural address on January 20, 1949, which is often regarded as the start of the development paradigm in international relations (cf. Sachs 1992a; Escobar 1995; Rist 1997). The *Four Point Speech* (Truman 1949) prescribed the vision put forth at the end of the WWII by Truman in four points: (1) to support the newly-established UN, (2) to continue with post-war economic reconstruction (particularly of Europe), (3) to continue protecting allies from (Soviet) aggression. Point four was about development:

> Fourth, we must embark on a bold new program for making the benefits of our scientific advances and industrial progress available for the improvement and growth of *underdeveloped* areas. More than half the people of the world are living in conditions approaching *misery*. Their food is inadequate, they are victims of disease. Their economic life is *primitive* and *stagnant*. Their poverty is a handicap and a *threat* both to them and to more prosperous areas. For the first time in history humanity possesses the knowledge and the skill to relieve the suffering of these people [. . .] I believe that we should make available to peace-loving peoples the benefits of our store of technical knowledge in order to help them realize their aspirations for *a better life* [. . .]

This should be a cooperative enterprise in which all nations work together through the UN [. . .] With *the cooperation of business, private capital, agriculture, and labor in this country*, this program can greatly increase the *industrial activity* in other nations and can raise their standards of living. [. . .]

The old imperialism – exploitation for foreign profit – has no place in our plans. What we envisage is a program of development based on the concepts of democratic fair dealing. [. . .] Greater production is the key to prosperity and peace. And the key to greater production is a wider and more vigorous application of modern scientific and technical knowledge.

This speech is recognized by development critics as having 'provided the cognitive base for both arrogant interventionism from the North and pathetic self-pity in the South' (Sachs 1992a: 2). By casting off of more than half of the world as *underdeveloped*, Truman transformed images of self and other, wherein over half of the world population

ceased to be what they are, in all their diversity, and were transmogrified into an inverted mirror of others' reality: a mirror that belittles them and sends them off to the end of the queue, a mirror that defines their identity, which is really that of a heterogeneous and diverse majority, simply in the terms of a homogenizing and narrow minority. (Esteva 1992: 6–7)

This is why for Esteva (ibid.: 9) the vernacular use of development metaphor 'gave global hegemony to a purely Western genealogy of history, robbing peoples of different cultures of the opportunity to define the forms of their social life'. This is no different from the experience of Chako; assuming uniformity of histories and a linear conception of development is similar in both colonial and developmentalist discourses.

At the same time, economic growth and techno-science have become the most important criteria of progress. For Truman, the 'miserable state' in which more than half of the world lived was a result of their 'primitive and stagnant' economic life: while the word *primitive* resonates with colonial discourses, the word *stagnant* points to economies that are not growth-oriented. The way out of this situation was the replacement of these economic systems with the growth-oriented capitalism, with a focus on industrial production. To modernize other spheres of life was possible through science, technology, and industry ('as these things go hand in hand' Havelaar would add). To receive US aid, however, depended on two conditions. One was apparently this capitalistic condition that the recipient countries would have to agree to. The second, subtler and implicit condition was the acceptance of this new category of being underdeveloped. In order to conceive the possibility of ending a situation, one has to agree with being in that condition. Hence, to call oneself 'developing' requires first the perception that one is underdeveloped, which brings with it 'the whole burden of connotations that this carries' (ibid.: 6–7). In this sense, Truman's speech was an intervention in the phantasmal order of what is desirable and how it could be attained, which had repercussions for the identity formation of the newly independent, post-colonial nations. It was not so much that a president of the United States was articulating a hegemonic world view that was the problem, but that this worldview recognized plurality neither historically nor into the future.

Historically this uniformity was manifest in the politico-semantic intervention which replaced the colonizer/colonized contrast (that expressed the inequalities rising from colonial domination) with a new one: developed/underdeveloped. The difference between these two couplets was the rhetorical vanishing of the relations of domination, which is indeed 'at the heart of the dialectic of development and underdevelopment' (Latouche 1989 [1996]: 82). This transformation not only naturalizes history to dismiss the ongoing effects of colonization and decolonization, but also conceals the question of how the 'development' of the already-developed countries had once taken place. In Esteva's (1992: 12) words, developmentalism 'displays a falsification of reality produced through dismembering the totality of interconnected processes that make up the world's reality and, in its place, it substitutes one of its fragments, isolated from the rest as a general point of reference'.

This new paradigm would not only universalize development, recognizing it as a sovereign right and duty for all nations, but also erase the extent to which Western development was built on (and by) colonial interactions. Hence, Esteva agrees with Said on the interdependence of histories, this time not between the West and the Orient (the colonizer and the colonized), but (as it causally follows) among countries whose different levels of development were interdependently shaped. Accordingly, by the 1980s, the east/west divide has been replaced by a north/south divide on the basis of development levels, assessed by presumably impartial development indicators. The Brandt line, suggested by the Brandt Commission in their report *North–South: A Programme for Survival* (Figure 6.1) visually depicts the economic split between North and South, encircling the world at the latitude of 30° N, with the exception of Australia and New Zealand. This gulf between economies was described with no reference to history; and the *impoverishment* caused by colonization was translated into an economic narrative of *poverty*, based on 'objective and calculable' indicators.

The second point refers not to the *historical* uniformity but to the short-term effects of this uniform world vision. Gilbert Rist argues that the development programme suggested by the United States and employed by the UN bureaucracy allowed for the deployment of a new 'anti-colonial imperialism' by keeping several national liberation movements in control

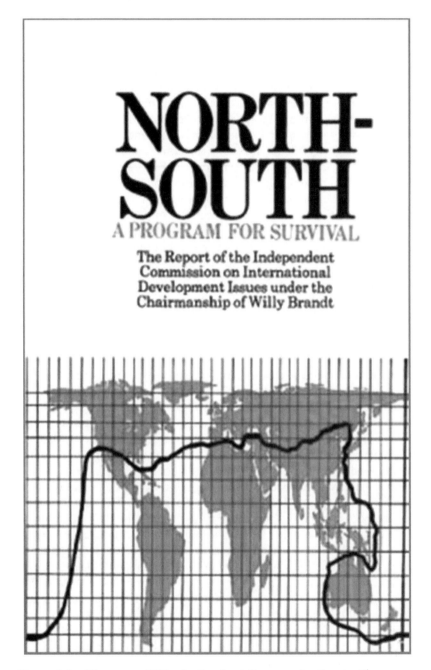

Figure 6.1   The cover of 'North–South: A Program for Survival'[4]

and gaining access to these new markets. Nevertheless, this does not, on its own, explain how the development paradigm has also been internalized by the modernist movements within the so-called 'developing' countries. In order to understand this, we need to retrieve Said's observation that the entire system of representation was monopolized by imperialism, which allowed for the colonizers to retain their former colonies *not only as markets*, but also through moral and intellectual influence after decolonization. In other words, before the realities, the fantasies were colonized. Truman was correct in his foresight that this new paradigm would be different from old imperialism ('exploitation for foreign profit'): development not only enticed the rulers, intelligentsia and the elite, but this time to a large extent the people of these lands. It was not a conspiracy theorized by the politicians of industrialized countries and the UN bureaucracy, it colonized the reality of developed and underdeveloped alike, once these categories were accepted by the categorized. But this internalization could only take place because of the fantasy that developmentalism evoked: the role of fantasy in politics is not to create a *false* illusion for the political subjects, but rather to allow for intersubjectively constructed realities to exist in, and at times dominate, the public domain.

Fantasies ensure that the radical contingency of social reality remains in the background and does not disrupt the worldview: only the objects of the political appear contingent. They save the political subject from intolerable fragmentation of 'reality', and entice them to the assumption that the difference between *what is* and *what ought* would diminish through a limited number of political actions. The logic of fantasy in the post-WWII developmentalist discourse, suggested that the difference between *what is* and *what ought* would diminish with the achievement of development, in some places through revolution, in others through independence, or careful alliance building.[5]

Finally, this vision placed a uniform goal in front of all nations *for the future*: to develop. As Roland Barthes (1957 [1987]: 117) reflects, myths are metaphors that 'transform history into nature', and the myth of developmentalism does so quite literally: development is a biological metaphor (Sachs 1992a). Underdevelopment is not the opposite of development, but its 'embryonic form' (Rist 1997: 74), hence the only logical or even possible route to take is those of the already 'developed' countries. The initial use of the word *development* in biology described a process wherein the potentialities of an 'organism are released until it reaches its natural, complete, fully-fledged form', the failure of which would be an anomaly; the concept was transferred to the social sphere only in the late eighteenth century, interweaving 'the Hegelian concept of history and the Darwinist concept of evolution' (Esteva 1992: 8–9). The implication of this biological metaphor is that neither returning to an earlier state is possible, nor to pause or stop this process is conceivable. Hence, the metaphor suggests that any society that is not growing ('developing') is dead or disqualified ('rogue states', 'axis of evil' or 'underdeveloped areas threatening the prosperous' depending on the political context). Yet, Truman also insisted on a non-expansionist form of growth, not through colonialism, but a constantly growing economy. In other words, economic growth is made the condition for development, which is in turn the condition of progress. Hence, the evolutionary metaphor contributed to the reification of developmentalism.

From this uniformity about the past, the present and the future emerged a new semantic constellation to which 'development' was tied: progress through techno-science, economic growth through industrialization, idealization of a system that merges liberal democracy with a capitalist economic system, and increasing control over the wealth, health and lifestyle of the population under a modernization project. Critics suggest that Truman's speech marked the beginning of this new ideology: the era of American hegemony (Esteva 1992: 6; Rist 1997: 75–76), together with an era of underdevelopment (Esteva 1992: 6–7). The former was because Truman transmogrified the meaning of development and made it the emblem of the era of American hegemony. With all its references to techno-science and industrialization, the speech placed the Western societies at the top of the global hierarchy. The US was 'pre-eminent among nations in the development of industrial and scientific techniques, [its] resources in technical knowledge constantly growing and inexhaustible' (Truman 1949).[6] However, the very existence of countries that 'achieved' industrialization outside of the capitalist order required yet another step in Truman's intervention – the justification of capitalism (Sachs 1992a: 2):

> Truman launched an idea of development in order to provide a comforting vision of a world order where the US would naturally rank first. The rising influence of the Soviet Union [. . .] forced him to come up with a vision that would engage the loyalty of decolonizing countries in order to sustain his struggle against communism.

Sachs' observation also indicates that Soviet socialism was similar to American capitalism in its relationship with nature, development and industrialization. Even before WWII, the Soviet Union put energy production as a top priority, constructing a network of thirty power plants between 1920 and 1931, with heavy environmental impacts. In the two decades following WWII, the Soviet economy largely relied on heavy and extractive industries. The aim of transforming an agrarian society to an industrial one was not so different than American industrialization, although its political organization had considerably diverged. In other words, although development as a hegemonic project was an American invention, development as a national economic strategy (characterized by industrialization, and increased levels of production and consumption) was by no means solely American, as the Brandt line graphically captured. Development as a fantasy was already becoming worldwide.

Ben Okri's prize winning novel *The Famished Road* (1992) provides a good counterpoint to Truman's narration of development. It details the spread of developmentalism during decolonization and successive nation-building/modernization processes. This is a story of development in a poor African village. The development of a small boy, Azaro, and his family (towards a deeper understanding of the world they live in) is made possible through their ceaseless journeys in a spiritual world, made up of dreams and nightmares, of witchcraft, healing, evil-doing and wisdom. As Azaro grows, his narration of their journeys in this real/spiritual/magical world gradually turns into an understanding of politics. At no point does the narration separate the real from the spiritual, other than immediate political events: the distribution of milk powder that poisons the whole village, the violence that political shambles give rise to, the riots against the white man, and the escape of the village photographer (who documented these events) from the corrupt policemen, and Mafioso politicians after him.

> We grew more afraid. Silence made it easier for us to be more powerless. The forms of dominance grew more colossal in the nightspaces. And those of us who were poor, who had no great powers on our side, and who didn't see the power of our own hunger, a power that would frighten even the gods, found that our dreams became locked out of the freedom of the air. Our yearnings became *blocked out of the realms of manifestation*. The battles for our destiny raged and we could no longer fly to the moon or accompany the aero-planes on their journeys through rarefied spaces or imagine how our lives could be different and better. So we had bad dreams about one another. (Okri 1992: 495)

The Famished Road is also a story of developmentalism: development aid comes in the shape of products and services (such as milk powder, electricity and roads); or political reform (such as elections and party politics). These 'developments' – sometimes indirectly, but often directly – bring with them violence, prostitution, deepening social stratification and impoverishment, while they take away the traditional and organic (albeit imperfect) ways of being, living and imagining a future. Once the 'real' aeroplanes of the white man (in collaboration with the Party of the Rich) arrive, it is no longer possible to fly to the moon on the wings of a cricket; the villagers can neither accompany the aeroplanes on their journeys through rarefied spaces nor can they imagine how their lives could be different and better. In this sense, Okri shows how developmentalism creates a radical monopoly, frustrating the ways of thinking that belong to the communities in question. He makes references to being blinded to 'the power of [their] own hunger', how their dreams 'became locked out of the freedom of the air' and how their 'yearnings became blocked out of the realms of manifestation' (ibid.). These references simultaneously indicate how reality is colonized, and how the Southern political subject is once more rendered without agency.

The similarity of the two Southern narrations depicting the hegemonic projects of colonialism and developmentalism is remarkable. Roy's locked-out native and Okri's underdeveloped villagers are both blocked out of history and representation. Both complain that their dreams are transformed by what happens beyond their reach. In *The Famished Road* myths and dreams are related, and different mythologies represent contesting hegemonic projects:

> The political parties waged their battles in the spirit spaces, beyond the realm of our earthly worries. They fought and hurled counter-mythologies at one another, [. . .] for the supremacy in the world of spirits. [. . .]
> The party of the Rich drew support from the spirits of the Western world. At night, over our dreams, pacts were made, contracts drawn up in the realm of nightspace, and our futures were mortgaged, our destinies delayed. In that realm the sorcerers of politics unleashed thunder, rain flooded those below; counter-thunder, lightning and hail were returned. On and on it went, in every village, every city of the country, and all over the continent and the whole world, too. Our dreams grew smaller as they waged their wars of political supremacy. (Ibid.: 496)

Okri implies a potential beginning to an 'African Renaissance'. As dreams get smaller the African political subject ends up in a vicious circle: when poverty becomes equivalent to underdevelopment, it implies a natural hierarchy. As a result the political subject is undermined and the cause of every problem becomes underdevelopment. On the other hand, the imperfections of pre-colonial nativity and pre-developmental social life do not provide the political agency needed to overcome oppression or reflect on these imperfections, either. The only power for Okri's political subjects comes from the power of their own hunger. It can be used to separate the two sets of problems (the imperfections resulting from traditional ways of living versus those resulting from inequalities generated by developmentalism), which do not necessarily require the same kind of solutions.

The two Western narrations can be juxtaposed to this background. Colonial and post-colonial discourses on developmentalism are represented by the two inaugural speeches (that of the fictional colonial administrator and the actual US president). The differences between the two speeches are clear: God is replaced by techno-science as the reason to (help) develop other lands. This change requires a new basis for the selection of who benefits from this charity. This was one of the reasons for the production of 'impartial' development indicators. The modern techno-scientific *épistémè* constructed a new vision on justice through these indicators. This has not only influenced the way the UN organizations have operated, but also solidified the inferiority of those sent to the end of the queue. In other words, techno-science became the only medium that was commendable in pursuing progress and development.

Another difference is the causality between war and production. In Havelaar's speech there is no war in Lebak, hence there can be abundant production. Truman reverses the causality: not only is greater production the condition for peace, poverty is a threat both to the poor and to the prosperous. This inversion is critical, firstly because reduction of poverty is made into self-interest for the rich; secondly, since it rests on the logical condition that the poor are a threat to the prosperous, and to peace. Then, Truman sets the condition that the benefits of knowledge will be made available only to peace-loving peoples. As greater production is the condition for peace, only those that aim at greater production (as opposed to, for instance, greater equality, universal employment or other socialist ideals) can be peace-loving. Hence, this inversion rhetorically marginalizes the poor and creates an antagonistic 'other', identifying the poor with the socialist.

A third difference between the two speeches is how they draw the boundaries of normality. Havelaar sees production in Java as normal; the soil is fertile and the people are willing. It is due to administrative injustices that abnormalities such as famine and immigration take place. In Truman's speech, this normality is inverted. The normal situation is not necessarily production; what exists as a socio-economic system in more than half of the world is primitive and stagnant. Only through the medium of technology can development be achieved, and its universal application to relieve human suffering is possible only for the first time in history. Historical achievements of these societies are cast aside by this narration unless they have acquired this medium Truman speaks of. Sharing it, however, depends on the conditions stated above.

The similarities in the contents of these two speeches are equally interesting: despite the decoupling of colonialism and development, colonial ideals such as increased production through the introduction of private property, interlinkage of cultural and economic development, as well as the will to expand (this time not to new lands, but to new areas of influence and/or markets) were retained. The discourse of colonization was sacrificed while the commitment to capitalist economy and political influence (through seemingly charitable action) was maintained. Both Havelaar and Truman use health, prosperity, production and abundance of food as the criteria to separate what is miserable from what is desirable. The duty to help 'people in misery' resonates in both speeches. Havelaar's feeling of responsibility is a god-given duty for which he appears thankful, whereas Truman's belief that human suffering should be relieved stems from the sheer possibility that it *can* be done, now that humanity possesses the knowledge and skill. Either dictated by a god or techno-science, they both speak from a position of *might*, which brings with it an assumed responsibility towards others.

Finally, both Havelaar and Truman call upon structural changes in societies to which they have some (unrepresentative) relation, which are in their perception in a miserable state. Havelaar asks for princes to moderate their demands from the peasants in Java. Truman does not make it as explicit, but refers to a certain democratic fair dealing and a condition of being 'peace-loving peoples'. The structural changes suggested by Truman are made much more explicit in a report by the United Nations Department of Social and Economic Affairs, titled *Measures for the Economic Development of Underdeveloped Countries*, in 1951 (in Escobar 1995: 3):

> [R]apid economic progress is impossible without painful adjustments. Ancient philosophies have to be scrapped; old social institutions have to disintegrate; bonds of caste, creed and race have to burst; and large numbers of persons who cannot keep up with progress have to have their expectations of a comfortable life frustrated. Very few communities are willing to pay the full price of economic progress.

Understandably, rapid economic progress was desirable for the reconstruction efforts in the post-WWII era. But the quote above suggests a very specific way of transforming societies, which was by no means the only option. The impediment between the existing situation and the fantasy of fulfilment (expectations of a comfortable life) is explicitly stated as the ancient philosophies, old social institutions and traditional bonds. Economic progress is 'impossible' unless they are given up. As discussed in the previous chapter in relation to globalization, narratives of inevitability are often employed as a discursive political strategy to establish hegemony. The suggestion that a radical transformation of traditional values is necessary is also identical to Tony Blair's depiction of globalization. Moreover, it shows that development is not a solely economic endeavour, but 'a perception which models reality, a myth which comforts societies and a fantasy which unleashes passion' (Sachs

1992a: v). The popular challenge to this powerful model of reality is the subject of the next section.

6.4 ENVIRONMENTALISM IN HISTORICAL PERSPECTIVE

> 'I hate that dam', Smith said. 'That dam flooded the most beautiful canyon in the world.'
>
> 'We know', Hayduke said. 'We feel the same way you do. But let's think about easier things first. I'd like to knock down some of them power lines they're stringing across the desert. And those new tin bridges up by Kite. And the god-damned road-building they're doing all over the canyon country. We could put in a good year just taking the fucking goddamned bulldozers apart.'
>
> 'Hear, hear', the doctor said. 'And don't forget the billboards. And the strip mines. And the pipelines. And the new railroad from Black Mesa to Page. And the coal-burning power plants. And the copper smelters. And the uranium mines. And the nuclear power plants. And the computer centers. And the land and cattle companies. And the wildlife poisoners. And the people who throw beer cans along the highways.'
>
> 'I throw beer cans along the fucking highways', Hayduke said. 'Why the fuck shouldn't I throw fucking beer cans along the fucking highways?'
>
> 'Now, now. Don't be so defensive.'
>
> 'Hell', Smith said, 'I do it too. Any road I wasn't consulted about that I don't like, I litter. It's my religion.'
>
> 'Right', Hayduke said. 'Litter the shit out of them.'
>
> 'Well now', the doctor said. 'I hadn't thought about that. Stockpile the stuff along the highways. Throw it out the window. Well . . . why not?'
>
> 'Doc', said Hayduke, 'it's liberation.'
>
> The night. The stars. The river. Dr. Sarvis told his comrades about a great Englishman named Ned. Ned Ludd. They called him a lunatic but he saw the enemy clearly. Saw what was coming and acted directly. And about the wooden shoes, *les sabots*. The spanner in the works. Monkey business. The rebellion of the meek. Little old ladies in oaken clogs.
>
> 'Do we know what we're doing and why?'
>
> 'No.'
>
> 'Do we care?'
>
> 'We'll work it out as we go along. Let our practice form our doctrine, thus assuring precise theoretical coherence.' [. . .]
>
> 'I'm thinking: Why the fuck should we trust each other? I never even met you two guys before today.'
>
> Silence. The three men stared into the fire. The oversize surgeon. The elongated riverman. The brute from the Green Berets. A sigh. They looked at each other. And one thought: What the hell. And one thought: They look honest to me. And one thought: Men are not the enemy. Nor women either. Nor little children.
>
> Not in sequence but in unison, as one, they smiled. At each other. The bottle made its penultimate round.
>
> 'What the hell', Smith said, 'we're only talkin.'

(Edward Abbey 1975[2006], *The Monkey Wrench Gang*, Philadelphia: Lippincott: 68–70)

Political connotations of 'sustainability' originate from the employment of the term by ecological, environmental, green movements and thought. As the excerpt from Edward Abbey's *The Monkey Wrench Gang* captures, despite their differences these movements share a common concern regarding the ecology/economy balance and the organization of modern societies. In Zoja's words, they remind us of the return of goddess Nemesis.

In the nineteenth century, worldviews concerned with these issues have already been formulated by various thinkers. But movements specifically concerned with the environment in the political sense (that aimed at polarizing the social space on the issue of environment, and politicize 'nature' which was previously an apolitical matter), emerged in the post-WWII period. This section focuses on *eco-political* thought and movements to understand sustainability.

6.4.1 Ideational Roots of 'Limits'

Daedalus: or, Science and the Future was a lecture given by biologist J.B.S. Haldane (1924) at Cambridge University in 1923, which was later published as a book. Although it had a rather liberal/progressive tone regarding the way science revolutionizes social life, it simultaneously expressed scepticism over some scientific advances of the time, most notably over the studies of eugenics. For Haldane, unless a scientific advance was accompanied by a corresponding change in ethics, it would not bring progress to mankind. Daedalus's controversial ethical choices made him the embodiment of this observation. Haldane regarded Daedalus as an interesting figure (far more interesting than Prometheus, for instance), also because it was not Daedalus himself who was punished, but it was his son Icarus who received divine wrath (*nemesis*) due to his father's hubris. Haldane's interpretation was novel: Greek myth often tells of the fates of families, rather than individuals; thus Icarus's death is often understood as the tragedy of Daedalus. 'The premises of the destiny to be suffered by the son are already present in the personality of the father [who] would seem to be nothing less than the incarnation of *hýbris*, and Icarus represents *némesis*' (Zoja 1993 [1995]: 133). Accordingly, Icarus is often not narrated at length as a separate individual, but in relation only to his father, highlighting this aspect of the myth. Haldane's (re-)reading of the myth reflected a certain cultural change (towards individualism) as well as a transformation of the imaginary of nature: the passing of the consequences of hubris and the potential catastrophe to the next generations, which later became a significant part of the sustainable development discourse.

Haldane was no ordinary biologist; he was a Marxist author, who befriended and influenced Aldous and Julian Huxley. His main body of work was on population genetics, crowned by his book *On Being the Right Size*, which focused on proportions (Haldane 1926 [1985]). The book demonstrated the way plants and animals are shaped by their size and sized by their shape. A species' proportions cannot exist outside a certain upper and lower limit: since the weight increases with the cube of its size, legs to carry this new weight would inevitably be beyond the recognizable properties of a species' proportions. This became known as 'Haldane's principle'. In the early 1930s, Max Kleiber's (1932) biological work was also becoming popular, which observed that most animals' mass correlated with their metabolic rate. Both 'Haldane's principle' and 'Kleiber's law' applied the laws of physics and geometry to biology, and are likely to have been influenced by an earlier and much more poetic inquiry into allometry (study of the relationship between size and shape):[7] D'Arcy Thompson's *On Growth and Form*, which was an inquiry into the form that fits the size in a more abstract way. Thompson (1917 [1952]: 205) challenged the scientific norm that assumed linear extension of proportions:

> An organism is so complex a thing, and growth so complex a phenomenon, that for growth to be so uniform and constant in all the parts as to keep the whole shape unchanged would indeed be an unlikely and an unusual circumstance. Rates vary, proportions change, and the whole configuration alters accordingly.

It was Leopold Kohr (1941, 1957, 1978) who translated this work on allometry to the language of economics. He made the biological morphology of Thompson and Haldane the starting point of a social morphology, by discussing that societies are shaped by their size and sized by their shape. Growth could neither be linear nor uniform in all societies, therefore plans of developmentalist scientists (particularly those of economists) should be rejected when they were time- and context-free. Later on, Kohr (1978) wrote about *overdeveloped nations*, a term that reflects his opposition to the dichotomy drawn by Truman between development and underdevelopment. It inspired several influential philosophers of green thought, such as Kirkpatrick Sale, Ivan Illich and E.F. Schumacher. Kohr was exceptional in his critique of limitless growth, at a time growth was the main goal of both capitalism and mainstream socialism.

Eco-political movements were only just emerging during post-WWII era, and were only to some degree influenced by the ideas of biologists. They were more clearly influenced by three other changes of the time. The first one was rapid economic growth, resulting in increased consumption. The distance between the site of production and the site of consumption also increased, delinking the consumer and the environmental consequences of her action, and consumption was 'depersonalized' (Hays 2000: 16).

Secondly, around this time, the US preservation movement was changing in two directions. The first one of these veins was marked by the Land Ethic of Aldo Leopold (1949 [1968]), which dealt with the relationship between humans and the land community, composed of living and inanimate members. It recognized humans as a plain member and citizen of this community. The second, neo-Malthusian streak was concerned with population growth. Two books were especially popular: Fairfield Osborn (1948), the President of the New York Zoological Society, published *Our Plundered Planet*, underlining the consequences of humankind's poor stewardship of the Earth. William Vogt (1948), an ornithologist, published *Road to Survival* the same year. Both books employed a sensational style, and an alarming tone regarding the impact of population growth on the environment. Neo-Malthusianism has become a dominant perspective in the eco-political issues of the next decade.

The third change that influenced the eco-political movements was the political conjuncture, which is the concern of the following section.

6.4.2 Logic of Equivalence: Sustainability as an Empty Signifier

The first decade of the Cold War was marked by the nuclear arms race. The Soviets developed their own atomic bomb by 1949, and both the US and the Soviet Union tested hydrogen bombs in the following three years. It was not until 1963 that the Nuclear Test Ban Treaty between the United States and the Soviet Union was signed. Hence, despite increasing soil, water, and particularly air pollution across the planet (for example the 1952 London smog killing several thousands), and despite new formulations such as Land Ethics and the alarming tone of population ecologists, it was the anti-nuclear movement that captured public attention.

By the end of the 1950s, anti-nuclear movements had started with a focus on peace and pacifism. In less than a decade, they became widespread eco-political movements across the US and Europe that simultaneously merged issues of health and environment, as well as an anti-consumerist tendency. The first reason for this expansion was the transboundary health and environmental effects of nuclear tests. The long-term health effects of radioactive fallout, particularly on children, were a major concern for groups such as Women Strike for Peace, founded in 1961. Another reason was that nuclear reactions were now used for power production, which intensified the ecological and health risks. The geographical expansion of the movement can be explained by the concerns over the Atoms for Peace Program of the Eisenhower Administration, which supplied equipment and information for civilian use of nuclear technologies throughout the world, and started the nuclear programmes of Iran, Pakistan and Israel. By the end of the 1960s, the anti-nuclear movement was a full-fledged political movement that mobilized peace activists protesting the American war against Viet Nam. On the other hand, it was in synch with a wide range of other movements ranging from the counter-culture and student movements to religious pacifism.

Another influential and popular book focused on the effects of chemical pollution (using the metonymy of chemical 'fallout'): *Silent Spring* (1962) by Rachel Carson is widely recognized as the book that inspired modern environmentalism. The book was influential not only because it scientifically demonstrated the thinning of eggshells due to the use of DDT (dichlorodiphenyltrichloroethane) in agriculture, but because it was a radical attempt to formulate ecology as a *subversive subject* (Shepard 1969; Kroll 2002). Although Carson used the 'rational discipline of ecology', she was also sceptical about the intensifying scientific control of both the body and the environment; and her critique of 'materialism, scientism, and the technologically engineered control of nature' transformed the discipline into a radical political project (Kroll 2002). Carson's critique of technological control of micro- *and* macro-biological systems thus symbolically linked the critiques of technology with concerns over health and environment.[8] Around the same time, Murray Bookchin (1962) was developing his theory of *social ecology*, and published *Our Synthetic Environment*. The book not only criticized the uses of pesticides and preservatives in modern production but also questioned the way through which science and technology was becoming a 'substitute for a balanced relationship between man and nature'. Throughout the 1960s, ecology as a subversive subject was advocated by a group of scientists, whom Carolyn Merchant (1992) suitably calls *the radical ecologists*.

This was a time when the environmental movement in the US made a legalistic turn. The local environmental causes were being adjudicated through law suits. In 1967 the Environmental Defense Fund was established to pursue legal solutions to environmental damage, and in 1970 the Natural Resources Defense Council was formed with a professional staff of lawyers and scientists to influence environmental policy in the US. The underlying assumption of such legalistic approaches was that the environmental problems could be solved within the existing social, economic and legal systems. Although the anarchist, socialist and other radical ecologist streaks remained powerful points of reference in the eco-political discourses until the mid-1980s, they increasingly coincided with less subversive and less critical versions of environmentalism.

Throughout the late 1960s and the early 1970s, environment-focused government agencies (for example the Environmental Protection Agency in the US) and NGOs (for example Greenpeace, Worldwatch Institute, Friends of the Earth) were founded. The NGOs started non-violent activism, information gathering and distribution, and international networking which resulted in several changes in the national and international legislations. It was by this time that Green parties started to emerge; deschooling, animal rights, anti-car movements began; environmentally concerned non-violent direct actions, publicity stunts and other forms of civil disobedience took place. The increasingly widespread articulation of these and various other demands reached its peak in 1968, which were later called 'new social movements'. The Green Parties (first in New Zealand, Australia and the UK, and then in Europe) started to merge these demands under pluralistic charters and manifestos throughout 1970s.

The eco-political movements of the 1970s directed a fundamental critique towards techno-scientific modernist industrial society, polarizing social space by linking the demands of feminists and homosexuals, anti-racist movements, pacifists/peace activists and the anti-nuclear movement. These groups united in their demand of an ecologically sustainable society, which was either threatened or made impossible by the patriarchal social organization, interracial injustice, war and the nuclear energy/arms race. The demand for *sustainability*, therefore, was a successful counter-hegemonic demand that allowed several other demands to be articulated *against* the industrial-military character of the modern Western state establishment.

The eco-political movements of the 1970s were simultaneously *popular* movements, in Laclau's terminology. The way these movements brought together various demands makes the demand for an ecologically sound and sustainable society a prime empty signifier. For the eco-feminists, this demand indicated a return to the feminine values that were forgotten in the patriarchal social organization; for pacifists, it was the articulation of anti-militarism and peaceful co-existence; for anti-nuclear movements, it was resistance against the expert rule, high technology and centralization of decision-making; for gay activists, it signified a celebration of sexual plurality.

In *Emancipation(s)*, Laclau (1996: 11–14) reaches the conclusion that each particularism has to appeal to the universal in order to become emancipatory. The first implication of this is that in its universality, the empty signifier represents various demands of the groups in the populist camp. Each must see its own identity represented by the empty signifier against the antagonistic *Other*, which in turn signifies several antagonistic forces (for example industrialism, militarism, capitalism, consumerism and so forth). The groups whose demands comprise an equivalential chain will regard all these forces 'as *equivalent* threats to their own identity' and this general negativity transcends the differences among these forces. Accordingly,

> the positive pole [the identity of the group] cannot be reduced to its concrete contents either: if that which opposes them is the universal form of negativity as such, these contests have to express, through their equivalential relation, the universal form of fullness or identity. [. . .] This constitutive split shows the emergence of the universal within the particular.

There is a second implication of the empty signifier 'mirroring' various identities: 'The agent of emancipation has to be one whose identity is prevented in its constitution/development by an existing oppressive regime' (ibid.). The identity of this agent must have been negated by the existing system, not merely produced by it, which resulted in an antagonistic dichotomy. The 'negated' dimension of this agent is also the universal, to which these groups appeal.

From this point of view, the eco-political movements and the radical ecologists attempted a universal emancipation. What was being negated was nature, and ecologists have traditionally constructed their 'self' in relation to it. Hence, preservationists like Aldo Leopold and deep ecologist philosophers like Arne Næss were identifying with 'the intrinsic value of nature', impossible to construct in the present system. Leopold's (1949 [1968]) Land Ethic placed humans amidst a land community, as an equal citizen that is dependent on all others, not for goods and utilities but for its very existence. Næss (1989: 164–165) brought insights from Gandhi's nonviolence and Carson's *Silent Spring*: he advocated Self-realization through not harming any other individual of the ecosystem. This (capitalized) Self was different from the ego-centric or the anthropocentric self: its realization depended on the Self-realization of other beings too. This position verges upon Laclau's description of an agent of emancipation: for Næss, one could only achieve her true ecological Self in a holistic way, by identifying with other elements, whose identity is prevented in its constitution by the existing oppressive regime.

Moreover, nature, being negated by the existing system, had a universal appeal: Edward Abbey would call it 'the bare bones of existence, the elemental and fundamental, the bedrock which sustains us' (in Cevasco and Harmond 2009: 4). In *The Monkey Wrench Gang*, Abbey's (1975: 87) best-selling eco-anarchist novel, the relationship between this element and identity is constructed by one of the gang's members as follows: '[T]he night and the wilderness belongs to us. This is [. . .] our country. Or so he assumed.'

The gang members related to the wilderness in various ways, but they all assumed it was theirs. As the quote opening this section shows, gang members unite in being threatened by developmentalism, industrialization and consumerism of the existing social order. Hence, they draw an antagonistic frontier (by only talkin'). On the one hand, their particular identities are oppressed by the equivalential chain they weave (as the disagreement on the littering of roads shows). On the other hand, several dimensions of 'The Enemy' are bundled together (ibid.: 107):

> When cities are gone [. . .] and all the ruckus has died away, when sunflowers push up through the concrete and asphalt of the forgotten interstate freeways, when the Kremlin and the Pentagon are turned into nursing homes for generals, presidents and other such shitheads, when the glass-aluminum skyscraper tombs of Phoenix Arizona barely show above the sand dunes, why then, why then, why then by God maybe free men and wild women on horses, free women and wild men, can roam the sagebrush canyonlands in freedom.

Against the universal appeal of the wilderness and nature Abbey places this bundle of enemies (referring to the existing system), which the gang calls *The Enemy*. Another gang member reflects 'the enemy. His enemy? Whose enemy? The Enemy' (ibid.: 274). The gang's identity forms against the antagonistic Other which unifies it. They unite to 'slow if not halt the advance of Technocracy, the growth of Growth, the spread of the ideology of the cancer cell'; but their *political demand* is in effect the radical emancipation of the society (ibid.: 225–229):

> 'I have sworn upon the altar of God', Hayduke bellows into the roaring wind [. . .] trying to remember Jefferson's words, 'eternal hostility against *every fucking form of tyranny*' – getting it slightly wrong but absolutely right – 'over the life of man.' [. . .]
> 'All you're asking for is a counter-industrial revolution.'
> 'Right. That's all.'

In sum, sustainability has come to reflect not only environmental but also other popular political demands, while 'The Enemy', the dichotomic frontier was defined through its negation of Nature's intrinsic value (Figure 6.2).

6.4.3 Logic of Difference: Sustainability as a Floating Signifier

In *The History of Sexuality*, Foucault (1976 [1990]: 95) presents his conception of power by the following statement: 'Where there is power,

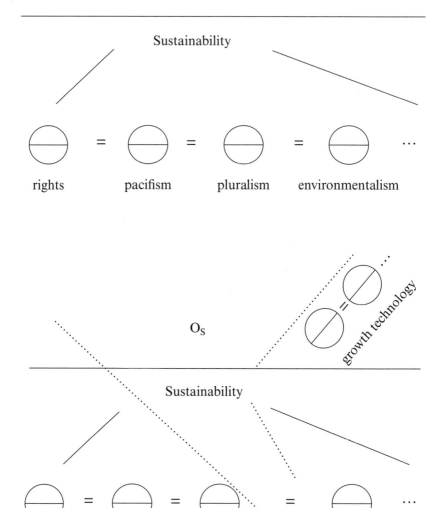

Figure 6.2   Transformation of 'sustainability' from empty to floating signifier

there is resistance, and yet, or rather consequently, this resistance is never in a position of exteriority in relation to power.' Laclau inverts this point by recognizing that where there is resistance, *the logic of difference* is, sooner or later, present. It was Herbert Marcuse's influential essay *Ecology and Revolution* (1972: 10) that applied these two points to eco-political movements for the first time. Firstly, for Marcuse, eco-politics was a radical way of 'attacking the living space of capitalism' as the 'ecological logic is purely and simply the negation of capitalist logic', most radically present in the anti-war movements of the time. A new 'revolutionary' identity between peace movements and environmentalism was being articulated. Secondly, he insisted that the eco-political movements were already being co-opted by commercial capitalism. Two events of 1970 in the United States supported his view: President Nixon's State of Union address in January, and the Earth Day on April 22 (Gottlieb 1993: 152–155). Nixon (1970) explicitly stated that the environmental cause was apolitical, and suggested a way forward, that was agreeable to the status quo:

> Restoring nature to its natural state is *a cause beyond party and beyond factions*. It has become a common cause of all the people of this country. [. . .] But clean air is not free, and neither is clean water. The price tag on pollution control is high. The program I shall propose to Congress will be the most comprehensive and costly program in this field in America's history. [. . .] We shall intensify our research, set increasingly strict standards, and strengthen enforcement procedures. [. . .] We can no longer afford to consider air and water common property [. . .] we should begin now to treat them as scarce resources. [. . .] This requires comprehensive new regulations. It also requires that, to the extent possible, the price of goods should be made to include the costs of *producing* and *disposing* of them without damage to the environment.

Gottlieb (1993: 152) suggests that challenged by potential presidential candidate Edmund Muskie, Nixon was seeking to 'pre-empt the environmental issue by putting forth a technology-centered, pollution control approach [which] appealed to [his] mainstream constituency'. Indeed, none of these demands belonged to the radical ecologists. Throughout his speech, Nixon made a number of points which were exact opposites of the ecological demands – in the name of environmental protection. Against the eco-political critique of capitalism and militarism, Nixon's argument was that environmental problems could be solved within the existing system: (1) production and consumption patterns need not change as long as the prices included environmental 'externalities'; (2) the dilemma between ecology and economy could be solved by the 'inventive genius' that created these problems. (In fact, the dilemma was a false one: echoing

Truman, he suggested that America pioneered in 'turning the wonders of science to the service of man'); (3) growth was non-negotiable:

> The answer is not to abandon growth, but to redirect it. [. . .] Continued vigorous economic growth provides us with the means to enrich life itself and to enhance our planet as a place hospitable to man. [. . .] I propose that before these problems become insoluble, the Nation develop a national growth policy. (Nixon 1972)

Finally, (4) the issue should be solved mainly by *individual* efforts: 'Each individual must enlist in this fight if it is to be won' (ibid.).

By constructing a metaphor of violence (through the use of words like 'enlistment' and regarding environmental degradation a 'fight to be won'), Nixon started establishing a different chain of equivalence. This was a language fundamentally different from that of the radical ecologists who not only would disagree with the violence it symbolized, but more importantly, very much specified the antagonistic other as the techno-industrial military character of the capitalist societies they lived in. Secondly, by 'enlisting' all individuals, Nixon insinuated that the cause of environmental degradation was not industrial production and economic growth, but the lifestyles chosen by individual Americans. His solution was geared towards reflecting this choice in the prices of products they bought, rather than reorganizing the production system in a fundamental way, as suggested by the radical ecologists.

Three months later, Senator Gaylord Nelson proposed celebrating the first 'Earth Day' across the US as a 'teach-in', inspired by the sit-ins protesting the American attack on Viet Nam. When the bill was accepted, Nelson selected a student, Denis Hayes, to coordinate the national activities. Hayes, resonating Nixon, suggested that the Earth Day should 'bypass the traditional political process' (in Nelson 1993). According to *Time* magazine (1970, my emphasis) this has been a successful attempt:

> Some radicals complained that the nation's relatively abrupt concern for the environment represented a distraction from the issues of war and racism. A few rightists noted darkly that Earth Day was also Lenin's birthday, and warned that the entire happening was a Communist trick. [Yet] Earth Day at least temporarily *gathered nearly all bands of the political spectrum*.

With almost 20 million participants, the 1970 Earth Day has been successful in making the environment an issue outside of the political sphere and pushed it back to the sphere of the social. This was partially the result of a shift in the discourse of environmentalism, from being the subversive subject of ecology into a matter of engineering (Kroll 2002):

> As environmentalism became a matter of political consensus dominated by professional environmentalists, ecology lost its subversive edge. Environmental science departments mushroomed in academia [. . .] but it was not a subversive ecology that questioned fundamental values of economics, consumer habits, and techno-scientific control. It represented an engineering mentality in which problems of waste, pollution, population, biodiversity and the toxic environment could be solved scientifically.

Such engineering and management approaches have already been proposed by two zoologists – Garret Hardin (famous for his sociobiological views and utilitarian ethics) and Paul Ehrlich. Hardin (1968) linked the idea of natural limits to population growth, in 'The Tragedy of the Commons', arguing that in a growing population the standards of living were bound to fall. Other than the obvious flaw in this argument regarding identical standards for everyone, the underlying liberal economic assumption of the article was also questionable: that human beings were all self-interested rational beings operating only with short-term rational calculations. On this basis, ultimate destruction of natural resources was inescapable unless common resources were secured through management, private ownership or enclosure. Hence, managerial and apolitical approaches were justified and 'naturalized' as several environmental problems were equated to resource depletion.

Paul Ehrlich's (1968) book, *The Population Bomb* was mainly inspired by the neo-Malthusians of the late 1940s and the continuing public debate about overpopulation in the 1960s. The book forecast famine and economic catastrophe as early as the following decade. Even though these predictions were largely unfulfilled, the book has been a great success, due to the public debate it created, with its alarmist tone and emotional style (Rubin 1994: 79). Despite its pessimism, the book suggested a number of actions for individuals to avoid the population disasters. The intellectual influence of the book has been described by historian Thomas Robertson (2005: 5–6) as giving Malthusianism an unprecedented attention, at the expense of other environmental issues. On the more practical side, the International Institute for Environment and Development was established in 1971 by renowned economist and policy advisor Barbara Ward, seeking to establish economic progress in line with environmental resource protection. The same year Ward was commissioned to write a policy document in preparation for the Stockholm Conference together with René Dubos (see below).

In sum, with the logic of difference, a contestation has emerged over the representation of environmental issues. First, the demand for sustainability became the empty signifier that brought different populist movements of the time together. Then, a second chain of equivalence was formed by the existing hegemonic project, based on technological solutions, capitalism, and individual responsibilities, which called for an apolitical environmentalism (Figure 6.2). This resulted in a division among the ecological movements: Some reinforced the existing chain of equivalence established earlier, and formed an increasingly more radical eco-political worldview throughout the 1970s. Others found it valuable that environmental values were becoming widespread and started increasingly to operate within the existing system.

Simultaneously, the existence of both chains of equivalence allowed for the formulation of new combinations of several demands, which incrementally caused shifts in the discourses of eco-politics. Two famous examples of such new formulations from the early 1970s were *The Ecologist*'s (1972) *A Blueprint for Survival*,[9] and the Club of Rome Report titled *Limits to Growth* (Meadows et al. 1972). It is worth looking into the contents of these texts to understand the change they have initiated in the discourse of sustainability and limits.

A Blueprint for Survival was also influenced by the concerns about overpopulation and overconsumption, predicting a 'breakdown of society and the irreversible disruption of the life-support systems [. . .] possibly by the end of the century' (*The Ecologist* 1972: vii). But the causality and the solutions suggested in this book were somewhat different than those of Ehrlich: the most critical cause of the ecological problem was perceived as 'the industrial way of life with its ethos of expansion' (ibid.: 3). Furthermore, the solution had to be a political one. The book suggested the foundation of a national movement, inspired by the ongoing work of the recently-established Club of Rome, which would assume political status and enter into the next elections, hopefully giving rise to an international movement. This political movement would ensure a highly controlled change that could only occur through a systemic reduction, substitution, and decentralization of industrial growth through mainly technological means and in a top-down approach. A radical counter-hegemonic political project was being suggested, even though a different one from the popular eco-political demand.

It was *Limits to Growth* (Meadows et al. 1972), a long-awaited Club of Rome report, that became the symbol of *the limits ethos* and the best-selling environmental book of all times. On the one hand, the report definitively established a causal relationship between ecological degradation and economic growth. On the other hand, it placed population growth as an equally important dimension for the logic of limits, as industrialization, through its choice of variables. Among the *five major trends of global concern* (population growth, industrialization, malnutrition, resource depletion and environmental degradation), only the first two were independent variables (causes of ecological crisis), while the last three were dependent variables (indicators of ecological crisis).

The methods employed in the report had further implications: According to critics, together with *The Population Bomb* and *A Blueprint for Survival*, the report 'made it seem natural to imagine the future of the globe as the result of the interaction of quantitative growth curves operating in five dimensions' (Sachs 1992b: 27–28). The reason for Sachs' critique is the methods employed in the report, which are very different from the contesting humanist and bio-centric perspectives of the time. These alternatives put more emphasis on the human condition or the intrinsic value of nature, which would inevitably require an end to the logic of growth and to the exploration of nature. However, *the global ecosystems approach* employed by the Club of Rome researchers,

> proposed the global society as the unit of analysis and put the Third World, by denouncing population growth, at the centre of attention. Moreover, the model rendered intelligible what would otherwise have appeared as a messy situation by removing resource conflicts from any particular local or political context. The language of aggregate data series suggests a clearcut picture, abstract figures lend themselves to playing with scenarios, and a presumed mechanical causality among various components creates the illusion that global strategies can be effective. And even if the ideal of growth crumbled, there was, for those who felt themselves in charge of running the world, still some objective to fall comfortably back on: stability. (Ibid.)

This twist was an early indicator of the Third World becoming the centre of attention in environmental discourses. Moreover, for the first time, sustainability was being equalized to stability. This was a very different definition of sustainability than that of the eco-political movements. For environmentalists, it was sufficiently interesting for challenging growth and suggesting its replacement with the ideal of equilibrium. The authors recognized how their own reality was colonized by the logic of growth as well. They made a modest claim regarding how to replace the logic of growth with logics of sustainability and equilibrium:

> We can say very little at this point about the practical, day-by-day steps that might be taken to reach a desirable, sustainable state of global equilibrium. Neither the world model nor our own thoughts have been developed in sufficient detail to understand all the implications of the transition from growth to equilibrium. (Meadows et al. 1972: 180)

Doing so, the report left a large gap between *what is* and *what ought* unaccounted for. This gap, which could be filled in many ways, is where politics takes place; how to fill this gap was indeed the focus of political contestation during the next decade. In the first instance, *Limits to Growth* has been praised not only by the environmentalists but also, as Sachs argues, by the international bureaucracy (which he calls 'the international development elite') of the United Nations for whom the report provided the cognitive base for viewing the world as an interrelated system, functioning under common constraints. Technological, liberal, expert-led, top-down approaches could be a way of ensuring this stability. But it could also be filled in a bottom-up fashion, based on sustenance, adequateness, minimalism and a deindustrialization effort. This ambiguity in the report made it eligible for discussion, for developmentalists and environmentalists, technocrats and activists, conservatives and liberals alike.

As Sachs suggests, *stability* was in the core of the logic that the report established: *sustainability* referred to a state of ecological *and* economic stability. In other words, the term *sustainability* pointed to the eco-*logical* impossibility of continuing with the trends of economic and population growth, assuming linearity. This assumption of linearity made the report very fragile and easily refutable, as has been the case since its publication (for example Sachs 1992b). But more importantly, it was this very assumption that lay at the core of developmentalism and had already been questioned by bio-centrists and humanists, and since Leopold Kohr, even by economists.

In 1973, Fritz Schumacher (a student of Kohr and an economist) published another best-seller and a highly influential book titled *Small Is Beautiful: Economics As If People Mattered*. It brought economic insights into why and how the transformations suggested by the eco-political movements of the time should and could take place, and challenged the notion of growth and the motto of 'bigger is better'. Instead, Schumacher argued for appropriate use of technology and small scale economic organization on the basis of *adequateness*. For Schumacher modern industrialism was irrational and inefficient as it required too much while accomplishing too little. It was immoral, as only 'greed and envy demand continuous and limitless economic growth of a material kind' which are the urges that 'the modern private enterprise system ingeniously employs [. . .] as its motive power' (Schumacher 1973: 222). In this sense, Schumacher's contribution was able to fill in the gap that the Club of Rome Report noted but did not address, between the suggested global transformation and the required day-to-day steps to reach this economic and social organization and value system.

Ideas mentioned in *Limits to Growth* could have been embedded in the values and economics of Schumacher. In fact, both sources have been formative in the discourses of Green political parties. But the signifier *sustainability* was also being incorporated to another chain of equivalence by the hegemonic developmentalist project. Manifest in Nixon's speech and the rhetoric of the 'international development elite' the logic of difference was linking sustainability to a new set of concepts (as shown in Figure 6.2). The contestation could have resulted either in a more radical and forceful articulation of the demands signified by sustainability, or their cooptation into the existing power structure. *Sustainability* was changing from being the *empty signifier*, that brought together several social demands, into a *floating signifier*, whose meaning is suspended between the equivalential chains of competing hegemonic projects. For instance, let's look into the opposite logics of development and sustainability on the basis of the biological metaphor they use (Table 6.2). While the logic of developmentalism used a biological metaphor based on a continuous process (the absence of which would indicate abnormality), the logic of sustainability employed a biological metaphor that suggested *limits* to such development: after a certain point growth would suggest abnormality (like cancer or obesity), if not prove impossible.

Compared to *developmentalism*, the logic of sustainability relies much more on the ideas of interdependence, communality and equality than that of freedom (in the form of free trade or unleashed economic growth). In its logical extreme, it counters the idea that man should freely derive personal possession from his labours and that this is the essence of freedom, which was shared by colonial and post-WWII notions of development. On this basis, *Limits to Growth* was a successful challenge to the development paradigm: its suggestion to limit growth (economically and biologically) came as a shock to neo-classical economics; and in the political context of the 1970s in Europe and the US, it was a political intervention. The demand to *limit growth* challenged the established developmentalist ideology, and was quickly picked up by eco-political movements to further politicize environmental issues. On the other hand, the report was both an attempt to *quantify* the ecological crisis and inadequate in filling the pragmatic gap. In the end, although the *logic of sustainability* established in the report was fundamentally different from *developmentalism*, it also set the scene for further cooptation.

This moment of floating (for the signifier *sustainability*) was a watershed. In a few years, eco-political movements have ramified into more radical and mainstream components. The second half of the 1970s and the early 1980s was marked by *transborder* industrial disasters with greater and better documented ecological impacts, which might have eased the practical turn many NGOs have opted for. The most (in)famous examples are the toxic dumping at Love Canal, the nuclear meltdown in Three Mile Island power plant, the industrial disaster resulting from the operations of Dow Chemicals in Bhopal, India, the explosion of the Chernobyl

Table 6.2   The biological metaphors of hegemonic and contesting logics

	Logic of developmentalism	Logic of sustainability
Basis of the biological metaphor	Development is a natural process wherein the potentialities of an organism are released until it reaches its complete, fully-fledged form.	There are natural limits to growth, as form fits size and size fits form.
Application to society	Social development is a natural and linear process; the failure to develop is an anomaly (underdevelopment). All societies develop in a more or less similar fashion. A growing economy is the condition for development, which is in turn the condition of progress. Economic growth can be endless.	Growth is not a linear function; just like the human body, when a certain size is surpassed further economic growth might have catastrophic effects. Social change is and should be determined by local conditions: applying one set of criteria reduces diversity. Production and reproduction are ongoing natural processes, but will meet natural limits and/or result in unsustainable situations (for example, malnutrition, environmental degradation, resource depletion, impoverishment).
Means	Increasing governmental control over the wealth, health, and lifestyle of the population is necessary to reach the aim of development mainly through a) techno-science; b) economic growth through industrialization; c) a system that merges liberal democracy with a capitalist economy.	To avoid these catastrophes, a balance between size and form should be sustained (a conceptual optimum, or equilibrium) through: a) form that fits the size: appropriate technology; b) natural limits on production and reproduction: small scale economic organisation on the basis of adequateness.
Agency	Nation states embedded in a global economy, global governance institutions, and markets.	Individuals in human-sized communities.

nuclear power plant, and the Exxon Valdez oil spill off the Alaska coast. Schumacher's arguments regarding the inefficiency and side-effects of large-scale techno-industrial organization on human freedom and wilderness were documented on the global media.

These events influenced the environmental movements: For the first time, environmental concerns were the cause of terrorism with the bombings of the so-called 'Freedom Club', better known as *Unabomber*. In 1977 and 1979, two NGOs were founded with more radical approaches and strategies than environmentalist movement to date: the Sea Shepherd Conservation Society and Earth First!. At the origins of both of these groups lay a critique of other environmental NGOs, which were becoming increasingly mainstream. Paul Watson, one of the founders of Greenpeace, unsatisfied with the organization's principle of 'bearing witness' to whale hunting, established Sea Shepherds, which uses direct action strategies including scuttling, disabling, 'stink bombing', non-violent but extralegal boarding of whaling vessels, as well as seizure and destruction of drift nets.[10] Earth First! was another radical action group; their most famous founder David Foreman decided to establish Earth First! as a consequence of his frustration with environmental lobbying and the general professionalization of the movement. The group separated itself from the mainstream environmental movement by tactics of 'monkeywrenching' – industrial sabotage traditionally associated with labour struggles. This was in sharp contrast with the cautious lobbying efforts of the established environmental organizations. Fittingly, the initial logo of Earth First! was a monkey wrench and a stone hammer.

The monkey wrench was not an arbitrary logo, and neither were the similarities between the two organizations: Paul Watson and David Foreman befriended each other, as well as Edward Abbey, who coined the term monkeywrenching for his novel dedicated to Ned Ludd. *The Monkey Wrench Gang* (Abbey 1975 [2006]) is a radical political critique of the social, economic and technological organization of the US (and modern societies in general), and it is a strategy against the co-option of the eco-political movement. For instance, the gang's members are all politically incorrect individuals: not only do they dismiss liberalism in terms of property law by sabotaging development projects, but also the way of life it brings. One of the characters is polygamous (with 'three happy wives'), mistrusts banks and chooses to live below the poverty level. Another likes excessive drinking and driving, big cars, weapons, swearing and makes a point against hygiene. As the quote at the beginning of this section demonstrates, the gang has several conversations regarding the amount of 'violence' they are willing to use. Pragmatic, symbolic and moral views intersect at the point of *deicide*: 'The murder of a machine' (ibid.: 86). No murder is committed and no one is intentionally harmed *physically*, but 'the person' is not identified with her property. Fittingly, the illustration on the cover of the paperback edition (Figure 6.3) depicts a caterpillar being crushed by a monkey wrench; the person hanging from the caterpillar is about to fall, yet appears insignificant.

Abbey's politically incorrect characters revealed how he regarded professional, mainstream environmentalism as forced uniformity and sacrilege towards nature. He was also deeply aware that apolitical references to and articulations of environmental values were prone to be co-opted through what he calls 'eco-porn'–the green wash activities of and the lip service paid by the very corporations that caused the damage (ibid.: 236). Mainstream environmentalists criticized his politically incorrect and 'highly opinionated style on the grounds that this is detrimental to the serious cause of environmentalism'; on which he would apologize from 'anyone still present whom [he] failed to insult' (quoted in Cevasco and Harmond 2009: 5).

Abbey's dismissal of the politically correct liberal environmental movements was shared also by Watson and Foreman, and shows the fracture between radical and (increasingly) mainstream environmentalisms: For instance, in the core of the gang's 'healthy hatred' was the Glen Canyon Dam (to which the quote at the beginning of this section refers), which was also one of Earth First!'s first areas of activity. The preface to the book's 2006 edition notes that Earth First!'s early actions there 'made Sierra Clubbers look like Junior Leaguers on a do-gooder field trip' (Abbey 1975 [2006]: xxiii). On the one hand, several changes initiated or inspired by environmental movements have been so influential that they have become mainstream values for most industrialized societies, in a variety of ways. On the other hand, the way environmental values have been increasingly internalized by the existing social system resulted in the emergence of environmentalisms that are even more compromising with the way the society is organized.

Earth First! and the Sea Shepherd Conservation Society (henceforth Sea Shepherds) were in this sense reclaiming the ground, operationalizing the logic of equivalence once again – by directing a radical critique towards the modern industrial society and its myth of growth – regardless of the limits ethos and the mainstreaming of the eco-political movements. Their political incorrectness might have protected them from co-option, but it also made them vulnerable to marginalization. Although their discourse was no more radical than that of Thoreau, the political background was different. As it happened with the anti-internationalist/nativist claims of decolonization discourses, while

Figure 6.3   The cover of 'The Monkey Wrench Gang'

some claims were internalized by the hegemonic project, others were marginalized. Eco-political activism against private property was significantly marginalized, while a general concern for the environment was internalized by the developmentalist project. Simultaneously, the

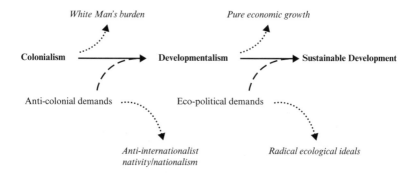

Figure 6.4   Marginalized discursive elements during the progression from colonialism to developmentalism and sustainable development

discourses within the hegemonic projects were changing as well: similar to the elimination of the colonialist conceit of civilizing other lands and societies, the ideal of constant and linear economic growth could no longer be maintained. A new political and discursive formulation was in the making: Sustainable development was the product of this political process, and found its most famous expression in 1987 with the report of the World Commission on Environment and Development, titled *Our Common Future* (Figure 6.4).

6.5   THE MERGER: SUSTAINABLE DEVELOPMENT

A year after Earth First! was founded, the term sustainable development appeared for the first time in a joint report by International Union for Conservation of Nature and Natural Resources (IUCN), UNEP and WWF (1980) titled *World Conservation Strategy: Living Resource Conservation for Sustainable Development*. It was the first report of its scope that fused the issues of environment and development, suggesting their equal significance: 'development and conservation are equally important for our survival and for the discharge of our responsibilities as trustees of natural resources for the generations to come' (IUCN et al. 1980: 1).

But the term 'sustainable development' became ubiquitous only when the World Commission on Environment and Development (WCED), authorized by the UN to sketch the future of environmental governance, published its report titled *Our Common Future* in 1987. With the mission of writing down the international political strategies for *environmental* protection, the Brundtland Commission took four years to publish *Our Common Future* (WCED 1987: 8), which has defined sustainable development, irrevocably, as 'development which meets the needs of the present without compromising the ability of future generations to meet their own needs'.

This definition was remarkably different from the way 'sustainability' was used by the eco-political movements to date. It was not only the exclusion of the term 'environment' that made the change paradigmatic, it was also the causality that 'sustainable development' signified. *Limits to Growth* reached two broad conclusions (Meadows et al. 1972: 27, my emphasis):

1. If the present growth trends in world population, industrialization, pollution, food production, and resource depletion continue unchanged, the limits to growth on this planet will be reached sometime within the next one hundred years. The most probable result will be a rather sudden and uncontrollable decline in both population and industrial capacity.
2. It is possible to alter these growth trends and to establish a condition of ecological and economic stability that is *sustainable* far into the future. The state of global equilibrium could be designed so that the basic material needs of each person on earth are satisfied and each person has an equal opportunity to realize his [potential].

The word 'sustainable' was employed several times in *Limits to Growth*, referring to a state in which ecological and economic stability could coincide. In other words, the term 'sustainability' was employed in order to point to the ecological impossibility of continuing with the trends of development and population growth. They had little to say about the practical steps to take for a desirable, sustainable state of equilibrium; nevertheless they thought it was possible to establish such a state of ecological and economic stability 'sustainable far into the future' by altering the growth trends (ibid.: 24, 180). In sum, the transition from *growth* to *equilibrium* could be achieved by limiting economic growth and mitigating population growth.

In *Our Common Future*, what was to sustain has changed: 'Humanity has the ability to make *development* sustainable' headed the Brundtland definition of sustainable development (WCED 1987: 8). The shift in emphasis, once again was critical in shaping how environmental politics and international institutions to date were going to frame the relationship between environment and development. We can rephrase the causality established in *Limits to Growth* as '[population- and economic-]growth-as-usual causes environmental degradation'. With the concept of sustainable development, this causality has been altered in *Our Common Future*, and it was postulated that growth as such can be limitless, and that 'economic development can be consolidated with environmental protection' (ibid.: 40). It was not development, but *under*-development that caused environmental degradation, and hence, it should be 'cured.' This revision is clearly articulated at the introduction of the report: 'We have in the past been concerned about the impacts of economic growth upon environment. We are now forced, to concern ourselves with the impacts of ecological stress [. . .] upon our economic prospects' (ibid.: 5).

Finally, the Brundtland Report established three 'interdependent and mutually reinforcing' pillars of sustainable development (economic and social development, environmental protection), which concealed the conflict between development and environment. In contrast, the report suggested that sustainable development would solve the dilemma between economy and ecology:

> The concept of sustainable development provides a framework for the integration of environment policies and development strategies – the term 'development' being used here in its broadest sense. [. . .] policy makers guided by the concept of sustainable development will necessarily work to assure that economies remain firmly attached to their ecological roots and that these roots are protected and nurtured so that they may support growth over the long term. (Ibid.: 40)

Development was used in its broadest sense, and policy makers could employ a wide range of strategies to ensure that their economies were growing. These economies should remain 'attached to their ecological roots', which could be interpreted in various ways. Environment was to be protected so that it could support further growth. Hence, the environment was linked to development. Economic growth, the limits of which were being constructed in 1972, was once again brought into the picture, this time as a viable and desirable *solution* to developmental inequalities and environmental degradation. The suggestion was not a contraction-and-convergence model which would ensure the so-called developing countries could create and maintain healthy economies, while the industrialized countries would slow down economic growth. On the contrary, the report prescribed 3 per cent annual per capita gross domestic product growth for industrialized economies (ibid.: 173). Through free trade, industrialization and technological innovation economic growth would be maintained *and* environmental problems would be solved. Industry was regarded as vital for 'human' needs, implying that social and economic models that are not based on modern machinery and technology (for example subsistence models) were inhumane (ibid.: 206, my emphasis):

Industry is central to the economies of modern societies and an indispensable motor of growth. It is essential to developing countries, to widen their development base and meet growing needs. [. . .] *Many essential human needs can be met only through goods and services provided by industry.* The production of food requires increasing amounts of agrochemicals and machinery. Beyond this, the products of industry form the material basis of contemporary standards of living. Thus all nations require and rightly aspire to efficient industrial bases to meet changing needs.

On the one hand the 'threat' embodied by the world's poor was changing. They were no longer a threat to the 'prosperous', in terms of economic activity and safety of private property (as Truman suggested), but to the environment. Since ecological stress had impacts upon the economic prospects of everyone, the so-called underdeveloped were once again fixed as the threat to economic prosperity of all. The difference was the indirectness of this threat, with the inclusion of yet another link to the chain: that link was environment. An immediate policy implication was the prioritization of developmental issues compared to environmental problems, which was supported rigorously by Southern governments and modernist intellectuals.

The position of Western societies was corrected once again: they were no longer to be blamed for environmental degradation or responsible for its correction; it was the 'developing countries of the South' that should protect their richly diverse ecosystems by refraining from their destruction. Industrialized countries would certainly aid this pursuit, providing them with the moral high ground. Pretes (1997: 1424) also notes that

> rather than jettisoning the notion of development, and rather than displacing development and infinite progress as social imaginary, Western society has responded [to the environmentalist critique] by mutating the discourse surrounding development, incorporating the arguments of its critics without fundamentally altering the nature of the conception. [. . .] This new discourse has emerged around the term 'sustainable development' [which is] not a new form of development [but] development that reaffirms the idea of the infinite.

In other words, to make development sustainable was to reaffirm a linear idea of infinite progress by way of technoscience, and thus, the idea of sustainable development was an inherently conservative one (ibid.). The report states: 'The concept of sustainable development does imply limits – not absolute limits but limitations imposed by the present state of technology and social organization on environmental resources and by the ability of the biosphere to absorb the effects of human activities' (WCED 1987: 9).

The effect of the Brundtland Report on environmentalist discourses can be traced in common arguments such as (adapted from Şahin 2004):

- development is the means to satisfy all basic needs of everyone;
- future generations, too, are entitled to satisfying their basic needs;
- poverty/underdevelopment is the reason for environmental degradation hence needs to be overcome; [ergo]
- issues of environment and development should be tackled together;
- the solution to these problems is to use resources rationally and ensure further development;
- this can only be achieved through liberalization of trade, technology transfer, and industrialization.

By doing so, the discourse of sustainable development and its institutions have quickly become radical monopolies. For instance, the Brundtland Report suggests that development through industrialization and growth is the only possible means to ensure basic needs (whereby autonomous alternatives are disqualified) and that these needs are the condition for a humane life (creating new standards that everyone must meet). It assumes that environmental protection can only be achieved through development which in turn requires industrialization and an integrated liberal economic system. It prescribes increased levels of the same 'cures', when smaller quantities have not yielded the desired results: when the so-called 'developing' countries were not 'developed' as a result of developmentalist efforts since the 1950s, what is prescribed by the Brundtland Report is 'more of the same'.

Hence, the radical conservationist ideal of an *ecologically sustainable society* was transformed into an industrialist social-democratic idea of the hegemonic developmentalist ideology. Now it was intertwined with other Western liberal ideals such as scientific and technological progress, free trade, and economic growth. In other words, a new equivalential chain was established that related growth-focused demands to the environmental ones. The most general and critical result of this paradigm shift was to marginalize ecological movements that demanded fundamental changes in the production and consumption models and the ideology of Western societies. This shift is the basis on which further neoliberal connotations would be attached to the concept, such as open markets as a solution to environmental *and* economic problems.

6.6   THE UN CONTEXT: CONFERENCES PRODUCE TEXTS AND PRODUCE INSTITUTIONS

6.6.1   1972: *Only One Earth* and the Stockholm Conference

In the 1960s the Southern governments were cautious about the environmental concerns of the North. When the United Nations Conference on the Human Environment (UNCHE) was announced, some Southern delegations made their negative stance explicit:

> Vocal arguments were raised, particularly by Brazil and Algeria, claiming that the Conference on the environment was a rich man's show to divert attention from the development needs in the underprivileged parts of the world. An influential seminar in Founex, Switzerland in the spring of 1971 concluded that there is no inherent contradiction between environment and development, and that these two concerns should be mutually supportive. This secured attendance from most developing countries, but the question could not be substantively settled at the Stockholm Conference. (Strong 2002)

This conflict needed to be resolved before international action and regulation was possible on environmental issues. Another attempt to bring together the conflictual claims of environment and development was a policy document commissioned to René Dubos and Barbara Ward by Maurice Strong, Secretary-General of UNCHE in May 1971. Strong asked the authors to draft a report that will 'represent the knowledge and opinion of the world's leading experts and thinkers about the relationship between man and his natural habitat at a time when human activity is having profound effects upon the environment' (Ward and Dubos 1972 [1980]: Preface). This would be a part of the preparations to the Stockholm Conference.

The resulting document was *Only One Earth: The Care and Maintenance of a Small Planet*, which was drafted by Ward and Dubos (1972), with contributions from 152 consultants. The consultative process was mainly for ensuring the support of Southern governments. Accordingly, *Only One Earth* reflected the concerns of scientists and opinion leaders over the bi-polar international order at the time. It put emphasis on the conditions for peace and the need for international cooperation, questioning the indispensability of national sovereignty in the face of global environmental problems throughout the text. The report (Ward and Dubos 1972: 66) asked challenging questions, and came up with a critical outlook of the existing social systems:

> If all man can offer to the decades ahead is the same combination of scientific drive, economic cupidity and national arrogance, then we cannot rate very

highly the chances of reaching the year 2000 with our planet still functioning safely and our humanity securely preserved.

This tone was maintained throughout the report. It problematized technology in its Part Three, titled *Problems of High Technology*. It challenged mainstream economic indicators, at times replacing the system based on gross national product with indicators for quality of life (for example 'little boys swimming in Delaware or Volga', ibid.: 201) or calorie calculations. It directly linked colonial relations with the origins of the developmental imbalances. The 'disguisedly subsidized consumption' patterns of modern urban societies (ibid.: 203) and 'the disease of growthmanship' (ibid.: 199) were questioned while the 'insufficiency of the market approach' was demonstrated (ibid.: 57). Alternative models of development were suggested for the South, replacing 'monsters of efficiency' with ecologically constructive man-power (ibid.: 233).

The relationship established by the report between development and environment is best summarized in the following paragraphs:

> Industry, often under foreign direction and ownership, introduces modern labour-saving technologies when unskilled labour is chiefly available. Markets overseas are blocked by the presence there of monsters of efficiency – Mitsuis, IBMs, Volkswagens – and by the tariffs raised to keep out cheap labour-intensive goods. Markets at home remain limited by local poverty or, often enough, by the extreme smallness of the post-colonial states. Such are the difficulties that make up a maze, a web, an obstacle race for developing governments which both intensifies their determination to break out of poverty and frustrates the efforts which they have to make.
>
> In developing, as in developed, lands all the pursuits and consequences of the only exits from poverty – greater productivity, the 'more for less' – have their impact on the environment. [. . .] Industry puts its effluents into the 'free goods' of air and water. (Ibid.: 210–211)

In this narration not only is the relationship between environment and development conflictual, but also the poverty in the 'developing' countries is regarded as a function of the colonial past, the existing market conditions and the efficiency-oriented industry. The report clearly recognizes that there needs to be different paths to development, but it does not suggest solutions. It limits its suggestions to the need for knowledge, delegating limited power to international bodies and a standard development aid of 1 per cent of the industrialized countries' gross national product. However, it is fundamentally different from its successors in placing the environmental problems as predominantly social issues. The report does not have a technocratic tone and does not go into the details of how a certain issue should be assessed, or what policies should be designed. Rather, it contours the historical roots of environmental degradation and developmental problems and calls for concerted action beyond concerns of national sovereignty, in the spirit of UNCHE.

Clapp and Dauvergne (2005: 55) notes that the initial focus of the Stockholm Conference was environmental problems arising from industrialization, but it was expanded to include developmental concerns so that the Southern governments too would join, and support the resulting documents. The Southern position on the matter was that: (1) exploitation by global capitalists caused poverty, which in turn caused environmental degradation; (2) the solution would be to reform the global economic system, which currently obliges the South to export cheap raw material in exchange for expensive industrial products (ibid.: 56). Accordingly, the so-called developing countries have made a suggestion to the UN to create a New International Economic Order, which would not only give more power to the South in the IMF and the World Bank, but also restrict the operations of the transnational corporations and reform the terms of trade for raw commodity producers (ibid.). This plan did not actualize, although it was a focal debate in the 1970s. The concerns of the South proved accurate in the following years: the oil crisis further increased the prices of industrial products relative to raw materials and, as the UN Chronicle suggests, the Northern countries showed little interest in global environmental protection (Strong 2002).

Although the resulting texts of the Conference did not reflect any suggestions regarding economic reform, they did reproduce the idea that environment and development were linked and non-contradictory issues. During the Stockholm Conference and in the follow-up events statements along these lines were commonplace. The most memorable articulation was made by Indira Gandhi, who suggested that the worst form of pollution was poverty and the reason for environmental problems in the South was not excessive industrialization but inadequate development.

6.6.2   1983–1992: *Our Common Future* and the Rio Conference

The Brundtland Commission and the resulting WCED Report, *Our Common Future*, were the third example of the UN tradition of asking social democratic prime ministers to establish commissions for creating overarching policy documents regarding global problems (after the Brandt and Palme Commissions). Like its 1972 counterpart, the Brundtland Report too has been written through a long (elite level) consultation process.

In the official document that established the Brundtland Commission

(UN 1983), the term sustainable development was used, and yet not defined. The text did not put as much emphasis on development as on environment.[11] As the South was at great unease regarding the environmental concerns of richer countries, the task of the Commission was to find a way to cooperate on issues of environment despite different levels of 'development'.

With the introduction of sustainable development the report circumvented the problem rather than solved it. Instead of producing a space for cooperation (across different development levels) towards an ecologically sustainable future, the report reified developmentalist discourse, rather than weakened it. As a result, sustainable development became a floating signifier, a signifier that can represent the environmental demand within the developmentalist hegemonic project. As the new equivalential chain formed by the logic of difference took hold, the contestation over the meaning of the floating signifier 'sustainable' was actualized. Development itself has become not more but less specific when merged with the adjective *sustainable*. Just as Wolfgang Sachs (1992a: 4) once observed development to be, sustainable development is a shapeless-yet-ineradicable concept: despite its lack of content it fulfils the function of gathering parties under the same banner by creating 'a common ground, a ground on which right and left, elites and grassroots fight their battles'.

This has been exactly the case with the Rio Conference. All the documents resulting from the summit referred to the Brundtland definition as the main reference point of all activities. *Agenda 21* (UN 1992b), which was drafted from 1989 and concluded at the conference, was a major document that would specify in 40 chapters the six dimensions of sustainable development (social, economic, conservation, resource management, participation and means of implementation). The Rio Declaration listed the 27 principles that would guide sustainable development around the world. The Commission on Sustainable Development, established by the UN General Assembly to ensure effective follow-up to the summit, was the first institution into which the sustainable development discourse sedimented.

6.6.3   2000–2002: the MDGs and the Johannesburg Conference

In September 2000, following the Millennium Summit, the General Assembly adopted the Millennium Declaration, out of which the MDGs were synthesized. The Declaration was based on certain principles and values, some of which I would like to cite so as to demonstrate the influence of the shift from sustainability (the empty signifier of the eco-political project) to sustainable development (a new nodal point in developmental-ist discourse):

> *Equality*. No individual and no nation must be denied the opportunity to benefit from development. [. . .]
> *Respect for nature*. Prudence must be shown in the management of all living species and natural resources, in accordance with the precepts of sustainable development. Only in this way can the immeasurable riches provided to us by nature be preserved and passed on to our descendants. The current unsustainable patterns of production and consumption must be changed in the interest of our future welfare and that of our descendants.

The Millennium Declaration regards development as a right, and respect for nature as in line with this right. In this articulation the conflict between the two demands is successfully concealed and environmental demands lose their primacy. For instance, from this point on, the adjective *sustainable* would be added to many more concepts related to developmentalism (sustainable finance, sustainable research, sustainable energy production and so forth). The MDGs reflected this change even further: out of the eight MDGs only one of them refers to environmental sustainability, while the rest mostly focus on poverty reduction. More significantly, from this point on, the Millennium Declaration and the MDGs have become central to the UN's broad sustainable development rhetoric, as *Agenda 21* was in the previous decade. The MDGs were more practical and specific than the long and detailed *Agenda 21*, and the place of environment was further demoted in the global political agenda.

On the issue of 'underdevelopment', the Declaration (UN 2002b, para. 11–16, my emphases) used a determined tone:

> We will spare no effort *to free our fellow men, women and children from the abject and dehumanizing conditions of extreme poverty*, to which more than a billion of them are currently subjected. We are committed to making the *right to development* a reality for everyone and to freeing the entire human race from want.
> We resolve therefore to create an environment – at the national and global levels alike – which is *conducive to development* and to the elimination of poverty. [. . .]
> We are concerned about the obstacles developing countries face in mobilizing the resources needed to finance their sustained development. We will therefore make every effort to ensure the success of the High-level International and Intergovernmental Event on Financing for Development, to be held in 2001. [. . .]
> We are also determined to deal comprehensively and effectively with the debt problems of low- and middle-income developing countries, through various national and international measures designed *to make their debt sustainable in the long term*.

The statement reiterated the position of international development elite on the issue of poverty. It also externalized extreme poverty from the societies experiencing it (so much so that its effect on the individual was described as abject and dehumanizing, rather than its effect on a community). Development was no longer a national right but now an individual one; and sustaining development was explicitly stated as a goal divorced from environmental concerns. While the success of this strategy was dependent on financial backing from the North, its aim was limited to making the economies of the so-called developing countries that were going bankrupt sturdy enough so that they could keep paying their debts. The Declaration revealed no traces of earlier colonial discourses and neither were there any insinuations that the global economic system was the root cause of the economic inequities among countries. The most global scientific and communication projects were being listed as the new trends in global economy, such as the human genome project and information technologies. Globalization was settling into the discourse of development. At the same time, environmentalist claims were universalized such that they meant little more than a general will to protect resources for future generations.

6.6.4   2002–2012: The SDGs and Rio+20

The Rio+20 Summit is widely regarded as a failure (ENB 2012; Pearce 2012; WWF in Centre for American Progress 2012). High hopes had been placed on the two main topics of the summit, the institutional reform agenda and the green economy, with little tangible effect. Despite calls for a transformation in global sustainability politics (Biermann 2012; Hultman 2012), the final document of the conference restates old commitments without delivering convincing answers to new challenges. The document, titled 'The Future We Want', illustrates the limitations of the consensus that can be reached internationally regarding critical environmental issues. Perhaps the most positive outcome of Rio+20 has been the proposed Sustainable Development Goals.

   The outcome of Rio+20 is partially the result of the broader systemic factors (such as the global economic and financial crisis) and partially the result of a deliberative strategy of the host country Brazil, which, faced with the thread of a final document that would not meet the approval of all summit participants, opted for presenting a document that was not more than a minimal consensus. This move ensured that a consensus document would be approved, but made it impossible for the arriving heads of state to reopen the discussion and enter into new bargains. The 282 paragraphs of the official summit declaration (UN 2012), 'The Future

We Want' dealt with the green economy and the institutional reform agenda in a total of only 36 paragraphs, while the chapter on addressing the remaining gaps and future challenges in the sustainable development agenda received close to 150 paragraphs. States seem to find it easier to agree on topics that need further attention (without detailing exactly how these problems should be dealt with) than on a new vision for change (the green economy) or the necessary organizational innovation (institutional reform). Furthermore, the proposals to upgrade the UNEP into a full-fledged UN organization and to transform CSD into a Sustainable Development Council with greater competences were both rejected. A more robust mandate for review and monitoring of existing commitments, a demand frequently made by both the NGOs and the scientific community, was also postponed. Finally, no real commitments were made to overcome the implementation deficit, the main concern of the summit (UNCSD 2012a). Governments have opted instead to pledge symbolic funds for various projects and goals, such as the US announcement of a USD20 million partnership with African nations on clean energy projects; Brazil and China's pledges to contribute to UNEP's projects in developing countries; Japan's commitment to disaster risk reduction (ENB 2012).

The most positive outcome of Rio+20 was the agreement to establish an 'inclusive and transparent intergovernmental process on sustainable development goals' (UN 2012: para. 248), and a working group comprised of 30 representatives nominated by the member states would be constituted. The SDGs were not concrete goals such as the MDGs, which make their achievement rather difficult to assess. However, the mandate of the working group and the general framing of the SDGs are broad enough to ensure a meaningful outcome on at least certain issues, providing ongoing public scrutiny.

With regards to partnerships, the summit used an explicitly positive rhetoric although there was little if any monitoring and assessment on the results of ongoing partnerships. Conference Secretary Sha Zukang underscored: 'This Conference is about implementation. It is about concrete action. The voluntary commitments are a major part of [its] legacy' (UNCSD 2012a: 1). Thus, the new partnerships emerging in the context of Rio+20 were not called CSD partnerships but voluntary commitments. While these commitments indeed show the mainstreaming of the sustainability agenda into civil society and business communities, Rio+20 failed to make them into a powerful governance mechanism. Just like CSD and Global Compact the Rio+20's voluntary commitments are also likely to suffer from lack of public scrutiny, lack of screening and monitoring, centralized organization at the global level, and most importantly, from the absence of any obligation towards democratic accountability or transparency: no screening or monitoring mechanism was introduced, whereas self-reporting remained the norm. Nonetheless, over 700 voluntary commitments were announced by the end of the conference, which initiated 'a new bottom-up approach towards the advancement of sustainable development' according to the UNCSD (2012b). The conference outcome is to register commitments as long as they deliver transparent and accessible information to the follow-up process. Furthermore, 'all commitments to be registered should be specific, measurable, funded, new [and that] at least one tangible deliverable is specified, along with the estimated timeline for completion' (UNCSD 2012b). These criteria are largely built on the Bali Guidelines; they are similarly non-binding and will remain largely unmonitored. The UN has already established a sustainable development knowledge platform, which disseminates information about the voluntary commitments. The information is provided by the institutions initiating these commitments, and many contain unspecific goals and deliverables. The large number of voluntary commitments is not a sufficient safeguard against these pitfalls, especially in the light of the following observations.

If voluntary commitments were an invitation for business and industry to join in the sustainability transition, this was not achieved. According to the UN website, 52 of the voluntary commitments are multilateral agreements, and 82 of them are categorized under UN/IGO initiatives. At first, these might appear marginal compared to the 611 commitments listed as major group initiatives. A closer look reveals, however, that 124 of these are Global Compact commitments, whereas 269 universities are currently listed as separate initiatives, despite being a part of the Higher Education Sustainability Initiative. In sum, the exact way of counting these initiatives is obscured as well as the amount of funds they already committed. If the private sector is in fact committing funds to sustainability, it is difficult to pinpoint the amount and there are certainly fewer initiatives by businesses than this categorization under major groups would suggest.

Secondly, 22 of the governmental commitments are the signatories of the Barbados Declaration, and 14 of them are the sustainable energy initiatives of governments under the UN Sustainable Energy for All Programme (SE4All). Of the 82 UN/IGO initiatives, 30 were IGO commitments to the SE4All, as well. This suggests that unlike the Type-II partnerships, voluntary commitments seem to signify commitments of state actors in the light of the recent stagnation in global environmental politics. However, unlike the coalitions of the willing or mini-lateral processes (Eckersley 2012), voluntary commitments are still non-binding declarations and statements of intent rather than legally binding multilateral treaties with measurable targets and timetables.

Notwithstanding these criticisms, there were minor improvements in the UN registration system in the sense that every initiative should specify the targets they expected to reach, and the resources devoted to this effort. This was an improvement to the earlier CSD partnerships database system and might provide some measure of output legitimacy and effectiveness to the partnership regime of the UN system. The requirement for naming a contact person, as opposed to the partnership contacting the focal points, was possibly another improvement in terms of follow-up and monitoring procedures.

6.6.5 The Conferences

The previous sections provide the fantasmatic and historical backgrounds for the two roots of sustainable development paradigm, followed by the UN context and documents as a political background. This section aims to summarize these shifts in the discourses of environment and development as reflected in the rights and responsibilities (and later 'opportunities') listed in the documents resulting from the three environmental summits that were held before the emergence of Type-II outcomes.

In the 1972 Stockholm Declaration (UN 1972: para. 2, my emphases), the rights and responsibilities coincide and are supported by the ideas of freedom, equality, and dignity: 'Man has the *fundamental right to freedom, equality and adequate conditions of life*, in an environment of a quality that permits a life of dignity and well-being, and he bears a *solemn responsibility to protect and improve the environment* for present and future generations.'

The Stockholm Declaration embodies an understanding of environment that is linked with rights *and* responsibilities, carefully carving the Southern and Northern demands into the text. The right to a healthy environment would ensure conditions for dignity and well-being, and is as fundamental a right as those of freedom, equality and adequacy. It is, however, balanced and restricted by the responsibility to protect and improve it. Adequacy and improving the environment were not articulated in international documents after 1972.

With the Brundtland Report and the establishment of the *sustainable development* ideal, the *requirement and right of aspiring to industrialization* was placed in front of all nations as a target. Similarly the rights and responsibilities of men and nations have changed in the UN documents resulting from environmental summits. The most immediate manifestation of this shift was available in the documents of the Rio Earth Summit. The Rio Declaration (UN 1992a) evokes states' 'sovereign right to exploit their own resources' and defines 'the right to development'. Simultaneously,

Chapter II of *Agenda 21* (UN 1992b: para. 2.3–7) is devoted to 'international cooperation to accelerate sustainable development in developing countries' and points at a requirement at the global level:

> The international economy should provide a supportive international climate for achieving environment and development goals by: [removing] tariff and non-tariff impediments, [. . .] substantial and progressive reduction in the support and protection of agriculture. [. . .] Trade liberalization should therefore be pursued on a global basis across economic sectors so as to contribute to sustainable development. [. . .] Enhancing the role of enterprises and promoting competitive markets through adoption of competitive policies.

After the Cold War, the UN texts tended towards liberal capitalism, as did the world. Fittingly, the documents of the Johannesburg Summit make direct references to globalization as if it is a force of nature: an objective, irreversible feature of the world, which can neither be disputed nor influenced or overcome. JPOI (UN 2002a: para. 47, my emphasis) devotes a chapter to 'sustainable development in a globalizing world', painting a very neo-liberal picture:

> Globalization offers opportunities and challenges for sustainable development. We recognize that globalization and interdependence are offering new opportunities for trade, investment and capital flows and advances in technology, including information technology, *for the growth of the world economy*, development and the improvement of living standards around the world. At the same time, there remain serious challenges, including serious financial crises, insecurity, poverty, exclusion and inequality within and among societies.

It is worth noticing that the opportunities are narrated as a direct consequence of globalization, while the challenges are a remainder, as if these are problems that globalization is yet to solve, rather than it caused or deepened. More importantly, the opportunities it represents are directly linked with the growth of a world economy, and advancing of technology. The introduction of JPOI (ibid.: para. 3), which emphasizes the importance of the Doha Ministerial Declaration and Monterrey Consensus for sustainable development, already contextualizes partnerships to the background of globalization: '[I]mplementation should involve all relevant actors through partnerships [to achieve] sustainable development. [. . .] [S]uch partnerships are key to pursuing sustainable development in a globalizing world.'

The main goal of partnerships and all other implementation efforts was the eradication of poverty, which was regarded as 'an indispensable requirement for sustainable development', and thus 'although each country has the primary responsibility for its own sustainable development and poverty eradication' global action and legislation too was legitimate and required (ibid.: para. 7). The paradigmatic shift that was initiated by the Brundtland Report in the constructed causality was even more strongly emphasized in the Political Declaration of the WSSD, which establishes the universal aim 'to banish underdevelopment forever' in the name of 'human dignity' through technology transfer and opening of markets (UN 2002b: para. 18). The policy implication of this change was the (re-)prioritization of developmental issues compared to environmental problems. As Table 6.3 shows, the changes in the documents relate to

- *causes* of environmental degradation, from growth to underdevelopment;
- *solutions* to environmental degradation, from a critique of industrialized society and technology to further development and technological advances;
- *policies for environmental protection*, from being based on responsibility to protect the environment towards trade liberalization, technology transfer and partnerships.

The conferences were titled accordingly: in 1972 the conference was on human environment, while in 1992 development entered the picture. Although most environmentalists refer to the Rio Conference as 'the Earth Summit', the official title was the UN Conference on Environment and Development. The global approach as well as the consolidation of sustainable development is reflected in the title of the Johannesburg Conference: the World Summit on Sustainable Development.

These changes were reflected in the end result of the WSSD: Type-II outcomes of the summit were largely geared towards developmental goals; they were semantically and politically linked to neo-liberal globalization; and partnerships not only reflected but also consolidated and institutionalized these narratives. They have become a new form of legality that keeps the environmental and developmental discourses in synch with financial and economic ones.

6.7   CONCLUSIONS: SUSTAINABILITY AS 'THE REMAINDER'

The discourse of sustainable development became the structuring variant of developmental discourses after 1987, and particularly following the Rio 'Earth' Summit in 1992. The same year, Esteva (1992: 8) observed that

*Table 6.3   UN summits on environment before the emergence of
            sustainability partnerships*

Date	Place	Conference	Rights emphasized	Environmental protection through. . .
1972	Stockholm Sweden	UN Conference on Human Environment (UNCHE)	The fundamental right to freedom, equality and adequate conditions of life.	The responsibility to protect and improve the environment.
1992	Rio de Janeiro Brazil	UN Conference on Environment and Development (UNCED)	Sovereign right to exploit natural resources. Right to development.	Trade liberalization across the globe and across sectors. Industrial growth.
2002	Johannesburg South Africa	World Summit on Sustainable Development (WSSD)	The right to development and the right of everyone to a standard of living adequate for their health and well-being. Intellectual property rights, and rights to self-determination. The right to utilize the opportunities globalization and technology brings for the growth of the world economy.	Global trade liberalization to further investment and capital flows. Partnerships among North and South as well as different sectors.

development is the strongest force in modern mentality guiding thought and behaviour, and that the term 'occupies the centre of an incredibly powerful semantic constellation'. Esteva simultaneously argued that development was a feeble and fragile word incapable of giving substance and meaning to thought and behaviour. With so many connotations and an overload of meanings, the term development 'ended up dissolving its precise significance' (ibid.). These features of the term can be replicated for sustainable development as well. The examination of issue areas on which CSD partnerships work further supported this observation (Chapter 4).

The ambiguity in the meaning of both terms brings to mind a number of questions. For theoretical purposes an important question is whether development, and later sustainable development, are concepts that can be termed as empty signifiers. Laclau suggests that the universal is an empty signifier. Nonetheless, he always refers to this process in the formation of popular resistance and the demands are articulated in this context. In other words, the universal is an empty signifier produced by an equivalential chain. Otherwise, when a concept is simply a buzzword, or as Esteva claims when a notion ends up 'dissolving its precise significance', I argue it is not an empty signifier. My answer to the question above is thus negative, as the process through which an empty signifier is established requires a radical political element – a characteristic that the conception of both development and sustainable development lacks. For sure, in the process that led to Western colonialism, development has acquired political connotations. But in the modern Western psyche, development is a structuring component of the social imaginary, rather than a polarizing universal, around which the many identities of resistance are reflected. By the same token, while the political project of an ecological society signified by *sustainability* was once an empty signifier, the term *sustainable development* never acquired such a status among environmental groups. On the contrary, it only came into existence through the logic of difference operating at the international level, which was successful in co-opting most eco-political movements and marginalizing the rest. Furthermore, the antagonistic dichotomy can only be established if the agent of emancipation has been prevented from constituting its identity by the oppressor in ways that are more than the product of the existing system (Laclau 1996). Neither the authors nor the followers of the sustainable development paradigm have this quality.

The logic of difference operates by including challenging demands into the hegemonic discourse. Radical elements in the eco-political discourses were thus integrated to the developmentalist ideology, or were marginalized. Professional environmental NGOs, consumer campaigns on environmental awareness and liberal environmental values have become the norm by the beginning of the millennium. The challenge posed by the eco-political movements has been instrumental in bringing this change, while the eco-political identity itself has been subjugated at the end of the process. As foreseen by the insightful article of Herbert Marcuse (1972), while *the ecological* was a negation of the capitalist logic, developmentalism was already redefining environmental values.

In discourse theoretical terms, '*all* struggles are, by definition, political'

(Laclau 2005a: 154) and so were populist eco-political struggles. The issue of nature moved from the sphere of the social to that of the political, creating a certain social *antagonism* among groups that would identify themselves with the ecological critique and the existing social and political system. Their conception of ecological sustainability has become the universal of a resistance movement, wherein it reflected the particularisms of all other demands in the equivalential chain. Later, with the conception of sustainable development, a logic of difference has been established between what was in the core of ecological critique (developmentalist, industrial modern social organization) and sustainability. *Sustainability* hence became first a floating signifier, the meaning of which was suspended until the contestation over it ended. The contestation could end in various ways (for example a revolution, wherein the oppressive regime is overthrown, or the dissolving of the equivalential chain and complete co-option). In case of the eco-political hegemonic project, most of the identities it reflects have become important components in Green politics, although the environmental demands were to a large extent co-opted into the sustainable development paradigm.

From the perspective of the signifier, the contestation could mean that it could signify radically opposing things for different political identities indefinitely. Or it may lose its importance in defining political identities altogether, in which case it was termed *the remainder*, that is what remains once signification is disrupted. In short, sustainability became *the remainder* of the hegemonic struggle between developmentalist and eco-political discourses. It has lost its particularism in becoming an empty signifier and its universal appeal was lost once the hegemonic struggle over its meaning was diffused. Its meaning is transformed as well as the hegemonic discourse; it has become a universal on which everyone agrees, but it does not define identities; it has lost its fantasmatic function. Unless defined more specifically (for example as 'ecological sustainability') it almost denotes nothing more than continuity.

The resulting managerial approaches to environment and development standardized and objectified issues that were once of political nature and relocated them into the sphere of the social. As a result, just as Mouffe (2000: 6–7) criticizes the national Third Way models that have 'simply given up the traditional struggle of the left for equality', discourses of voluntarism and expertise undo the political nature of environmental issues, which originally aimed at the negation of capitalist logic.

From the perspective of the hegemonic discourses, it has been a contestation they have successfully integrated to their social imaginary. As Figure 6.4 describes, this has taken place twice in the discourses studied here. Firstly, the colonial discourses based on developing the land for the sake of human well-being and civilization has been internalized by the developmentalist discourse. The notion of god-given duty in Max Havelaar's speech was translated into sharing of the benefits of technology with 'peace-loving peoples', as Truman put it. As a result while the white man's burden was eliminated from the hegemonic discourse of development several notions regarding its developmentalist ideas were maintained. On the other hand, the radical elements such as the anti-internationalist/nativist claims of the decolonization discourses were excluded and marginalized from the hegemonic developmentalist discourse as well.

A second shift took place with similar characteristics when developmentalism was re-articulated as sustainable development. So far I have only mentioned that when faced with the challenge of eco-politics, the developmentalist discourse has successfully internalized some of its environmental values while ridding it of radical elements. Like the previous shift, this one too had marginalized both 'pure economic growth' arguments of the earlier developmentalist discourse and of radical ecologists. The invention of sustainable development maintained the developmentalist logic and the existing social order, while representing the environmental demand within the existing hegemonic project.

But there is an equally important similarity between these hegemonic discourses regarding the political subject. The Orient, the South, the 'developing' countries, or the Third World is always external to the Western identity. It is 'a screen for the Western projections of otherness, the mirror by which the West can see itself as a positive unitary subject; [therefore] Western discourses on development and the Third World, can be understood [. . .] as another means by which the West represents its own ideal of itself to itself' (Tuathail 1994: 230). This externality and otherness implies a profound Western 'fear of "the shadowy outside" which must be made safe through penetration and assimilation' (Slater 1993: 422). This allows for interventionism exemplified in the 'democratization efforts' in Iraq, transition to market economy in Eastern Europe, transfer of technology and know-how to Africa. What Said observed as the ontological absence of the Orient continues in the developmentalist discourse, and it is continuously reified by sustainable development.

NOTES

1. Two tenets of Western developmentalism distinguish it from earlier versions of development: the focus on unlimited growth and the assumption of universal desirability of development.
2. In ancient Greek mythology, each powerful human emotion was represented by a corresponding deity. Each deity was jealous of the faculties and qualities s/he represented

and would only to a limited extent share it with the mortals. The transgression of such limits would mean to 'threaten the primacy or privilege of the deity, [thus] abandoning that deity as a point of reference' (Zoja 1995: 46–47).

3. For Said, the West was *the colonizer* and the Orient was *the colonized*. The references to these overtly broad categories are reproduced here to depict his analysis of the colonization process, rather than assuming a Western and Eastern geographical space for these categories. The reinvention of these categories in the developmentalist discourse, as the North/South divide is nonetheless noteworthy (Section 6.3.2).

4. *North–South: A Program for Survival* was published in the English language by The MIT Press, 1980.

5. Even in countries that have never been colonized, modernization, industrialization and economic development were powerful fantasies, for example Japan's Meiji Restoration and Turkey's Kemalist Revolution. These modernization efforts were mostly in response to the military dominance of the Western powers. However anti-imperialist these reformations may appear, they carried all the industrialist, modernist and Westernist connotations of the developmentalist fantasy. In other words, these examples do not controvert the colonialism–development link, but show the extent to which the development paradigm was able to monopolize systems of representation ('colonize reality') with this change in the semantic constellation around it.

6. The discursive interplay of industrialization and Westernization has been noted by Serge Latouche (1989 [1996]: 76), who regards Westernization as 'a cultural cladding for industrialization', which in turn is 'deculturation [by way of] destruction of all traditional structures, economic, social and mental'.

7. It is unlikely that Haldane and Kleiber were unaware of Thompson as a decorated fellow Cambridge graduate.

8. Otherwise, much more expansive and radical critiques of technology were already present, such as Jacques Ellul's and Lewis Mumford's.

9. *A Blueprint for Survival* was published in January 1972, occupying all of *The Ecologist* Vol. 2, No. 1, in advance of the 1972 Stockholm Conference, republished by Penguin books due to its popularity.

10. Sea Shepherd Conservation Society website: http://www.seashepherd.org/whales/sea-shepherd-history.html, accessed: 12-10-2010.

11. A simple word count shows that the word 'development' was only used four times in the text (as 'sustainable development' twice), as opposed to 31 repetitions of the word 'environment'.

7. Partnerships and the discourse of participation

---

either to pay some respect to or show their awareness of the rules of the game: women in power suits, indigenous peoples' representatives in feathers speak perfect U-N-glish, the youth delegates speak only when it is their 3-minute turn and most evidence-oriented natural scientists employ terms like 'sustainable science', which they call 'diplomatic language'. Major groups are sometimes represented in the big meetings, but there is hardly reciprocity: delegates rarely join the meetings of the major groups.

Underneath the surface, resistance is omnipresent. A youth delegate spoke of a game youth representatives play when there are long, back-to-back speeches, which they call 'bullshit bingo'. They prepare lists of buzzwords like sustainable, peace, international cooperation and so on; then as the speeches go on, and as the speakers utter these words, they cross the words in their cards. 'Whoever crosses them all first whispers "bingo" and wins the game!' Over coffee, an NGO worker tells me that her boss became a 'bouncer', holding the doors to international funding for development projects, only after being deeply disillusioned with his earlier development work. (Even the concept of development doesn't go completely unquestioned. Nothing does. It's a constant pull and push of meaning: tug of war with multiple strings, being pulled in all directions. There are differences in thickness of strings and the strength of groups. Maybe that's the secret of *status quo*, or maybe this is how institutionalization could be graphically represented . . ..)

In the big meeting room, several opinions are raised – all in good time and a particular order. This is a strictly symbolic level of representation. Yet, voices are much less resonant or permanent than texts in this building. Delegates reify their stances in turns, in front of a big screen on which 'the text' is projected through a non-identifiable beamer. Each comment is counteracted by another delegate or coalition, opposing the change of some sentence, clause, or principle. 'The text', already imbued with the usual UN concerns in italics and bullet points, becomes heavily burdened with paraphrases and disagreements symbolized by various types of parenthesis and highlights. The meaning behind these rather complicated textual signifiers is hidden from uneducated eyes. Another respondent said, 'one must come prepared [as] conferences are exams' for those who actually have a stake but not the necessary formation. The repercussions of subtle changes may be critical for some groups, represented by a single individual in this big room: the small difference between singular and plural may mean the legal distance between recognition of existence in all plurality versus the tacit agreement on the lack of any particular identity of the 'indigenous peoples'. It is unimaginable to benefit from a lack of understanding of this cramped and faltering text, its workings and terms, its grammar and its lexicon once inside this building of modernist order and structure, reflecting an ideal of an international system from some time ago.

7.1 INTRODUCTION

Even in much of today's progressive politics, the danger is not passivity, but pseudo-activity, the urge to be active and to participate. People intervene all the time, attempting to 'do something', [while] the truly difficult thing is to step back and to withdraw from it. Those in power often prefer even a critical participation to silence – just to engage us in a dialogue, to make it sure that our

ominous passivity is broken. Against such an interpassive mode in which we are active all the time to make sure that nothing will really change, the first truly critical step is to withdraw into passivity and to refuse to participate. This first step clears the ground for a true activity, for an act that will effectively change the coordinates of the constellation.
(Žižek 2006: 26–27)

The discourse of participation is the last discourse of this analysis on sustainability partnerships. Participation is one of the most elusive concepts also in democratic theory, and relates to several (at times even opposing) ideological perspectives: Participation as a political right is a fundamental tenet of classical libertarianism, whereas social democratic arguments for participation involve bringing about social justice. In the context of development, it is regarded as a non-ideological criterion to judge or improve the efficiency of development projects by most development economists, while the empowerment arguments of the 1970s regarded participation as a radical political project to alter social stratifications, political systems and institutions through class struggle. In short, participation is a fuzzy concept; therefore to study participatory discourses to understand partnerships, it is necessary to focus on the partnerships regime, the partnership projects and their political environments.

Participation of civil society in international governance platforms, such as the UNCSD, is regarded as an important means to make these platforms and processes more democratic. As mentioned in Chapter 4, the partnerships concept was introduced to the UN texts for the first time, after the Rio Earth Summit, as a means to advance the democratic quality of global environmental governance. Twenty years later, it is difficult to suggest that civil society participation in global environmental governance enhanced its democratic quality. The extent to which participating in UN platforms helps advance the aims of vulnerable and/or radical groups in civil society is also questionable. The exclusively positive and democratic connotation of the term *participation* is one of the main reasons for this paradox. Political science literature on participation focuses mostly on the problem of inclusion/exclusion. Who has the power or privilege to make decisions? Who is included and who is excluded from citizenship or the public sphere? If a political system actively prohibits or indirectly impedes most of its citizens from the governing mechanisms, it is regarded undemocratic (and often, therefore, illegitimate). However, as the quote from Žižek aptly puts it, participation is not necessarily meaningful, and does not always serve the democratization of a political process. Moreover, at the global level, where there is no specified *demos*, territoriality, or representation, the habitual questions and solutions of democratic theory are less pertinent.

Robert Chambers (1997) suggests that participation has become the new paradigm in governance and development discourses: at the local level, even the smallest of development projects is legitimized on the basis of community involvement. At the global level, the concept of *good governance*, developed by the World Bank and taken up by the UN, is built on participation as a fundamental criterion (UNESCAP 2011). In turn, the Bretton Woods institutions themselves are repeatedly challenged and invited to reform themselves, towards being more inclusive (Hardt and Negri 2004: 290–291; UNESCAP 2005). It is notable that in all these contexts the terms *participation* and *inclusiveness* are regularly used interchangeably.

In an attempt to link the discourse of participation as an important context to sustainability partnerships, this chapter begins with a discussion of the problem of scale in democratic theory (as opposed to the uses of the term in governance literature) as the fantasmatic background. Then, it focuses on the level of global environmental governance, specifically on the way wherein the participation of civil society has changed since the Rio Conference. This was a transformation of civil society into major groups, which could participate in the CSD platforms. Subsequently, when partnerships were initiated as Type-II outcomes of the WSSD, *major groups* were asked to 'participate' in environmental governance by establishing partnerships to implement policy. Finally, since stakeholder participation has come to be regarded as an indispensible aspect of the 'good governance' paradigm, community participation in development projects is examined, both historically and in the context of CSD partnerships.

7.2 FANTASMATIC LOGICS: ON BEING THE RIGHT SIZE

Inclusion/exclusion is at the heart of democratic theory. The ancient meaning of democracy was that the power to rule (*kratos*) rested in the people (*dêmos*), indicating a more inclusive system than its alternatives, and a relative emancipation from elitism and dicta. The immediate question that follows is, naturally, who constitutes *a people*. In fact, what differentiates modern democracy from its ancient precursors is the inclusion of most of the citizenry (especially after the abolition of both slavery and the legal subjection of women). Most of the adult population can participate in politics – at least through voting in the elections. Thus, participation is almost always regarded as a positive quality in politics.

In the historical formation of nation-states (particularly after the First World War, and the following period of decolonization), the question of who constitutes a people was a complicated matter. How were the borders to be drawn, if certain terrains did not have a 'nation' claiming to be the rightful rulers? On countless occasions 'a people' entitled to self-govern were determined by earlier colonization experiences. Robert Dahl (1989: 3) argues that political philosophers deal with this problem by presupposing that 'a people' already exists, as a creation of history, even though this presupposition is problematic since nationhood is often established 'not by consent or consensus but by violence'.

The myth of popular sovereignty is also in the roots of the contemporary international system, particularly the UN, which is based on the idea of sovereignty linked to nation-statehood. This is partially because there are few powerful political imageries comprising *a global demos*. If a world government is out of question, then, inclusiveness at the global level can be an attribution only of decision-making processes. Inclusiveness of a process can be defined as *the extent to which those who are affected by a decision participate in its making*. There is but one problem with the application of this definition to *global* governance: global issues (such as environmental problems) influence all of humanity. Would this mean that every person should somehow be included in every decision-making process? If not, what are the boundaries of the citizenry that should participate in which decision? As the number of persons involved in a decision-making process necessarily influences its character and form, this problem is about size. In other words, the problem of participation/inclusion in global governance is simultaneously *a problem of scale*.

Dahl (1989: 4–5) makes the problem of scale central to his study of democracy: his starting point is the change in the scale of democracy from the *polis* (with only a small part of society enjoying rights and duties of citizenship) to the nation-state (with an extensive *demos*), which resulted in a magnification of 'the already significant utopianism of the democratic ideal'. By this, he refers to the problematic assumption that 'today's large-scale democracies [. . .] can still possess the virtues and possibilities of small-scale democracy' (ibid.).

Early political writings on the best political system (regardless of its democratic quality) has been characterized by considerations of scale, which in both Plato and Aristotle was no bigger than the city-state. For example, Plato's ideal society in *The Laws* ([1984]) was located in a small, long-abandoned Cretan harbour. Similarly, most ideal commonwealths and utopias have taken on this idea of seclusion as a literary strategy (such as Thomas More's *Utopia*, Tommaso Campanella's *La città del Sole*, Francis Bacon's Bensalem and James Hilton's Shangri La). The point is that, except for some of the Christian imageries, the utopian genre is full of imagined lands situated outside of the bounds of other societies, whichever time they were written in. This also applies to actual utopian experiments, almost all of which were placed in geographically isolated landscapes, particularly in North America. The reason for so many 'seclusion utopias' to have been written is probably not that the authors decided not to explain how control of the population took place. (Indeed, as a literary strategy, seclusion might have this impact for if the author focuses on the control mechanisms of the population the genre is called a *dystopia*.) When a utopia is located far away from the existing societies, the more insidious problem of scale is circumvented.

Secondly, the utopianism that Dahl is referring to is related to the question whether *representative* democracy sufficiently includes all the citizenry (in qualitative terms). The re-invention of democracy as a desirable and applicable model of government for nation-states has taken place amidst contestations regarding the best system of rule, the virtues of direct democracy put against the virtues of republicanism. The question was whether representation could transform a republic into a democracy.

Representation was a monarchic tradition before it paradoxically became the solution to the problems of a nation-wide democracy. It was Montesquieu (1748 [1989]) who first observed that separation of powers could make a democratic republic possible. In other words, creating checks and balances between the executive, the legislative and the judiciary, the drawbacks of the transformation from small- to large-scale democracies could be remedied. What needed to be remedied, Dahl explains, was the romanticized idea of direct democracy in the writings of many political philosophers, particularly Jean-Jacques Rousseau. Throughout the French Revolution, Rousseau was significant in the transformation of the discourse on democracy from connoting disunity and decadence to implying harmony and regeneration (Miller 1996: 202–203): 'Before Rousseau democracy was, at best, an admirable but obsolete pure form of government; [. . .] after him it became a name for popular sovereignty, [. . .] a conviction that all human beings possess, in their own free will, the capacity and desire to govern themselves'. In sum, Rousseau's imagery was categorically opposed to representation.

The French Revolution was unique in its affirmation of the absolute power of the people, producing new forms of legitimacy and a political culture based on popular sovereignty, which later formed the democratic imaginary (Laclau and Mouffe 1985: 155). The revolution therefore indicated a great discontinuity and opened up the space in which texts on several possible democracies were brought into the spotlight, with their pros and cons, all the risks and promises involved. In other words, democracy had become an ideal during the Revolution, and there was contestation among different types of democratic projects.

The most important of such projects were Robespierre's dictatorial democracy, *sans-culottes'* direct democracy and Paine's representative democracy. Miller (1996: 205–206) notes that this moment of dislocation, wherein various political projects contested the meaning of democracy and legitimate rule, gradually disappeared. For example, Robespierre changed his position and defended representative democracy 'as the only feasible form of modern democracy'; then Bentham and Mill argued for universal suffrage and parliamentary representation; simultaneously, the example of self-government set by the United States reduced the worries regarding violence of the masses. Finally, it was Alexis de Tocqueville's (1835) influential book, *Democracy in America*, that delinked representative democracy from the French Revolution and created an imaginary of its potentials on the basis of the experiences in the United States: his idea that democracy could be tamed if 'the most powerful, intelligent, and moral classes [. . .] gain control of it in order to direct it' made representative democracy safe for liberalism.

It is critical at this point to recognize the fundamentally different roots of liberal and democratic traditions. This does not necessarily mean that the two traditions are incompatible. Following Carl Schmidt, Mouffe (2000) points to the paradox of democracy resulting from the merger of liberalism (with its emphasis on freedom) and democracy (with its emphasis on popular sovereignty and equality). Acknowledging this paradox is the starting point for her conception of radical democracy based on agonistic pluralism. But for the purposes of this chapter it is sufficient to recognize the tension between direct democracy and representation as the restrictive myth for participatory discourses in global governance. In other words 'direct participation of all affected citizens in decision-making' is the participatory ideal in democratic discourses, which serves as the ultimate and unreachable fantasy. On the other hand, as the scale of national or global democratic decision-making does not (in practice) allow participation of all, representation has long become the tradition that replaces participation.

For the application of democratic principles at the global level, various procedures and principles are proposed. Most importantly, new, hybrid governance mechanisms such as partnerships are often seen in this light by proponents of deliberative democracy and governance. 'Environmental politics and sustainable development has emerged as an experimental arena for new modes of governance' with democratization goals, such as partnerships (Bäckstrand et al. 2010: 15). These new mechanisms are almost always introduced as a means to enhance the democratic quality of environmental governance by more inclusive, participatory processes. Still, their democratic potential is found to have repeatedly been compromised by economic incentives (cf. Stripple 2010). Furthermore, democratizing elements such as deliberation are employed in processes with little policy relevance, or at the implementation phase after decisions are made. As Nikolas Rose (1996) pointed out they become a means to delegate responsibility for environmental performance to various 'partners' or consumers. In the context of neo-liberal globalization that shifts power from the political to the economic sphere, these mechanisms often defuse the radical potential of civic critique, and function as a legitimizing strategy of global capital (Paterson 2008; Bäckstrand et al. 2010). However, at national, local, and even supranational levels, whenever there is the shadow of hierarchy, hybrid governance mechanisms are more responsive, transparent and accountable (cf. Brinkerhoff 2002, Hagberg 2010). This suggests that their democratic quality depends on the level of governance they operate in. At the global level, there are very few and only fragmented mechanisms to ensure their democratic qualities, nor is there a legal authority to petition in case of undesired consequences or governance failures. Hence, these new mechanisms do not increase the democratic quality of global governance by simply making governance platforms more inclusive. On the contrary, they require new mechanisms of checks and balances, specifically designed for *global* environmental governance.

The next section examines the way the United Nations system has operated on and responded to challenges posed by the assumption that representation can ensure democratic participation. Especially illustrative in this regard is the transformation of civil society into major groups that were invited to participate in the CSD. Later, their participation has come to be regarded as indispensable for 'good governance' and became critical for the implementation of MDGs through sustainability partnerships.

7.3   POLITICS OF PARTICIPATION

7.3.1   NGO Participation in the UN

The UN defines itself as an all-inclusive forum and its outreach as the whole globe:

> Due to its unique international character, and the powers vested in its founding Charter, the Organization can take action on a wide range of issues, and provide a forum for its 192 Member States to express their views, through the General Assembly, the Security Council, the Economic and Social Council and other bodies and committees. The work of the United Nations reaches every corner of the globe.[1]

The assumption that representation can ensure democratic participation has been questioned by the transnational civil movements – their participation in and demonstrations around UN summits displayed the existence and political presence of various systematically underrepresented minorities. Distributed across national borders, these minorities are unlikely to ever gain the representation that is needed for governing nation states and be represented in the UN's governance platforms. Nevertheless, they amount to a sizeable minority among the population of the globe. Furthermore, their activities in global summits challenge not only the legitimacy of solely nation-state-based negotiations but also the UN's self-image of global outreach.

In global governance, only state actors have guaranteed access to negotiations (Clark et al. 1998: 4–6; Wolf 2002: 40; Dingwerth 2007: 38), although there are instances of state exclusion, such as the G8 or the G77. The UN, with the notable exception of the Security Council, applies this rule in most of its institutions. However, the democratic legitimacy of solely intergovernmental rule-making is being challenged as well. Klaus Dingwerth (2007: 39) notes that

> the exclusive participation of governments is problematic where affected communities are incongruent with national constituencies. Where the interests of the domestic constituencies are heterogeneous and fall into identifiable subgroups, the view that governments can best represent the interests of their citizens is challenged. As a result, when specific interests are systematically underrepresented by national governments, other actors – such as transnational advocacy coalitions – may be better representatives of the interests of communities affected by a decision-making process.

Dingwerth (ibid.) includes *scope of participation* (how constituencies and participants are defined), *quality of participation* (access different constituencies have to different modes of participation, ways of representation and so on) and *discursive balance* (how the dominant discourse shapes the decision-making process, and whether alternative discourses can play a part) among conceptual dimensions of democratic legitimacy in transnational governance institutions.

Specifically, masses of crowds demonstrating their disagreement with the decisions of an international summit challenge the democratic legitimacy of the ongoing negotiation platforms on all these three dimensions. The protesters and the participants to the external/alternative events challenge the scope of the participation, while internal participants of civil society – by their mere presence – challenge the quality of participation, as governments are the main actors in the decision-making process. Moreover, the positions of these two groups (and other relevant civil society that might not be physically present) substantiate the existence of alternative discourses which are absent in the negotiation platforms. Hence, they highlight the ways in which dominant discourses shape the political agenda. This is why the massive civil society participation in Rio was so significant for the practice of international relations and resulted in a sharp and steady increase in the number of NGOs registering with the ECOSOC since 1992.[2]

In fact, in a 2004 article, Tony Hill, by then the coordinator of the United Nations Non-Governmental Liaison Service (UN NGLS), wrote that the first major change in UN–civil society relations was the result of such participation (particularly in the Rio Earth Summit). Notably, Hill was not only referring to issues of environment and development, but also of a general change in the quality *and* scope of participation that civil society enjoyed within the UN. According to Hill, the first generation of UN–civil society relations, lasting up to the end of the Cold War, was formal and ceremonial rather than political in nature, and involved professional and business associations in the form of international NGOs. These were granted formal consultative relations with the ECOSOC, but remained autonomous.

The second generation of UN–NGO relations, starting with the Rio Earth Summit, were 'essentially political and reflect[ed] the motivation of NGOs to engage with the UN as part of the institutional architecture of global governance' (ibid.). NGO presence in Rio further polarized societies on environmental problems, which were previously not regarded as global political issues. Simultaneously, these groups represented a wide range of demands from environmental groups but also from the poor, from the underrepresented, from the politically excluded (for example workers, indigenous peoples, women, youth and so forth). Such representation of demands as an intervention can best be understood as the logic of equivalence, wherein all these demands could be represented in a singular platform.

The UN's response shows how the myth and the three dimensions of democratic legitimacy mentioned above were being challenged. Firstly, with *Agenda 21* civil society had been compartmentalized into major groups and enlarged to include groups with fundamentally different political aims (for example techno-scientific networks, local governments, workers and corporations); secondly, the UN invited *national* NGOs to apply for a consultative status. In other words, civil society had been asked to join only on condition that other sectors also would. Thirdly, they were encouraged to participate in the national decision-making processes rather than the international ones. Hill's (ibid.) note on this suggests a deep conflict:

In 1993, partly in response to the experience of NGO participation in the Rio Conference, [an ECOSOC] working group began a review and evaluation of relations with NGOs and Civil Society, leading three years later to the adoption of Resolution 1996/31 as the formal, legal framework for UN–NGO relations. [This] explicitly open[ed] up UN consultative status to national NGOs – despite the efforts of some of the first generation of INGOs [international NGOs] who allied with some of the most reluctant UN Member States to try to prevent this opening up to national (and regional) NGOs.

According to Hill, this second generation of relations was marked by an increasing cooperation, not only in collective funding of NGO projects, but also 'voluntary – as opposed to contractual – cooperation' between NGOs and UN secretariats. But this had also been a process in which the business actors were officially included in civil society and were invited to participate in the same fashion. As this quote suggests, 'non-governmental' started to mean *any* non-state actor. This process of instrumentalization of civil society and its consequences for the potential of political action are the focus of the next section. This topic is approached from the viewpoint of Hannah Arendt's observation on the meaning of political action.

7.3.2 Post-Rio Instrumentalization of Civil Political Action

With word and deed we assert ourselves into the human world. [. . .] This assertion is not forced upon us by necessity, like labor, and it is not prompted by utility, like work. [. . .] The innermost meaning of the acted deed and the spoken word is independent of victory and defeat. [. . .] Action can be judged only by the criterion of greatness because it is in its nature to break through the commonly accepted and reach into the extraordinary. (Arendt 1958 [1998]: 176–205)

In *The Human Condition* Hannah Arendt has a conception of *action as freedom* that constitutes 'the political' (or the public sphere). Human activities, in her thought, are separated into three spheres: *labour*, which includes endless and repetitive activities to sustain life; *work*, activities that produce an enduring artefact; and *action*, political activity undertaken in the public sphere and among equals. These three facets of the human condition stand in an ascending hierarchy of importance, action being 'the most *human* of all'. This is not only because action requires being among other persons, nor because it is the only realm in which one's agency is disclosed (to reveal *who* she is, as opposed to *what* she is: identity as opposed to function). Action is the most human of all, because it is the realm of freedom: 'to be free and to act are the same' (ibid.).

The quote asserts that the meaning of political action is not its outcome. Firstly, utility is a function of another realm, the realm of work, which aims at the production of artefacts that will endure and/or be of use. Secondly, political action is necessarily out of the ordinary: it is in its nature to break through the commonly accepted and reach into the extraordinary (in Laclau's terms to 'polarize' and 'dislocate' the discourses that have sedimented into accepted social norms and institutions). Otherwise it is not 'great' action: change is possible through political action, and contingency is thus accounted for. Simultaneously, for discourse analyses, 'great actions' often provide heuristic markers during which frames and narratives are most highlighted; points of reference that predicate the future changes.

The Rio Earth Summit is a moment of such 'great' action in global environmental politics, that reached into the extraordinary and transformed the commonly accepted. Many of its participants remember it as an 'exceptional' moment due to the unforeseen civil society participation and public interest in the summit – 2400 NGO representatives and 17 000 people attended the Rio Conference and/or the simultaneous NGO Global Forum, which had a consultative status to the summit.[3] Such massive participation of civil society was neither overseen by the organizers, nor had a precedent. For a moment, it put the environmental issues at the top of the global political agenda. This overwhelming crowd was instrumental in the formation of major groups, as a senior programme officer at UNEP[4] who took part in the organization of the summits recalled:

> It's not clear where the major groups idea came out. Everybody agrees that it came out partly in reaction to the numbers of people in Rio, and the diversity in Rio. These communities never participated at that level and complexity in any other conference before. It was a creative response to go and ask specific communities for issue papers. That partly laid the foundation: [Instead of] asking professional consultants to write papers on women and indigenous people, going to the networks of women, youth groups, indigenous groups et cetera and asking them what they think about the issues, about their role, and how they want to engage . . . There is no one person that came up with the 'major group' term but it evolved out of a process. These entities were already playing a role, so you had to acknowledge them.

In Rio, the UN addressed the role of all social groups in the achievement of an internationally agreed programme, for the first time. For an instant of 'creative response', their opinions were asked, and immediately afterwards a process emerged: the UN started to institutionalize their role, categorizing them into major groups. *Agenda 21* defined these groups and their specific roles, dedicating a section to 'issues of how people are to be mobilized and empowered for their various roles in sustainable development' (IISD 1996: 9). After the massive participation of civil society, it was still deemed necessary that people were mobilized, even empowered for this goal. While civil society represented a variety of discourses, sustainable development had to be fixed as the single goal around which all groups would be mobilized.

In Dingwerth's terms, the formulation of major groups would be an act of re-establishing the discursive balance. Alternative discourses were acknowledged and some components of these were even included in the documents resulting from the Rio Summit. On the other hand, the political character of these actions was ignored and instrumentalized for the greater goal of sustainable development. Thus, the participation of civil society was no longer a spontaneous result of their choices and activities. To summarize, the overwhelming participation of civil society in Rio with their variety of demands, was now subject to *logic of difference*, which invited them to take part in the governance process but simultaneously made them a *means* towards the end-goal of sustainable development.

For instance, in *Agenda 21* (UN 1992b: para. 23.1–2) civil society participation in decision-making was narrated in purely functional terms: '[participation of all social groups is] critical to the effective implementation of the objectives, policies and mechanisms agreed to by Governments in all programme areas of *Agenda 21* [. . .]. One of the fundamental prerequisites for the achievement of sustainable development is broad public participation in decision-making'. At first, there seems to be a contradiction in terms: civil society is invited to participate in the decision-making, while the decisions are already made by governments. This is, in fact, a double operation: the first movement is the suggestion that these intergovernmental decisions are globally accepted, and they can only be successfully implemented if all social groups committed to them. Hence, the myth of representation (of all citizens based on national sovereignty) is reiterated. Secondly, new ways of participation for major groups in the decision-making process is detailed:

> In the more specific context of environment and development, the need for new forms of participation has emerged, [including] individuals, groups and organizations to *participate in environmental impact assessment procedures* and *to know about and participate in decisions*, particularly those which potentially affect the communities in which they live and work. (Ibid., my emphasis.)

This statement does not entail civil society participation in global decision-making, but to policy processes at the national or local levels, specifically by understanding and knowing the decisions that the governing elite has made. By doing so, the text lets the governments decide the scope of civil society participation in their countries, as it suggests no specific or binding procedures for inclusion. While these indications are piecemeal, they also provide a certain point of view wherein *Agenda 21* does not make two conflicting statements, but affirms UN's sovereignty-based decision-making model.

At this point, civil society was necessary for a goal to be achieved, not the reason for its existence. Its polarizing force was already transformed into a means to the goal of sustainable development. As they institutionalized into major groups, their political identities were also played down: they were compartmentalized and categorized (mostly on the basis of their economic functions) into workers, scientists, farmers, municipalities, business, or women, youth, and so forth. On the other hand, the importance of civil society participation in environmental politics was being repeatedly highlighted in the texts that brought about this change. However, as Arendt (1958 [1998]: 200) suggests, it is of great importance that the momentum of such political action is not lost:

> Power cannot be stored up and kept in reserve for emergencies, like the instruments of violence, but exists only in its actualization. Where power is not actualised, it passes away, and history is full of examples that the greatest material riches cannot compensate for this loss. Power is actualised only where word and deed have not parted company, where words are not empty and deeds not brutal, where words are not used to veil intentions but to disclose realities, and deeds are not used to violate and destroy but to establish relations and create new realities.

Arendt calls this characteristic of power its potentiality or dynamics. From coming together with fellow humans emerges the public sphere, and power keeps it together. Only then (before they institutionalize and subsume disagreements) do words disclose reality and deeds create it anew: action precedes institutionalization.

At this point, Arendt is juxtaposing the logics of equivalence and difference: when words and action are one, the words disclose reality; political demands are articulated. Through political action different demands conjoin in a chain of equivalence and form bigger collectives. Once the logic of difference successfully sets in and institutionalization takes place, the dynamics change and the words are used to veil intentions. This does not suggest that any of these documents are false or intentionally misleading. Nevertheless the process of institutionalization necessarily demotes the radical political dimension of collective action. Institutions become more inclusive so that their deeper structures remain the same. As the next section demonstrates, it would require a decade of institutionalization and another environmental summit before civil society's place in global environmental governance was properly redefined.

7.3.3   Post-Johannesburg Institutionalization of Major Groups

In terms of major groups' participation in the CSD process, perhaps the most telling evidence pointing to the instrumentalization of civil society was the 2004 statement of the major groups, titled *CSD-12: Historic Statement by 9 Major Groups*. Evaluating the twelfth session of the CSD, the major groups noted that the Chair of the session as well as the secretariat has been open and encouraging, which was not the case with other chairpersons, sessions, or UN platforms. Yet, the session failed to address their concerns, particularly 'on involving and empowering the local communities, local governments and indigenous peoples', or the need for different platforms (intersessional or regional working groups for major groups), and for ground rules to ensure meaningful participation (SDIN 2004). The complaints in the statement were revealing: the discussion papers of major groups have received little attention, the groups 'did not get a sense that they played a significant role', and they demanded their representatives to be 'seated as experts' on panels, 'to be questioned and challenged by the governments' (ibid.). In sum, both the scope and the quality of major group participation were unsatisfactory.

The same year, Tony Hill (2004) described a 'possible third generation of UN–Civil Society relations' emerging with the Type-II outcomes. On the one hand, this process raised questions on 'the role of the UN as a broker of partnerships, the future of multilateralism as a form of global governance and the future of the UN's relations with [NGOs, who] view these latest developments with scepticism'. On the other hand, it transformed the UN from being an intergovernmental platform to one that 'brings together the political power of governments, the economic power of the corporate sector, and the "public opinion" power of civil society'.

This win–win narrative is employed quite often regarding partnerships; it suggests division of labour, cooperation and economies of scale, bringing the various competencies of all three sectors together. Yet, there is no unified goal in this narrative: 'win–win' refers to the simultaneous achievement of *different* goals of different actors. In the introductory chapter, I argued that not only does this narrative translate the reduction of transaction costs to effectiveness, but it also uses this economic definition of effectiveness to legitimize a governance model. But for the purposes of this chapter, I would like to juxtapose this narrative to Hill's last two statements in his article. Firstly, he invites civil society to continue 'invest[ing] its "public opinion" power in UN fora both to influence and empower governments and counter [. . .] the private sector' (ibid.). Secondly, he notes that the international community has largely accepted that good governance 'demands the participation of independent groups and organizations of civil society, and representatives of the private economy, in governance processes' (ibid.).

Hill's first point suggests that civil society aims at countering the power of corporations, which is only partially true – civil society involved in the UN processes is hardly uniform, and includes many NGOs with no such aim. Nonetheless, the way civil society is perceived by most UN technocrats is similar: a bloc of NGOs with different priorities and yet with the main goal of opposing deepening corporate power and influence. This categorization is employed often and it can be understood as a coping mechanism with the complexity of civil society's demands. It could also be seen as an overly-unifying and oversimplified understanding of civil society, dismissing the several political dimensions of these groups and their work. Accordingly, the business community is aware of these dimensions, and funds several pro-business environmental groups or initiates partnerships with them. Hill's second point sends a rather direct message to civil society: good governance incorporates civil society *and* business at once; and this is not negotiable. The goal of countering corporate power is only allowed into the system by cooperating with corporations, only if the corporations are also allowed in. Hence, he points to one of the paradoxes of partnerships.

The win–win narrative gains a new meaning when juxtaposed against this background. When understood with this message and the contradictions involved, Hill's article is a rather accurate historical account of UN–civil society relations. Whenever civil society expands or deepens its participation in the operations or the processes of the UN, this new participatory principle is also applied to corporations as the 'third pillar' of liberal democracies.

This was once again the case, during the negotiation of partnerships in the Bali PrepCom. Two crucial changes took place regarding the discourses of participation, which constitute the next two sections. The first one is about the function of partnerships: the Bali Guidelines redefined their goal by substituting *participation* with *implementation*. Secondly, the meaning of the participatory principle guiding major groups has changed from 'participation of all social groups', to 'participation of stakeholders'.

7.3.3.1 From participation to implementation

The concept of 'partnership' in the context of sustainable development first appears at the end of the Rio Earth Summit, with the Rio Declaration (UN 1992a, Annex I) and *Agenda 21* (UN, 1992b). At the time, the word partnership was not defined, and was mainly used as a means to ensure the involvement of civil society in decision-making and policy implementation. As the previous section shows, throughout the text there were references to the importance of their participation to the decision-making processes, particularly at the national level. Chapter 27 of *Agenda 21* explicitly defined NGOs as 'partners for sustainable development', and their participation was qualified as having a democratizing value: '[NGOs] play a vital role in the shaping and implementation of participatory democracy' (ibid.). It is important to recognize that regardless of the later developments, these documents had certain democratic elements and reflected such intentions.

This emphasis on the participation of major groups and NGOs in decision-making, and the democratic value of such participation disappears in the documents of 2002. By the time they were being negotiated in the Bali PrepCom, sustainability partnerships were defined by Bali Guidelines (UNCSD 2002b, my emphases) as 'specific commitments by various partners intended to contribute to and reinforce the *implementation* of the outcomes of intergovernmental negotiations of the WSSD and to help the *further implementation* of *Agenda 21* and the MDGs'.

How can this shift in the focus be explained? The first set of reasons relate to the separation of state and non-state authority in the international system. The state actors are generally reluctant to share their authority, to some extent because of the sovereignty-based organization of the UN system. One respondent's account of the process was revealing:

> [*Agenda 21* required participation in decision-making,] and not in the symbolic. But it was very unusual that an intergovernmental summit like Rio agreed to that language in the first place. It's never happened [before or] since then; because member states are very sensitive about the term 'decision-making'. It's their domain. They don't like to share [it]. And if there is any hint that there may be a reason or process that would be open about decision-making you immediately see statements that start with 'this is a membership-driven organisation' [meaning] 'This is our organisation; we make decisions here. We can consult with you if we want [but we don't have to] take it. It's our decision'. When the issues are not difficult or politically sensitive, they may go up and down in terms of where they stand on that dimension, but if you ask [straightforwardly], everyone will [say] 'We don't want to share [decision-making power]'. The states at the CSD are falling into line; you see this a lot less in the General Assembly, where the stakes are high.[5]

Moreover the inclusion of non-state actors into decision-making processes immediately raises questions of democratic legitimacy in the UN, as they are regarded as having little representative power *vis-à-vis* state actors. While at the CSD the legitimacy of non-state actors is generally acknowledged, several respondents indicated that when non-state actors assume a role in decision-making, their democratic credentials are questioned.

Another reason was a more general change from Rio to Johannesburg, in the way the participatory ideal was framed and/or perceived by state actors:

> After the nineties, NGOs were getting more [finances and] were the most trusted institutions. Some governments didn't appreciate this [since] the polls [suggested] they are not responsible enough. Their reactions limited the whole participatory spirit which defined CSD since '92. Before, whatever musing was taking place in CSD was slowly adopted by other commissions. CSD [was] the best participation example. [Recently] it became exclusive to CSD. (Ibid.)

The second set of reasons relate to specific non-state actors and the way they are perceived by other state and non-state actors. In other words, although 'inclusion of *all* social groups' to the decision-making can be regarded as a democratic ideal that needs to be upheld, in the process of negotiating which specific major groups will enjoy inclusion to decision-making, contestations began to emerge. First of all, some national delegations were very reluctant to include NGOs or indigenous peoples in the decision-making process even on paper, as these groups were understood as a threat to the sovereign state. For example, the Chinese delegation to the WSSD was persuaded on condition that each Chinese NGO in the process would be approved by the delegation.[6] This was not only due to the nature of the international system. Many governments resented the democratization process that was being forced from the global down to the national level.

Business involvement was also questioned regarding their unenforced procedures of transparency and lack of democratic accountability. Early in 2002, arbitrations of this nature started to appear in the documents. NGOs and trade unions were sceptical of the inclusion of business groups in decision-making. One reason for their concerns was the General Assembly resolution analyzed in Chapter 5, *Towards Global Partnerships* (UN 2001a), that encouraged businesses to take part in partnerships, without mentioning any liability on their side. To alleviate these concerns, two criteria were proposed: a code of conduct and a strict commitment to CSR, which were both declined.

To conceptualize partnerships as implementation mechanisms remedied some of these legitimacy questions. As long as partnerships were implementing the inter-governmentally agreed decisions, they could be no threat to national sovereignty. If any of the non-state actors fundamentally challenged the authority of a nation state or touched upon sensitive issues, the state actor could have the upper hand on the basis that they never agreed to 'that specific partnership' as technically state actors only agreed to the Johannesburg partnerships, and not the partnerships registered afterwards. The concerns about the inclusion of business actors remained largely unresolved. Some even argued that they had relative gains from the process: their participation in the CSD had been in the form of NGOs like all other non-state actors, and not as separate corporations. In the partnerships scheme, however, they could use their own names, form, lead and finance their own projects and so on. Although symbolic, some respondents found this problematic.

The third set of reasons for the shift in emphasis from participation to implementation relates to the implementation deficit. As early as the 'Rio+5 meetings' in 1997, the inadequacies in the implementation of Rio commitments were articulated, for instance, in the *Programme for the Further Implementation of Agenda 21*. As I have earlier quoted a Southern country representative, the binding agreements of Rio were 'not very binding'.[7] This was a critical observation: the three conventions resulting from Rio took several years to operationalize, which shed doubt on the effectiveness of the processes. More importantly, governments (particularly the US government) failed to ratify the treaties they signed, and even when they did, some of the conditions were simply not implemented. Moreover, despite the increase in the number of platforms that address environmental issues, most of them could not produce agreements, or solutions to these problems.

In contrast to UNCED, the focus of WSSD was implementation. Aiming at implementation of intergovernmentally agreed outcomes which were poorly implemented gave partnerships the legitimacy that they could enjoy for projects which could be funded by governments and corporations alike, even when they were focusing on rather controversial issues. As a result, the implementation focus of the WSSD became central to what partnerships are.

7.3.3.2   From political inclusion to social exclusion

What happened, then, to the democratic ideal of participation and inclusion, once partnerships were negotiated as 'implementation mechanisms'? According to the *Secretary-General's Report on Partnerships* (UNCSD 2008: 10) and the GSPD, less than one per cent of all partnering organizations are from five (out of nine) major group categories: farmers, workers and trade unions, indigenous peoples, women, youth and children. Around four per cent of all partnerships include any of these groups. More institutionalized major groups are represented in more partnerships and by more partners: eight per cent of all partners are from scientific and technological community, 11 per cent from business and industry, and 18 per cent from NGOs. On the other hand, governments make up 28 per cent and intergovernmental organizations make up 17 per cent of

Number of partners from...

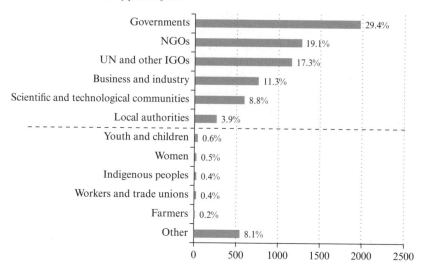

Figure 7.1   Distribution of partners from different sectors

all partners involved. This picture of partnerships is in strong contrast to their conceptualization, in terms of ensuring participation in decision-making or implementation.

Even before the WSSD, the imbalances in the actor constellation were obvious. According to UN Secretary-General's Report (UN 2001b):

> Major Groups' participation in sustainable development continues to face numerous challenges. Among them are geographical imbalances in participation, particularly at the international level, growing dependence on mainstream major groups as intermediaries, the need for further work on setting accountable and transparent participation mechanisms, lack of meaningful participation in decision-making processes, and lack of reliable funding.

Major group participation has been limited to institutionalized actors such as transnational NGOs and corporations, as well as scientific and technological communities and local governments (Figure 7.1). Traditionally the most vulnerable and/or the most underrepresented major groups do not become partners. A youth representative openly stated, 'Nobody wants to partner with us!'[8] This was put more decisively by a respondent in Buse's (2004: 232) study of health partnerships 'If you don't have some money on the table, some time, and expertise, you are not a partner'.

The exception to this argument is the case of workers and trade unions, which are organized and institutionalized, but not party to any partnerships. According to the labour unions engaged in the CSD process, the concept of partnerships was drawn from neo-liberal economic discourses; the tri-partite system that has traditionally been employed in all UN-level negotiations was being abandoned in a way to disempower the labour unions (Ottaway 2001). A union representative suggested:

> We have over two million legitimate agreements that would qualify as partnerships, as a collective agreement, as a partnership in every sense of the word, except we refuse to call them partnerships, because we know that [. . .] a collective agreement takes away power from the employer to make decisions arbitrarily when it comes to labour relations. Without this collective agreement or collective bargaining relationship we are in a master–servant relationship. And a master–servant relationship isn't a partnership. [. . .] we refuse to call it that because we are weary of the concept: we know it's a smoke screen; it's what I call a stocking horse.

This account openly challenges the win–win narrative, and instead uses a zero-sum game metaphor: the role the labour unions played against corporations has not been one of cooperation but rather conflict. When they bargained on issues such as wages, working conditions, regulations and so forth, the gain of one was the net loss of the other. Labour union representatives insisted that partnerships were 'a corporate vocabulary', and as mentioned earlier, business delegates agreed to this conception. But unlike other major groups, the unions had more experience with possibilities of co-option, and refused to take part in any such initiatives, in an attempt to regain power over the meaning of the term.

While partnerships were immediately agreeable to the business actors, and disagreeable to the unions, there were a number of relative gains: Quarless highlights this aspect when she says partnerships 'gave [NGOs] the recognition that they didn't have before and legitimized their participation'.[9] DESA's conceptualization of partnerships would indeed allow for this recognition, which is important for NGOs that demand representation at the UN level. The recognition of their work by the UN could also help their projects, affirm the importance of their work, and possibly help them find funds.

Finally, other than these major groups, there were less institutionalized major groups, such as women, indigenous peoples, youth and children, or farmers. Unlike business actors, building partnerships is obviously not the way they operate. Neither would they particularly benefit from UN-level recognition of their projects. On the contrary, their demand to be represented at the UN is not a project-based issue, or a problem to be solved as such but rather more ambiguous. Furthermore, many of their demands are often impossible to reduce to 'interests'. Major groups such as women, or children and youth, do not demand solutions to a specific problem for the benefit of *all* women or children: their demands cannot be fulfilled by creating projects in which they can take part, but only by the representation of various groups they embody, and their continuous participation in decision-making. In other words, for those groups that had little interest or stakes in gaining such recognition but were necessarily influenced by the decisions, partnerships were merely a new way of reproducing their exclusion from decision-making.

This is what Rahnema (1992: 116) describes, when he differentiates between the transitive and intransitive forms of the word 'participation'. The *transitive* form signifies goal-oriented participation, mediated, if not manipulative, wherein people are 'dragged into partaking in operations of no interest to them'. The *intransitive* form means partaking in the course of daily life, spontaneously and with no particular objective. Thus, he deconstructs the assumption that traditional societies are not participatory, and points to the various ways in which the oppressed participate, resist, or exert power. By being repetitively invited to participate (in the transitive sense) in a structure that does not allow for their participation (in the intransitive sense), most major groups have been socially and politically excluded from processes that they have 'stakes' in. By not taking part in partnerships, these major groups articulate a negative opinion regarding a process they might not be able to stop, or influence in a meaningful way: as Žižek advises, they refrain from pseudo-activity. The next section concludes, however, that this first step is insufficient to clear the ground for effectively transforming the distribution of power and character of global governance.

This is most often the case with participation in the context of development, which is the subject of the next section: firstly, regarding the history and ideological connotations of participation in the context of development, and secondly, its relation to partnerships in the context of sustainable development in today's global politics.

7.4 PARTICIPATION IN THE CONTEXT OF DEVELOPMENT

Participation as a democratizing element of global governance requires further inspection in the particular context of development, both because of the dependency relationship generated by developmentalist project and because of the specific focus of this book. In the previous section I aimed to show the problems pertaining to participation in the context of CSD partnerships. This section aims to further problematize existing practices. This is necessary for two reasons. The first and practical reason is to reveal the intersection of earlier debates on developmentalism and its discontents with debates on participation. This can reveal that some of the issues pertaining to major group participation to the CSD are in fact related to problems of contemporary developmentalist ideals. The second and more general reason is to show that participation does not connote the same democratic promise in this context as it does in other spheres of governance.

7.4.1 Good Intentions as 'Empty Gestures'

In 1961, Ivan Illich established *Centro Intercultural de Documentación* in Cuernavaca, Mexico. This centre offered language courses both to missionaries from North to South America and to the volunteers of the *Alliance for Progress* programme, initiated by the US President John F. Kennedy that year, offering development aid to South American countries in an attempt to block the influence of the Soviet Union and the Cuban Revolution. This gathering of (religious and non-religious) missionaries might appear unusual at first, but for Illich (who was also a priest) the roots of religious institutionalization and modernization were interlinked: 'Wherever I look for the roots of modernity', he stated, 'I find it in attempts of the churches to institutionalize and manage Christian vocation' (Illich 2000). Hence, through the work of the centre he witnessed and documented the role of the Vatican in the exportation of modernization and developmentalism to the so-called Third World. Illich also lectured on the inherent paternalism in development aid. Owing to these efforts he had to resign from priesthood.

His work remains relevant to the problem of inclusion/exclusion that concerns this chapter. Similar to Žižek, participation in development projects was problematic for Illich both from the perspective of the recipient community and from the perspective of the development worker. Development projects represented the formation of modern, industrialist hegemony in South America, and he suggested that the missionaries should not impose their own cultural values (originating from Enlightenment and industrialism) to the South American communities. They should rather regard themselves as guests of these communities. While these points are repeated themes throughout Illich's work, they are exceptionally lucid in his address to the 1968 *Conference on InterAmerican Student Projects* in Cuernavaca. After expressing his surprise regarding the invite, Illich (1968) makes a speech titled 'To Hell with Good Intentions', wherein he deconstructs the narration that justifies development aid with community involvement. He forces the volunteers about to move on to the Mexican villages to notice their symbolic and ideological position for these communities: an American salesman, advertising the American middle-class lifestyle to those who have no option but be exposed to their developmentalist idea(l)s.[10] He emphasizes the inequality and injustice of such an act. It is not involvement as such that Illich rejects, but the notion of external aid as a politically neutral phenomenon since it is instrumental in establishing the hegemony of industrialism, modernization and development.

Instead, Illich suggests that such 'good intentions' should be directed to the communities in the home country of the volunteers, where they know what they are doing, how to communicate with those they are trying to help, and where they can be refused by the receiving party. Most important for this book is his observation regarding the subject positions of the donors and the recipients: working for the poor in their own community, the volunteers would know the ground rules of communication (in Lacanian terms, the symbolic order), as would the recipients of their aid. This allows for a certain equality and reciprocity between them. More crucially, their aid can be rejected, which saves the volunteer from the position of a 'salesperson' as the other party is no longer a passive recipient. Similarly, in development projects whether the community participation is meaningful depends not only on the 'quality' of participation but also on the possibility to refuse the project all together. Otherwise, community participation becomes no more than 'an empty gesture', which forces the subject to 'choose freely what is in any case compulsory' (Žižek 2006: 12–13). The invitations for the recipient communities to participate in development projects often are empty gestures, as they have not chosen (or even wanted) the project and neither is there the possibility of rejection. In this process, the development worker safely positions herself where she can 'help' the poor, transforming the poor into what she imagines them to be, without reflecting on, or learning from her own subject position.

This point is crucial, not only from the point of view of development aid as such, but for the participants in the developmental projects. When exercised with financial backing and advertisements of sorts, development aid invites participation while it compromises free will – not of individuals that participate but of those communities that choose not to. In this context, the democratic credentials of participation are questionable, from both perspectives.

As partnerships are geared towards developmental goals, it is important to recognize that the participatory promise at the project level has significantly different implications than at the UN level. The connotation of inclusiveness and democratization at the global level (however limited) should not be presumed at the project and community levels. Secondly, the presence of local partners does not guarantee that recipient communities are participating in the project or that they are better off as a result of partnership activities. In what follows these two points are linked with the conjuncture in development aid.

7.4.2   Participation in Global Politics through Partnerships

Of all tyrannies, a tyranny sincerely exercised for the good of its victims may be the most oppressive. It would be better to live under robber barons than under omnipotent moral busybodies. The robber baron's cruelty may sometimes sleep, his cupidity may at some point be satiated; but those who torment us for our own good, torment us without end, for they do so with the approval of their own conscience. (Lewis 1953: 58)

The popularity of partnerships is closely related to the assumption that development projects provide better outcomes with than without community participation. This would however be simplistic: the inclusiveness of a development project is restricted to the parties that accept its ground rules. Imagine a situation in which product X is introduced to community A, through a partnership project. The participants from the community will be those groups that will benefit from (or at least not suffer from) the introduction of X, have no radical opposition against X (or what it symbolizes), against the partnership itself, or the partners involved. Even if the recipient community has an overwhelming opposition to the installation of X, those that oppose radically are likely not to become partners at all. It appears sufficient in most cases to include a few groups or individuals that do not oppose, as 'representatives of the recipient community'. Whether the product is a vaccine, genetically modified seeds, or an institution of neo-liberal capitalist system makes little difference for the argument: this is about agreeing with the basic tenets of the project. Naturally, the situation is more complex when the project has mixed or positive effects on the community in question, and a part of the community support the introduction of the product, institution, or technology.

How should community participation be ensured, then, in the decision-making process? Moreover, is it possible that communities refuse the 'help' offered by the partnerships, or channel it to their own perceived needs?

A telling example of such an experience took place in the aftermath of the devastating earthquake and tsunami in 2004. According to development workers[11] when the state of emergency was over and life was to some extent normalized, around 500 international NGOs arrived in Aceh and Sri Lanka, the two worst-hit islands. With India and Thailand (the lesser affected countries) refusing most of the aid provided, an unprecedented amount of international aid flowed into Aceh (the initial promise of USD13.6 billion is likely to have been exceeded). As the international aid agencies flooded the island with projects, the communities started to be increasingly selective in the aid they accepted. If, for instance, the development agency required a structural change in the community (for example more gender equality in the *shariah*-ruled island), the community would choose the aid provided by another agency. On the one hand, the development workers were aware of the ethical problems of making demands in return for much needed aid. On the other hand, they regarded it normal that such a long recovery process resulted in structural changes in the aid relationship. The disaster ended the 30-year-long conflict between the Indonesian government and the Free Aceh Movement: during the recovery programme the structure of the economy changed significantly and an 8 per cent economic growth was achieved in 2006 (World Bank 2007). The mere presence of so many international development workers considerably increased house prices to the international scale, and caused a higher inflation rate than anywhere else in Indonesia. All these important structural changes were related to the continued development aid in Aceh, which received its autonomy in the process and elected a new provincial governor.

At the end of 2009, four assaults were made, shooting and wounding international aid workers by 'unknown militants' (*The Times* 2009). These events (often blamed either on the unequal distribution of the received aid to subcontractors, or on the Indonesian military) support the argument that over time the international aid organizations 'become enmeshed in a deeper way in the conflict dynamics', as Rajasingham-Senanayake (2009: 7) finds out about Sri Lanka – the other conflict zone that received much post-tsunami reconstruction aid. In Sri Lanka, too, 'the development cart was put before the conflict resolution horse' and not only did this result in several attacks on the aid workers, but also endangered the peace process: the improvement in the financial capacities of both parties to the civil war resulted in an arms race and heightened conflict (Srikandarajah 2005).

Secondly, a more general example of how hegemony is established through development aid is provided by the website of the United States Agency for International Development (USAID). The webpage titled *This is USAID* shows how aid is perceived and narrated from the side of the hegemonic project. The institution establishes its origins and role as follows:

The United States has a long history of extending a helping hand to those people overseas struggling to make a better life, recover from a disaster or striving to live in a free and democratic country. It is this caring that stands as a hallmark of the United States around the world – and shows the world our true character as a nation. U.S. foreign assistance has always had the twofold purpose of furthering America's foreign policy interests in expanding democracy and free markets while improving the lives of the citizens of the developing world.[12]

In line with this goal, after the US attacks on Afghanistan and Iraq, USAID reported on its involvement in establishing free market economies and minimally democratic governments in these countries. In the case study reports of 2008, while the US occupation is not mentioned, the absolute poverty caused by the Soviet invasion and the Taliban rule in Afghanistan does find a place. In Afghanistan USAID praises itself for having achieved the development of 'a market-driven agricultural sector', 'strengthening property rights' and building 'transportation and electricity networks' (USAID 2008: 57–58). The same report notes that these have been achieved through management and business training, providing loans and financial services, constructing roads, and supporting the operations and maintenance of Afghan electric utilities. The report omitted controversial issues related to aid and politics, such as the distribution of leaflets 'calling on people to provide information on al-Qaida and the Taliban or face losing humanitarian aid' (*The Guardian* 2004). According to *Medécins Sans Frontières*, this was a major threat to aid workers, as 14 were killed the year before (ibid.).

USAID's work in Iraq also involves CSD partnerships. The agency reports that it 'helped' Iraqi people by promoting entrepreneurialism, stimulating private sector growth, strengthening counterinsurgency efforts and so forth. To complement these efforts, new institutions were established such as the CSD-registered partnership Global Initiative Towards a Sustainable Iraq (GITSI), which aims to 'have a sustainable, stable and prosperous Iraq where all present and future generations can live in peace and harmony with other nations and where all resources are utilised in a sustainable manner catering to the well-being of Iraq's current and future generations and ecosystems'.[13] GITSI aims to achieve this rather ambiguous goal mainly by capacity building, technology transfer, awareness raising and subcontracting. In other words, GITSI aims to provide the necessary institutions, human resources, technological means, economic resources as well as the public opinion for Iraq's modernization such that a pro-American, capitalist system can flourish. Although it was not possible to find a contact person to verify this assumption, it would not be too farfetched to expect that NGOs or citizens that disagree with this kind of a modernization process will not be included in the partnership as decision-makers.

Thirdly, it is a misconception that these examples are exceptions, and should not be generalized regarding the reality of *development* or *sustainable development*. These are exceptions that prove the rule: aid is always in the name of development and progress through modernization, industrialization and economic growth. Even if the immediate issues are reconstruction after war or disaster, development is the main frame of reference in both cases. Therefore, development aid always operates in a political setting, with political aims and results.[14]

This is critical in relation to participation in development; indeed, the developmentalist ideology has benefited considerably from participatory approaches employed by most development projects. This new understanding of participation submerged the political element of emancipation and focused on the utility of participation, turning it into a managerial tool. Frances Cleaver (2001: 36–55) highlights the lack of reflexivity in participation as understood and applied in development projects, and argues that it has become 'an act of faith in development [on the basis that] participation is intrinsically a "good thing" (especially for the participants); that the focus on "getting the techniques right" is the principal way [to success]; and that considerations of power and politics [are] divisive and obstructive'. Furthermore, participatory methods ignore informal institutions; they fail to recognize more subtle methods of participation; they categorize people without understanding 'the non-project nature of [their] lives' and the complexity of their social networks; and they have a foundationalist understanding of culture and community (Cleaver 2001: 38). While some of these problems are shared by all anthropological methods, participatory methods in development projects affect the very livelihoods of people.

Cleaver lists another set of problems that are intrinsic to development projects in general: they see individuals as inputs (as the human resource), based on a model of *homo economicus*. They might have the opposite effect of what they intend to do, resulting in the further marginalization of the poor; and they are 'infected by the pervasive functionalism and economism of development thinking' (ibid.: 48).

Finally, Cleaver recognizes a shift in the discourse of participation from its roots in radical democracy and emancipation to managerial toolboxes. She regards this as the paradoxical relationship between developmental focus on efficiency and the presumed empowerment through participation:

> The predominant discourses of development are practical and technical, concerned with project-dictated imperatives of efficiency, with visible, manageable

manifestations of collective action. These, however, are commonly cloaked in the rhetoric of empowerment, which is implicitly assumed to have a greater moral value. Radical empowerment discourse (with its roots in Freirean philosophy) is associated with both individual *and* class action, with the transformation of structures of subordination through radical changes in law, property rights, the institutions of society. [. . .] Such ideas, associated with structural change and with collective action facilitated by and in opposition to the state, are rather out of fashion in development [. . .] As 'empowerment' became a buzzword in development, an essential objective of projects, its radical challenging and transformatory edge has been lost. The concept of action has become individualized, empowerment depoliticized. (Ibid.: 37)

While the relationship she describes is indeed paradoxical, more importantly it points to incommensurability: the developmentalist ideology is so powerful that any new social project (environmental or democratic) can be internalized, depoliticized and used for its own further legitimation. As Rahnema (1992: 123–128) suggested, 'the notion of empowerment was intended to help participation to perform one main political function – to provide development with a new source of legitimation'. In this sense participatory development is one more version of developmentalism, carrying all its prejudices and arrogance. He claims that planned, top-down macro-changes are often an indirect outcome of numerous micro-changes at the bottom, which threaten 'the dominant knowledge/power centres at the top' once they reach a critical mass. Then, they are co-opted and used for 'turning the potential threat to the top into a possible asset for it':

Hence, major projects of change from above generally represent an attempt, by those very forces under threat, to contain and redirect change, with a view to adapting it to their own interests, whenever possible with the victims' participation. [. . .] This is how the pioneering participatory mendicants of early development years were also robbed of their participatory ideal, as the latter was transmogrified into the present-day manipulative construct of participatory development. (Ibid.)

Rahnema describes the logic of difference par excellence, wherein participation is made safe for developmentalism. This works both at the individual and the systematic levels: Freire's (cf. 2004) radical ideal involves the transformation of the field worker, joining the oppressed for a collective emancipatory project. In 'development aid', however, the field worker's own emancipation is completely taken out of the picture, and the reciprocal process of empowerment and learning is reduced to a one-sided, educational project. Moreover, a collective emancipatory project is achieved when not only the institutions and the discourses of oppression but also the legal and economic structure of the society are transformed. When the participatory demand is merged into a different semantic constellation, it becomes managerial without being revolutionary. Henceforth, it carries all the positive connotations of participation without being emancipatory.

A clear example of this transformation was documented by Action Aid, in an article that analyzed the results of the *Poverty Reduction Strategy Paper* (PRSP) of the IMF and the World Bank (Rowden and Ocaya Irama 2004). An increasing number of citizens and protestors demanded participation in the decision-making of national economic policies as well as a change in the mandatory set of economic reforms (based on privatization, financial deregulation/liberalization and removing trade protection for domestic companies) that the agencies commanded in exchange for new loans. PRSP was the 1999 response of the IMF and the World Bank to these demands, and promised some new loans and debt cancellation for the countries that would draft a national poverty-reduction strategy based on participatory practices.

According to Jane Ocaya Irama, Policy Coordinator of Action Aid Uganda, when PRSP was introduced, 'we thought we had finally been given a real opportunity to discuss these controversial policies in public and to advocate for alternative policies, but that has not been the case' (in Rowden and Ocaya Irama 2004). The national PRSPs had to be approved by the executive boards of both agencies, before borrowing governments could access any loans or debt-relief. As the governments were aware of this condition, they self-censored and 'carefully regulat[ed] what is allowed to be discussed in the consultations for drafting the PRSPs' (ibid.). In other words, the restrictions to participation were pushed down to the level of national governments, saving the agencies from a negative public image. Four years after the initiation of the process it was reported that participating citizens' groups were given no real authority or power regarding economic policies neither at the national nor at the agency levels: 'The high-profile effort to use "participation" rhetoric to get citizens' groups to stop protesting in the streets and sit down at the table has now run aground because, after four years of attempted participation in the processes, no major policy changes have resulted in the key World Bank and IMF loan conditions' (ibid.). As Rick Rowden, Action Aid USA's policy analyst suggested, citizens' groups were 'back to square one: the true participatory process they were promised by the World Bank in 1999 has not materialized' (ibid.).

To conclude, the democratic demand of participation has been co-opted in many levels in the context of development. At the global level, bottom-up demands for participation were transformed into guiding principles in the handbooks, principles and programmes of development banks as well as the United Nations. Participation at the individual and local/community levels has become an integral part of the developmentalist strategy, supported by official development aid and partnership projects.

In short, with its roots in colonialism, developmentalist ideology had no problem with the internalization of the demands for a more democratic and participatory global governance, so long as these demands could be articulated with the hegemonic developmentalist project.

7.5 CONCLUSIONS: PARTICIPATION AS MANIPULATION

This chapter aimed to investigate the discourse of participation historically, in order to provide a deeper analysis of its sedimentation to the partnerships regime. After an initial problematization, Section 7.2 described the fantasmatic logic that makes participation a part of the democratic imaginary and ideals. Section 7.3 focused on the political logics: it explained the different processes of participation in the UN, the CSD, the partnerships regime and individual partnership projects. At the same time, it contextualized the participatory discourse to the changes in global environmental governance, from the Rio Earth Summit onwards. Finally, Section 7.4 explained the development–participation nexus, with the aim of revealing their relationship, and the use of particular participatory practices to further the aims of developmentalist hegemonic projects on the one hand, and for foreign policy goals on the other.

The Rio Summit was crucial for the various demands of civil society to be articulated in a chain of equivalence. As a result, environmental issues that were previously not regarded as significant in global politics were polarized across the world. At the same time, the event opened the space for the participation and inclusion of previously unrepresented groups. Similar to the developments towards the end of the French Revolution, a hegemonic struggle took place, regarding the inclusiveness of the governance architecture, after the conference. There was a demand for open, participatory, bottom-up decision-making at the global level. But there were also concerns about loss of sovereignty. The UN bureaucracy was sympathetic to participatory processes in environmental governance after UNCED. The CSD had become the platform wherein civil society would be introduced to the UN. Between 1992 and 2002 non-state actors were gradually institutionalized into major groups and were given limited space in meetings. Until 2002, major groups appropriated this position, and the CSD was regarded as the platform that would gradually set the participatory rules for all UN institutions.

On the other hand, when the radical potential of civil action was transformed into major groups, the numerous, plural and diverse demands articulated in 1992 were unified under the ambiguous end goal of sustainable development. The overwhelming participation of civil society in Rio was thus internalized into the governance process, such that participation would not further challenge state-based negotiations and representation at the UN. This greatly limited the major groups in participating, contesting and exerting power. This was also the moment that partnerships were introduced to the UN texts, whereby the concept was associated with the participation of social groups, democratization, inclusiveness and so forth. By the time of the Johannesburg Summit, partnerships as implementation mechanisms aimed to mobilize major groups towards sustainable development in a co-operative mode. With their endorsement in 2002, partnerships were transformed from a concept that enables democratic participation, to one that keeps the status quo. This is why they are regarded by many NGOs as co-option mechanisms: when the logic of difference succeeds, the dominant discourse retains its hegemony, and earlier social exclusions are replicated.

An analogy can be drawn between the US volunteers in Mexico and partnerships as implementation mechanisms: the 'good intentions' of development aid limited the non-developmentalist alternatives of South American communities, once it institutionalized. Similarly, the good intentions of building partnerships as inclusion mechanisms, once institutionalized, were reduced to implementation goals. In Illich's terms, when an initially beneficial process turns into a harmful one after it institutionalized, *counterproductivity* sets in. Instead of transforming itself to fit its purpose, the institution starts to invent ways of keeping itself intact and frustrating other ways of achieving the same result (creating *radical monopolies*). For instance, it creates professional experts, starting licensing procedures to disqualify other practitioners, increasing the bureaucracy through which one can influence the strategies of the institution and so on. All of these are the case regarding the UN accreditation of major groups as well as development aid practices. With the partnerships regime, the role of civil society has been further restricted to efficient implementation of decisions made at the global level. Moreover, participation became counterproductive in the sense that any intervention by civil society could be incorporated into an institutional process that can no longer be questioned by the participants.

The environmental demands civil society articulated at the Rio Summit is similar to the developmental demands of various local groups that challenged the World Bank in 1999, which were also frustrated. In the context of development, the participatory appraisal programmes internalized the participation into a project-based, efficiency-oriented paradigm. This situation is further complicated by the problems inherent to development aid, specifically the alliance of foreign policy goals with those of development projects, the transfer of alien institutions, technologies and paradigms.

To conclude, both at the local and the global levels, the fantasy about community involvement blends and becomes indissociable from imaginaries of a global *demos*. Illich's example of a local intervention in Mexico and the institutionalization of CSD partnerships are both examples that reveal the inaccuracy of these positive associations. Nevertheless, in the existing sovereignty-bound UN system, there are few options for democratization at the global level. This is also about the *problem of scale*. What goes unnoticed in democratic theory is the critical change in the scale of participation these developments infer. On the one hand, refusal to participate is reenacting the logic of equivalence: when unions openly refuse to list their contracts as partnerships or when other major groups refrain from forming any, they are resisting the change of meaning in the governance platforms they partake. On the other hand, greater stakeholder participation does not guarantee consensus over state-based rules or decision-making processes. Even though the rules advocate participation and community involvement, civil society is instrumentalized in this process. Responses to this counterproductivity are manifest in the demands for a different, more democratic global governance architecture, both in the UN and in other platforms such as the World Social Forum.

The ultimate democratic fantasy of direct involvement might once again require political action, articulated and acted upon. The final chapter reflects on such utopian imageries and factual possibilities.

NOTES

1. The UN website: http://www.un.org/en/aboutun/index.shtml, accessed: 26-10-2011.
2. The UNDESA website: http://www.un.org/esa/coordination/ngo/about.htm, accessed: 12-07-2014.
3. The UN website: http://www.un.org/geninfo/bp/enviro.html, accessed: 5-12-2010.
4. Interview with UNEP representative, and organizing committee member of the UN environmental summits; New York, 2008.
5. Interview with UNEP representative, and organizing committee member of the UN environmental summits; New York, 2008.
6. Interview with UN representative to the WSSD process; New York, 2008.
7. Interview with Southern country delegate to the WSSD process; Denpasar, 2006.
8. Youth group representative to the CSD process; May, 2007.
9. Interview; New York, 2007.
10. An interesting juxtaposition is George W. Bush's justification of the wars his administration launched on Iraq and Afghanistan in terms of protecting the 'American way of

life'. His father, George H.W. Bush expressed his disagreement with the decisions of the Rio Summit by saying: 'The American way of life is not negotiable'.

11. Interview with NGO workers; Bandah-Aceh, 2006.
12. The USAID website: http://www.usaid.gov/about_usaid, accessed: 26-11-2011.
13. The UNCSD website: http://webapps01.un.org/dsd/partnerships/public/partnerships/ 2407, accessed: 9-1-2011.
14. In 2011, the CIA ran a covert vaccination scheme that helped locate Osama Bin Laden, which later resulted in his killing. Consequently, development aid workers in Pakistan were heavily threatened. According to *The Guardian*, InterAction, 'an alliance of 190 US-based NGOs, has called on the spy agency to stop using humanitarian work as a cover for counter-terrorism', as it endangers both local populations and legitimate aid workers. My aim is not to equate actual development aid efforts with covert operations, but to reveal that different aims can be found closely associated at times, wherein the credibility of NGOs is often at stake. Available at: http://www.guardian.co.uk/ world/2011/jul/11/cia-fake-vaccinations-osama-bin-ladens-dna, accessed: 20-11-2011.

8. Conclusions

In the introductory chapter it was noted that any myth is 'to some extent reality' if sufficient number of people with sufficient temporal, financial and human resources believe and act upon it. Through the mediating discourses abstractions and concepts such as partnerships cease to be 'solely myths', and 'make sense' to individuals. The aim of this book has been to better understand sustainability partnerships through a study of discourses mediating our understanding of them, which sedimented into projects and into the logics of the partnerships regime of the United Nations. The UN was an important context in this regard, as the partnerships regime acquired the endorsement of temporal, financial and human resources at global and transnational levels, at the end of WSSD.

The various accounts regarding the conception, negotiation and actualization of sustainability partnerships provided by contributors and observers of these processes revealed two important points. Firstly, partnerships are not governance phenomena the utility or even benevolence of which is regarded similarly by all parties. Secondly, they have changed considerably from their conception to their negotiation, and then again during their actualization. These transformations were influenced by historical social and political processes and reflecting and contributing to the present transformations in governance.

Accordingly, Chapters 1–4 focused on the various narratives that revealed the first conclusion, as well as the tools and assumptions through which this research was carried out. The second part (Chapters 5–7) consisted of the three discourses analyzed; namely, privatization of governance, sustainable development and democratic participation. This part focused on the historical development of each of these discourses, shedding light on present narrations of partnerships. It also served to reveal how 'myths' have become discourses through which governance is practiced, how these mediating discourses implicated the formation and actualization of partnerships and the characteristics of the partnerships regime. Without studying these mediating discourses, the following conclusions would have remained – at best – abrupt observations.

This chapter aims to conclude this inquiry by summarizing the findings of earlier chapters with a specific focus on sustainability partnerships, pointing towards the challenges and potentials of the partnerships regime, and suggesting a continuation of this research agenda. In what follows, I aim to demonstrate how neither the functionalist/neo-institutionalist arguments (such as the win–win narrative and organizational flexibility argument) nor analysis based solely on international political economy dynamics are sufficient to reveal the changes sustainability partnerships represent, in the context of global governance. Accordingly, the following section focuses on the mediating discourses and the findings resulting from the discourse analytical part of this book. Section 8.2 summarizes the transformations that the practice and discourse of partnerships have gone through since their conception. It also looks into the discourse theoretical implications of the concepts developed in the earlier chapters. The final section aims to open up a debate regarding the political function of partnerships at the global level, and contextualize their future implications by linking the various meanings of partnership to imaginaries of perfection and the contemporary democratic paradox.

8.1   MEDIATING DISCOURSES

This volume has started with the suggestion that to compose different and more desirable governance institutions one needs to analyze the discourses that sedimented into the logics of sustainability partnerships. Recognizing the contestations, their results, and what has been eliminated from the resulting hegemonic discourse has in fact been informative for the purposes of this study. The three mediating discourses of privatization of governance, sustainable development and participation have constructed the fantasmatic and political backgrounds for sustainability partnerships.

8.1.1   Partnerships as Private Governance Mechanisms: New Forms of Legality

In Chapter 5, I placed partnerships in the context of globalization by critically approaching privatization of governance. In this context partnerships are representative of private governance institutions in general and their analysis reveals the implications of their employment in global environmental governance. Firstly, partnerships appear to operate in a process that can be described as 'delegalization'. While the negotiations of new international treaties have failed since 2002, new governance mechanisms are increasingly characterized by voluntary and unbinding sets of rules outside of the legal system. This is reflected by the lack of agreements and memoranda of understanding between the UN and CSD partnerships, and among partners of partnership projects. The end result is a shift from public law to private governance. While there are legal elements to it, the core problem is a diminishing role for the public, democratically controlled law.

Secondly, the application of the term partnerships to mechanisms of private governance points to a change towards the limitation of legal liabilities. This is partly because CSD partnerships are voluntary mechanisms, and partly due to the way the partnerships regime institutionalized: failure of individual partnerships or the regime itself is difficult to detect, and it is unclear which party is accountable or responsible in such occasions. In this context it is difficult to disregard the historical development of business partnerships, which has implied limited liability from the beginning. This is also the case for partnerships and other private governance mechanisms. In examples such as carbon markets, forest conservation schemes, or councils without public oversight a pattern is emerging that makes them problematic for actual problem solving; not only are failures difficult to detect due to the voluntary, unmonitored nature of these arrangements but in case of failure, the responsibility is so diffused that no party can be held accountable.

Thirdly, Type-II outcomes are what I have called 'new forms of legality' in the context of global transformations. Narratives of globalization and markets consolidate homogenization in financial governance across the world. Capital markets and the increasingly flexible transfer of globally accumulating capital comprise the final step in what Marx called 'socialization of capital', which started with the invention of partnerships as an ownership model with limited liability. Although state actors have arguably lost power relative to global capital markets, the international state system copes with the market order by inventing new governance mechanisms that are in line with the dominant narratives of globalization. Partnerships are one example of these new forms of legality. This does not contradict with the statement above, concerning delegalization. Delegalization is a process that characterizes global environmental governance, wherein partnerships provide an illustration of its end result. Nonetheless, partnerships do acquire legal personas; they are in line with international and often with national laws.

On the one hand, the continued fragmentation and deregulation of social/environmental governance allows for state actors to maintain some degree of control over their economies. On the other hand, as market failures are no longer corrected by the states and are often regarded as inevitable results of globalization, they are transformed into narratives of *state failures*. Whenever the state system fails to regulate, implement, or democratically govern global issues (which are often called governance deficits), markets, global financial institutions and corporate actors are summoned to solve the problem. In this process, the corporation becomes both a legitimate stakeholder in global politics and the medium between hypermobile capital and the public sphere. Hence, its social influence is consolidated.

In other words, the hegemonic discourses of neo-liberal globalization underlie the dominant frames of reference, while other possible solutions are discredited if conceived at all. This is the case not only in social and environmental governance but also with financial governance. All together these processes can be called the privatization of global governance, wherein corporate actors are increasingly included in the political decision-making – either by state actors willingly relinquishing some of their functions, or unwillingly, when sidelined by private authority – and in which regulatory approaches based on state coercion are replaced by market-based and voluntary mechanisms.

Finally, addressing governance deficits through private governance mechanisms presumes that global financial markets can correct state failures. Sustainability partnerships are mechanisms to implement what states failed to implement and (self-)regulate where states fail to regulate. Furthermore, they keep legislations on social/environmental issues analogous to those of financial governance, operating within the same frames of reference. Yet, legality does not assume legitimacy; while partnerships are not disputed in terms of being legal entities, their legitimacy is challenged by various parties. Firstly, their output legitimacy is questioned as the results of their activities are limited in terms of developmental and environmental achievements. Secondly, their input legitimacy is questioned in terms of their accountability and inclusiveness. These are the concerns of the next two sections that summarize the analyses of the two other discourses.

8.1.2 Partnerships in Environmental Governance: Shifts in the Discourses of Sustainability

As Chapter 6 aimed to show, social and environmental issues have exclusively been represented by the sustainable development discourse within the UN, since the publication of the Brundtland Report in 1987. Sustainable development has become the structuring variant of developmental discourses particularly following the 1992 Rio Earth Summit. Discursively, the concept brought together the conflicting needs for economic growth and ecological conservation. In other words, sustainable development suggested a harmonious resolution to the dislocation generated by various environmental problems resulting from economic development. By doing so, it has successfully disrupted chain of equivalence gathered around the popular demand for ecological sustainability. Inversely, the story of once radical demands of the eco-political discourses being integrated to the developmentalist ideology is a demonstration of how the logic of difference operates by including challenging demands into the hegemonic discourse.

From the point of view of the signifier sustainable development, it has become overloaded with various meanings, and ended up dissolving its precise significance. However, it has successfully co-opted most eco-political movements, and marginalized the rest. In the long run, most environmental discourses previously articulating more radical viewpoints conformed to this new understanding. Professional environmental NGOs, consumer campaigns on environmental awareness, and liberal environmental values have become the norm. Yet, the ecological was no longer a negation of the capitalist logic at the end of this process; environmental values were being redefined by developmentalism. Managerial approaches to environment standardized and objectified issues that were political and relocated them into the sphere of the social. Emerging discourses such as voluntarism, expertise and win–win situations negated the political nature of environmental issues. The remnants of this hegemonic struggle are manifest in green politics: most of the identities eco-political movements represented became important components of green ideologies. Even when Green parties fail to re-assert the ecological ideal (for example in contemporary Western Europe) their founding principles still reveal the importance of the first chain of equivalence formed in the 1970s, such as pacifism, feminism, gay and minority rights, and ecological sustainability.

At the international level, environmental conservation has become a part of official development aid. Development aid has been instrumental in establishing the hegemony of industrialism, modernization and development. Through ODA, environmental principles defined strictly within the confines of these hegemonic discourses were introduced to the recipient societies. It is critical to assess the extent to which these projects, funds, institutions, technologies and values can be refused or transformed by the recipient community, when designing and assessing development aid.

This pattern is also manifest at the global level. Since the 2000 Millennium Declaration, the MDGs have taken the place of sustainability in the UN's discourses of environmental governance. Furthermore, since the beginning of the global financial crisis, economic growth and sustainability are once more being articulated in non-contradictory terms. For instance, one of the two main themes of the 2012 Rio+20 Summit was green economy. This is likely to further instrumentalize green values for the purposes of neo-liberalism.

8.1.3　Partnerships as Participatory Mechanisms: Shifts in the Discourses of Democracy

Chapter 7 focused on the discourse of participation. During the Rio Earth Summit the demands of eco-political movements were articulated in a chain of equivalence. The event opened the space for the participation and inclusion of previously unrepresented groups in governance platforms. Civil society was invited to join certain UN platforms, such as the CSD, in the form of major groups. When the radical potential of civil action was transformed in this fashion, the plural and diverse demands articulated in 1992 were unified under the ambiguous end goal of sustainable development. This greatly limited the major groups in participating, contesting and exerting power.

The categorization of civil society into major groups coincides with the conception of partnerships in the UN texts, wherein they are associated with the participation of social groups, democratization and inclusiveness. But their actual institutionalization and endorsement in 2002 rendered partnerships as institutions of the status quo, replicating earlier social exclusions. At the Johannesburg Summit, partnerships were redefined as implementation mechanisms aimed to mobilize major groups towards sustainable development in a cooperative fashion. Once institutionalized the power of partnerships to intensify participation was restricted to implementation, and they were regarded by most civil society actors as co-option mechanisms. Their demands for alternative rules for governance, and their reluctance in joining partnerships demonstrate their frustration.

Participation in (or through) partnership projects is further complicated in the context of development. The developmentalist ideology succeeded in internalizing and depoliticizing the demands for a more democratic and participatory global governance, so long as these demands could be articulated within the hegemonic developmentalist project. Accordingly handbooks, manuals, principles and paradigms were produced in order to ensure the limits and the place of such participation. In short, participation has become an integral part of developmentalism, without being able to remedy the democratic deficit in the most significant platforms of global governance.

8.2　TRANSFORMATION(S)

As Chapter 4 aimed to demonstrate, CSD partnerships have undergone important transformations after their conceptualization. Their meaning, aims, expanse and participants have gradually developed and then were redefined. The negotiations that converted the rather vague concept of partnerships into the official outcomes of the Johannesburg Summit were a process of contestation. Various ideas about partnerships were excluded from the official text (the Bali Guidelines) defining and delimiting partnerships. Later, in the actualization stage, there were other ideas that did not materialize, that were not successfully implemented, or that were taken advantage of. Thus, the current partnerships regime has also become unlike what was negotiated. I tried to understand these changes by examining their emergence, endorsement and actualization using the concepts of 'sedimentation of conflict' and 'institutional spectrum'. The next two subsections summarize the findings and reflect upon the use of these concepts.

8.2.1   Negotiations and the Sedimentation of Conflict

Examining the emergence and endorsement of Type-II outcomes through in-depth interviews and text reviews have revealed various definitions, narrations and points of view among the parties involved. Not all of these views have been integrated into the final definition in the Bali Guidelines. The contestations centred on the inclusion of non-state actors (both NGOs, and business and industry), the possible results of a partnerships regime (such as substituting international regimes) and blue-washing (the abuse of the UN credibility). Various accounts of these contestations are detailed in the previous chapters. For the purposes of this section, it is necessary to focus on the production of the partnerships regime. Looking into contested elements through the lens of sedimentation of conflict has proven useful in identifying elements from competing hegemonic projects settling into the logics of a single institution.

According to Hajer's (1995) definition of discourse institutionalization, a successful discourse almost always sediments into institutions. I have argued that during the negotiation of international institutions, it is not only one discourse that sediments into the logics of an institution. Demands from various competing hegemonic projects have sedimented into partnerships as well as conflicts among these projects. The first time partnerships were proposed as a part of WSSD's agenda, the aim was to form a partnerships regime that would not only bring in corporate funds to sustainable development projects, but also to include multinational corporations into the accountability frameworks of environmental governance. Organizers of the conference hoped that this would also reduce the pressure on delegations, and increase the likelihood of reaching agreements during the summit. This would give DESA some power over the monitoring of business activities already taking place in the name of sustainable development and CSR. Creating norms and standards for CSR projects in line with the UN's developmental ideals was one part of this conception. It would also attempt to change the existing rules of sustainability politics. Internationally, DESA hoped for a change within the UN by providing more platforms for the small countries and civil society. Transnationally, development work would have to change, as it often failed to address the problems of these actors. DESA's proposal comprised the following steps: corporations would sign a code of conduct and a commitment to CSR, which would secure recognition, credibility and international support for their CSR activities. When corporate funding for profitable projects was secured, nation states would focus on issues they could agree on, and sign binding treaties. As discussions on Type-II outcomes started in the PrepComs, the demands of many groups were articulated in a more general framework and DESA's suggestions were ultimately turned down.

The PrepComs ensured the support of the business groups, the EU and the US for the Type-II concept, but also raised the suspicions of civil society and the countries that received ODA. In other words, the partnerships proposal was not an empty signifier, representing many demands in a bottom-up fashion and bringing different groups together against the hegemonic order. No chain of equivalence was formed; and partnerships were almost immediately accepted and supported by the existing hegemonic project. The business lobby, some NGOs and governments of the global North redefined the concept and fixed its meaning such that with mere surface changes, the existing practices of development governance could be maintained. Furthermore, during the summit the newly negotiated partnerships regime had become a pretext for not signing regulatory treaties. As partnerships could be designated to address environmental problems, no timetable was agreed upon for the North to provide the means for greening the economies of the South.

Nonetheless, neither the explanations of sustainability partnerships as privatization mechanisms, nor international dependency arguments are sufficient to explain this process, as it was not only the dominant neo-liberal ideology that defined partnerships. During their negotiation, contestations were severe between supporters of the new partnerships regime and the opposition. Moreover, hegemonic struggles took place among the supporters of different conceptions of partnerships. These different interpretations of the concept were based on various hegemonic projects, and numerous particularisms belonging to incommensurable hegemonic projects have entered the official documents establishing the rules. We could categorize different particularisms according to their success during this process: the first three PrepComs served as platforms for the articulation of several suggestions as to how to understand, define, form and monitor partnerships. Many of these proposals were rejected or nullified, so they can be called 'the rejected particularisms'; for example, the European Union's support for partnerships as an unofficial means to achieve specific emission reduction targets until a global agreement was reached. A more comprehensive list of rejected particularisms was provided at the beginning of Chapter 4.

During the PrepComs, concerns about the potential repercussions of endorsing partnerships were more forcefully expressed once the concept received the support of dominant actors. This second group of demands can be called 'the sedimented particularisms', as they were listed in the Bali Guiding Principles. Despite their internal contradictions, these concerns were included in the guidelines so that an agreement could be reached. However, they never gained a binding status, and hence, the definition, description and framing of partnerships encompassed various contradictions, tensions and inconsistencies. For instance, partnerships could not substitute MEAs, although no party had the authority to prevent such a development. Partnerships should address all dimensions of sustainable development, but remain within the realm of MDGs. They should be restricted to implementation of intergovernmental agreements and yet be in line with national sustainable development policies. They should be transparent and accountable, although they would be self-reporting projects and no overseeing body would be established that could influence their operations. Neither the principle of self-reporting nor the caution against substitution of treaties achieved the desired result.

Other contradictions in the Bali Guidelines were increasingly conspicuous as the partnerships regime developed. The guidelines also contained conflicts pertaining to the organization of the partnerships regime: the elimination of the participatory function of partnerships, the alienation of the less powerful major groups, or the choice to limit the scope of partnerships to inter-governmental outcomes were all a result of this process. In the end, imbalances in actor constellation, geographic dispersion and in issue areas have been unavoidable.

Finally, 'the dominant particularisms' (or sediments) were present in the definition and formation of partnerships, in both official texts and their application. For instance, the voluntary nature of partnerships was mentioned in the Bali Guidelines, while the practice of partnership formation also supported this principle. As a result, even parties strongly supportive of Type-II outcomes had no obligation to initiate them once they were endorsed.

In sum, the texts and principles on which sustainability partnerships were built reflected the contestations over their meaning and carried the residues of conflicting interests and interpretations. This was also the case with the UN partnerships regime. The demands of several country delegations as well as bureaucrats from the UN and other agencies of global governance influenced the end result. Their different hegemonic projects were present in the agreed framework in a piecemeal fashion; hence, several hegemonic struggles settled into the logics of the regime.

8.2.2   Institutionalization and Actualization of Partnerships

Despite the sedimentation of conflicting discourses into the Bali Guidelines, partnerships have nevertheless been defined in a particular way. The guidelines were a partial fixation for the term 'sustainability partnerships'. Reaching an agreement on the definition of an institution results in homogenization; a reduction in the differences among articulations and narratives, if not among subject positions. Therefore, the scene after discourse institutionalization is often less diverse in terms of contestations and alternatives. Contestations do not cease to exist, but are different and more subtle in nature. As the partnerships regime started a life of its own, different hegemonic projects asserted themselves as different manifestations of the same architecture – in the specific forms of initiated partnerships, or the lack thereof. For instance, despite their opposition to the concept in the beginning, some environmental NGOs have decided to form partnerships and affect their quality. By the same token, business and industry supported the concept during negotiations, but did not initiate major partnerships. Several practices and technologies, previously unable to secure UN recognition in their issue areas, have found their way into the UN system and have been 'blue washed'. The introduction of controversial technologies and institutions attests the influence of specific partnerships on their respective issue areas, such as nuclear energy, biotechnology and vinyl. Finally, certain actor constellations, issue areas and organizational models were popularized through partnership governance, while others were not.

These observations can be generalized to some degree. The idea that institutions are sedimented discourses can be supplemented with a more dynamic view recognizing different cycles of formation. The dynamics of international institutions are fundamentally different in the first two stages of their existence. The first one, in which an organization is only beginning to form, can be called *discourse institutionalization* as suggested by Hajer (1995). Sometimes this is in fact the sedimentation of a successful discourse into an institution through the repetitive social practices it implied. When there are negotiations involved, institutions often contain sediments of a number of available discourses, at times in conflict with each other. These sediments solidify into the logics of the institution. In this second stage, the success of an institution depends on the speed and ease with which these conflicts are resolved in a consistent discourse. If it succeeds, these practices become increasingly commonplace, and start forming standards, rules, excellence criteria and so forth to consolidate the specific social practice. In the case of partnerships, a consistent practice and discourse has not emerged: the partnerships regime failed as the momentum was lost in the few months after the WSSD. While a limited number of individual partnerships have considerable influence, the WSSD resulted in a weak partnerships regime. So far it has not only failed to address governance deficits, but it is also extremely unlikely to accomplish the Millennium Development Goals, or the Sustainable Development Goals.

Simultaneously, the institution can operate so as to exclude other ways of producing the same results, for instance by assuming complete authority over an issue, by producing licensing procedures, by insisting that its services or products are actually needs previously considered redundant, or by discrediting communities that resist its rationale. The emergence of radical monopolies through such practices often coincides with the creation of new 'needs', and with the tendency to be socially addictive (by prescribing increased doses of the treatment when smaller quantities have not yielded the desired results). Thus they become *manipulative institutions*, as opposed to *convivial* ones that enable autonomous ways of being, living and working (Illich 1970). With their developmentalist resolve, the partnerships regime already fulfils the conditions of being a manipulative institution. Their widespread use in various levels and spheres of governance as well as the increasingly popular employment of their main logic, the win–win narrative, also suggests that they are forming a radical monopoly despite the diversity of their issue areas and the lack of a central authority to standardize their activities.

8.3   PARTNERSHIPS: THE NEXT GENERATION

A second objective of this study was to use partnerships as a resource to better understand global environmental governance, its historical and future transformations, and particularly its most recent institutions with private and hybrid compositions. In line with Bruno Latour's idea of compositionism, this would enable a study that goes beyond critique and reformulates premises that serve as building blocks of a more desirable partnerships regime.

Compositionism aims to go beyond the 'superficial' difference between what is and is not constructed, towards an understanding of what is well

or badly constructed (Latour 2010: 3–4): This could bring about the reconstruction of a common ground 'built from heterogeneous parts that will
never make a whole, but at best a fragile, revisable and diverse composite
material'. In this context, compositionism is an alternative to critique.
While it has been successful in 'debunking prejudices', critique acquired all
the limits of utopias: its intellectual usefulness depends on the existence of
a world of reality beyond the veils of appearances, whereas compositionism is 'all about immanence' (ibid.).

To go beyond critique and reformulate more desirable partnerships, I listed the potentialities of partnerships that were not fulfilled
(Box 7.1), that is the suggestions excluded from the Bali Guidelines,
or the later governance of CSD partnerships. These *rejected particularisms* provide some pieces for composing partnerships anew, and the list
serves as one of the various possible compositions of a more coherent
and desirable partnerships regime. Components of the mediating discourses analyzed in the earlier chapters could give further direction to
this composition.

Regardless of the influence of individual partnerships, the *partnerships
regime* has been unsuccessful in addressing the implementation deficit
and the environmental crisis. In effect, the partnerships regime was never
actually a promise to address these issues but only a partial component
that could assist in addressing them. Moreover, the sustainable development discourse has never been a radical political project to transform
the human-nature relationship. The same is true for the discourse of
privatization of governance: even if partnerships are private governance
institutions promoting voluntary and market-based solutions to environmental problems, they have not been successful in consolidating their
form as a preferable, desirable, or singular one. Neither has the partnerships regime been successful in reducing the controversies around public–
private cooperation. Within the UNCSD, most major groups oppose the
partnerships regime, albeit unofficially and often through their reluctance
in forming new partnerships. In short, privatization was never an openly
discussed aim of partnerships.

Participation, however, was the one ideal that produced the pretext for
partnerships. Although it was excluded or restricted during the negotiations, it is still the main promise of partnerships that every supporter of
the concept brings up both within and outside of the UNCSD. The ideal
of inclusive, participatory governance mechanisms has been consistent
with the assumption underlying the win–win narrative: bringing together
the comparative advantages of each sector would produce effective
governance mechanisms. It is also consistent with the flexibility argument: partnerships are regarded as promising mechanisms of governance

because they can be flexible, both in terms of their actor constellations (across partnerships) and through time (in the lifetime of a single partnership).

The empirical results suggest that partnerships are failing to fulfil their participatory promise. One reason for this failure has been explained earlier as the shift from a participatory to an implementation-focused definition. However, as Andersen (2008: 1) explains, the promise of partnerships is greater than this rather limited and practical goal: not only do partnerships seem to unite the political centre and the political left by overcoming 'the dilemma between public shared responsibility and independent social criticism' but they also appear to solve the dilemma between 'the logics of cooperation and competition in and among public and private sectors'. This makes them a uniting principle, regardless of their practical influence. Various parties keep working together with other partners regardless of the difficulties, problems and impediments. This is a powerful imaginary, and perhaps it is accurate for some of the bottom-up, local partnerships. Introducing partnerships to global and transnational environmental governance, particularly by inviting major groups to cooperate in these projects, is assuming that these groups *can* work towards consensual goals. However, there is no identity of goals between the UN and the private sector, or among major groups. Therefore, partnerships have the effect of 'wishing antagonisms away' in *transnational* governance, inadvertently depoliticizing the governance platforms. On the other hand, this is not the case in *international* governance as state actors secured the perpetuation of the UN's present sovereignty-based operation. This perpetuation, however, is unlikely to produce better environmental governance: while the UN remains sovereignty-based, transboundary environmental hazards intensify at the global level, where the influence of the corporations and financial governance institutions is intensified *vis-à-vis* the state system. With fewer regulatory mechanisms in place the protection of the environment appears to be on the agenda of very few transnational or global actors, often with limited means. This may (to some degree) explain the intensification of *global* activism on environmental issues, while expectations from international summits such as Rio+20 have weakened if not completely dissipated.

The final section is comprised of reflections regarding the promise of partnerships as a unifying mechanism and the place of antagonisms in democratic theory. To complete a circular narration they link 'what has been' to 'what can be': from *myths*, which have been an important component of the fantasmatic logics throughout this work, to *utopias*.

8.3.1   Final Reflections: Partnerships as an End to Antagonisms?

> [Myths] are almost all rooted in death and the fear of extinction. Nietzsche, in
> The Birth of Tragedy, sees myths as dreamlike shapes and tales constructed
> by the Apollonian principle of order and form to protect humans against
> the apprehension of the Dionysian states of formlessness, chaos and gleeful
> destruction. (Byatt 2011: 157)

Friedrich Nietzsche (1872 [1956]: 23) wrote that 'without myth every culture forfeits its healthy creative natural power: only a horizon surrounded with myth completes the unity of an entire cultural movement'. Individuals interpret their lives and struggles through the lens of myths, and 'even the state knows no more powerful unwritten laws than the mythical foundation' (ibid.). In sum, myths unify a culture and represent order in the face of our constant fear of conflict and dislocation that surround the social as they narrate historical and abstract versions of dislocation and its resolution. Every social order, every hegemonic project must represent an explanation to dislocation and antagonism, and suggest a viable alternative order. In the sections pertaining to the fantasmatic logics, I have paid attention to the myths around various hegemonic projects, the narrations of *the past* so as to guide and unify *the present*. In order to complete the cyclical narration as promised in the introduction chapter, this section reflects on imageries of cohesion, unity and order directed towards *the future*: utopias.

Utopias are imageries that represent an end of societal formation: perfect harmony among citizens and a general lack of discontent and dislocation characterizes the societies described across the genre. In the next section a number of utopias are depicted regarding this characteristic. I aim to reveal that there is an anti-democratic element in the heart of most utopian imageries, which can be compared to the win–win narrative that partnerships operate in, in the way they disregard opposition, antagonism and democratic resolution of these situations.

8.3.2   Imageries of Perfection: Socialist Utopias and the End of History

The French Revolution opened a brief window of endless possibilities regarding the organization of communities. In the five decades following the revolution many authors and philosophers were concerned with imagining and founding new communities. Most famously, Charles Fourier invented the concept of *phalanstère*, self-contained communities working together based on the military formation of a phalanx. Socialist businessman Robert Owen organized a community of workers in a Scottish textile factory based on shorter working hours, basic labour rights and schooling for children. Later, he set up another community called 'New Harmony' in the United States, which eventually dissipated. Alternatively, Saint-Simon suggested that science and international struggle were the means to reorganize societies.

In *Socialism: Utopian and Scientific*, Friedrich Engels (1880 [1999]) grouped these thinkers as 'utopian socialists', as they were interested in the emancipation of the whole of humanity rather than the proletariat. Saint-Simon's breadth of view and Fourier's criticism of the existing conditions of society inspired almost all later socialists, whereas Owen demonstrated the possibility of creating a model colony from workers 'in which drunkenness, police, magistrates, lawsuits, poor laws, charity, were unknown [. . .] by placing the people in conditions worthy of human beings' and educating the young (ibid.: 68). Yet, they were not aware of the slowly forming antagonism between the bourgeoisie and the proletariat, as class formation was not complete. But more important than any of their achievements and failures, Engels (ibid.: 66) notes that already in 1816 Saint-Simon

> declares that politics is the science of production and foretells the complete absorption of politics by economics. The knowledge that economic conditions are the basis of political institutions appears [in Saint-Simon's Geneva letters] only in embryo. Yet what is here already very plainly expressed is the idea of the future conversion of political rule over men into an administration of things and a direction of processes of production – that is to say, the 'abolition of the state'. (Ibid.)

Still, for Engels it is a problem that there are many different interpretations of socialism in the utopian socialist thought. This might not only divide the working class but also results in an 'eclectic, average Socialism' while what is needed is a singular reality: 'To make a science of Socialism, it had first to be placed upon a real basis' (ibid.: 70–71).

This 'real basis' was historical materialism, on which *scientific* socialism was to be founded. It would construct the detailed and sufficiently powerful analysis to support Saint-Simon's idea that economic contradictions produce political antagonisms. Accordingly, the next generation of utopian socialists paid less attention to ethical issues and the education of the working class than did Saint-Simon, Fourier and Owen. Engels' suggestion that Saint-Simon correctly observed the necessity of politics being absorbed in economics became commonplace: once the economic hardship (under which the working classes lived) was eliminated by the abolition of private property, political antagonisms would wither away.

Hence the next generation of socialist utopias focused on the qualities (how) and the benefits (why) of an equitable economic community. In these narrations politics was something of the past, which did not belong to these ideal societies. To demonstrate the extent to which the utopian socialist literature of the late nineteenth and early twentieth centuries dismissed politics, I would like to quote three important novels of the time: Edward Bellamy's *Looking Backward, 2000–1887*, William Morris's *News from Nowhere* and H.G. Wells's *In the Days of the Comet*.

One of the first utopian novels published in the US, Bellamy's (1887 [1951]), *Looking Backward, 2000–1887* was a big success both in terms of sales and following.[1] The main character in the novel, Julian West, wakes up from a hypnosis-induced sleep in the year 2000, in the same place (Boston) but a completely changed world: the US is transformed into a socialist utopia with reduced working hours, equal respect for all jobs, lack of a leisure class and an infinitely more efficient production system owned by the whole nation. When West asks his host Dr. Leete whether the new system has 'done away with the states', he learns that this was indeed the case as governments have become superfluous (ibid.: 168):

> Almost the sole function of the administration now is that of directing the industries of the country. Most of the purposes for which governments formerly existed no longer remain to be subserved. We have [no] military organization, [no] departments of state or treasury, no excise or revenue services, no taxes or tax collectors. The only function proper of government, as known to you, which still remains, is the judiciary and police system, [although the absence] of crime and temptation to it [made] the duties of judges so light [and reduced] the number and duties of the police to a minimum. [. . .]
> We have no legislation [as] we have nothing to make laws about. The fundamental principles on which our society is founded settle for all time the strifes and misunderstandings which in your day called for legislation. Fully ninety-nine hundredths of the laws of that time concerned the definition and protection of private property and the relations of buyers and sellers. There is neither private property, beyond personal belongings, now, nor buying and selling, and therefore the occasion of nearly all the legislation formerly necessary has passed away. Formerly, society was a pyramid poised on its apex. All the gravitations of human nature were constantly tending to topple it over, and it could be maintained upright, or rather upwrong (if you will pardon the feeble witticism), by an elaborate system of constantly renewed props and buttresses and guy-ropes in the form of laws. [. . .] Now society rests on its base, and is in as little need of artificial supports as the everlasting hills.

England's most influential utopian novel, William Morris's (1891 [1970]) *News from Nowhere*, focused less on efficiency and more on aesthetics, reverting to an economy based on agricultural and handicraft production. Nevertheless, private property was replaced with common ownership and communal living, similar to Bellamy's imagery. The protagonist William Guest, too, falls asleep (on his return from a Socialist League meeting) and wakes up in a future society. Guest's host, Hammond, an old man with expansive knowledge of 'the old times' informs him about the wonders of this new society, until he is asked how they manage politics, to which he responds (ibid.: 72):

> I believe I am the only man in England who would know what you mean; and since I know, I will answer your question briefly by saying that we are very well off as to politics, – because we have none. If ever you make a book out of this conversation, put this in a chapter by itself, after the model of old Horrebow's Snakes in Iceland.

Hammond argues that politics is unnecessary (ibid.: 73–74), as 'differences of opinion about real solid things need not [. . .] crystallise people into parties permanently hostile to one another'. In the old times, politicians pretended that there were serious differences of opinion in the society so as to 'force the public to pay the expense of a luxurious life' or otherwise 'they could not have dealt together in the ordinary business of life'. Since this is obsolete, there is no political platform other than the neighbourhood meetings in the new society. Accordingly, Parliament House in London is transformed into the Dung Market so that it would prove useful. International relations have also changed considerably, as 'the whole system of rival and contending nations which played so great a part in the "government" of the world of civilization has disappeared along with the inequality betwixt man and man in society' (ibid.: 72). On personal matters that did not affect the welfare of the community, there could be no difference of opinion and everybody did as she pleased. When Guest asks further about the general differences of opinion within communities, Hammond describes the decision-making process (ibid.: 74–77, my emphases):

> 'Amongst us, our differences concern matters of business, and passing events as to them, and could not divide men permanently. *As a rule, the immediate outcome shows which opinion on a given subject is the right one; it is a matter of fact, not of speculation.*' [. . .]
> 'And you settle differences, great and small, by the will of the majority, I suppose?'
> 'Certainly. [When] the doing or not doing something affects everybody, the majority must have their way; unless the minority were to take up arms and show by force that they were the effective or real majority; which, however, in a society of men who are free and equal is little likely to happen; because in such a community the apparent majority is the real majority, and the others [. . .] have plenty of opportunity of putting forward their side of the question.' [. . .]
> 'There is something in all this very like democracy; and I thought that democracy was considered to be in a moribund condition many, many years ago.'
> The old boy's eyes twinkled. 'I grant you that our methods have that drawback. But what is to be done? We can't get any one amongst us to complain

of his not always having his own way in the teeth of the community, when it is clear that everybody cannot have that indulgence. [. . .] A terrible tyranny our Communism, is it not? Folk used to be warned against this very unhappiness in times past, when for every well-fed, contented person you saw a thousand miserable starvelings. Whereas for us, we grow fat and well-liking on the tyranny; a tyranny, to say the truth, not to be made visible by any to seek for troubles by calling our peace and plenty and happiness by ill names whose very meaning we have forgotten!'

Finally, H.G. Wells (1906 [2004]) resorts to the extraordinary powers of a comet passing by the Earth to bring about the change that is needed for the creation of an equitable society, in *In the Days of the Comet*. William Leadford, a socialist with upper-class roots narrates everyone being swallowed by the soporific fog and waking up in a world of *Great Change*. Humanity has entirely changed and has a greater understanding of itself, and therefore not only are all 'petty titles' such as ranks and ownership eradicated but wars, borders and military forces are also antiquated. Ministers reflect that they never did anything worth doing, that they have been fools, and that they have to forgive even themselves. Finally, one politician professes (ibid.: 309):

[We lived] creating nothing, consolidating many things, destroying much. [Our] self-conceit has been monstrous. We seem to have used our ample coarse intellectuality for no other purpose than to develop and master and maintain the convention of property, to turn life into a sort of mercantile chess and spend our winnings grossly. [. . .] We have had no sense of service to mankind. Beauty which is godhead – we made it a possession.

Leadford reflects:

This group of men who constituted the Government of one-fifth of the habitable land of the earth [. . .] had no common idea whatever of what they meant to do with the world. [. . .] That great empire was no more than a thing adrift, [. . .] inordinately proud of itself because it had chanced to happen. It had no plan, no intention; it meant nothing. And the other great empires adrift, perilously adrift like marine mines, were in the self-same case. [. . .]
One thing struck me very forcibly at the time, the absence of any discussion, any difference of opinion, about the broad principles of our present state. [At the time of] awakening those barriers and defences had vanished [. . .]. They had admitted and assimilated at once all that was good in the ill-dressed propagandas that had clamored so vehemently and vainly at the doors of their minds in the former days. It was exactly like the awakening from an absurd and limiting dream. They had come out together *naturally and inevitably* upon the broad daylight platform of obvious and reasonable agreement upon which we and all the order of our world now stand. (Ibid.: 311–312, my emphasis.)

While this abhorrence of politics might be related to the political conduct in their societies, the way differences of opinion are played down by all authors is remarkable. Even for Morris, who details communal decision-making, issues are only practical and not ideological or ethical. All authors refer to certain democratic principles in the *management* of the communities, but almost exclusively in a *managerial* manner and particularly in relation to the decisions made about production. What is most striking in the responses of the utopian hosts is their resort to either reason, or to forces of nature in their defence of their ways: after the comet, men 'naturally and inevitably' find a reasonable agreement regarding the order of the world; Hammond establishes that the decisions people take are verified immediately and as 'a matter of fact, not of speculation'; and for Dr. Leete it is a gravitational force that ensures that society stands on its base, not on its apex – which would need 'artificial supports'.

That politics naturally (or out of common sense) vanishes with the abolishment of economic inequality echoes Engels and Marx. It also points to a shared paradox; while a revolution, a supernatural event, or long transformations were needed for the new economic system to emerge, none of this was necessary for politics to disappear. The hegemonic struggle was so definitively about economics that the authors could not envision politics once equality was established: in effect, they were insinuating an 'end of history' of their own inclination.

There are some common points among these novels that would describe utopian socialism. First, what *constitutes the change* between the societies in which these novels were written and the society they idealized: in all cases, the ideal society is based on a just and equitable distribution of livelihoods, common ownership of either all property or the modes of production and communal living. This results in differences of opinion to be solely about either personal issues, which are in all cases left to individuals' free will, or matters of public management, which are solved without serious conflicts. This simplification of difference and the total lack of antagonism is a feature of the whole genre.

A second common point is how this change into the ideal society comes about, that is *what constitutes the 'revolution'*: Bellamy suggests a completely rational and peaceful transition to the nation-scale production 'simply' brought about equitable distribution. Wells limits his revolution to the influence of the comet passing by. Morris (1891 [1970]: 87–111) in the chapter titled 'How the Change Came', describes a working-class revolution with surprising accuracy. The initial use of force against the revolutionaries is followed by attempts by the ruling elite to support a counter-revolutionary fascist movement. The crucial role of the media and the final consolidation of power as the original leaders are replaced by a more vigorous and decentralized government are described in detail. Despite these observations, Morris leaves a certain temporal gap between the time that his protagonist falls asleep and the time that class consciousness becomes widespread. Although the utopian system is narrated as more natural, rational and appropriate for human nature, neither narration reaches it from within the social circumstances they were written in, but through a supernatural event or dream.

The final common point among these imageries is the complete lack of an explanation – or even contemplation of what constitutes a people and their identity, which in turn would constitute *the political*. Accordingly, no further structural change could take place in these utopian societies: the lack of contingency is the rule for a continuous state of perfection unanimously agreed upon since Plato, for whom democracy was undesirable to begin with. In this sense, socialist utopias narrated the end of politics by imagining societies with no antagonism. The assumption was that circumstances (as opposed to identities) and upbringing made people antagonistic. In an equitable society, harmony would replace all antagonisms.

The utopias precluded further identity formation/transformation among their citizens, and (as a result) assumed the end of antagonisms. The lack of antagonisms, however, insinuates not only the end of politics, but that of democracy. Democracy requires antagonism; issues are politicized on the basis of antagonisms originating from social identities. Inversely, only a *pluralist* democracy can accommodate continuous identity formation. As Mouffe (1996: 25) suggests, 'a society in which all antagonisms have been eradicated, far from being a truly democratic one, would be its exact opposite. Pluralism is constitutive of modern democracy, and it precludes any dream of final reconciliation'.

Furthermore, Mouffe (1993: 5) observes that the contemporary political processes alienate citizens, by avoiding antagonisms related to their identities. Thus they discourage meaningful participation and collective identities are increasingly formed on more traditional platforms, such as religious, nationalist or ethnic forms of identification, instead of democratic political platforms. She also notes that the left, having inherited the idea of 'common good' and the 'end of politics' from socialism, is restricting its potential to influence the participation of a diverse citizen body (ibid.: 7):

> Nowadays, the crucial issue is how to establish a new political frontier capable of giving a real impulse to democracy. [. . .] There are currently many attempts on the left to recover the idea of citizenship but [. . .] it is important not to aim at a neutral conception of citizenship applicable to all members of the political community. This is why, while being attentive to its critique of liberal individualism, I am wary of many aspects of a substantive idea of the communitarian approach. Its rejection of pluralism and defence of a substantive idea of the

'common good' represents, in my view, another way of evading the ineluctabil-
ity of antagonism. There will always be competing interpretations of the political principles of liberal democracy, and the meanings of liberty and equality will
never cease to be contested. Citizenship is vital for democratic politics, but a
modern democratic theory must make room for competing conceptions of our
identities as citizens.

For Mouffe, both the principles of democracy, and the idea of (our own)
citizenship is contingent; hence the suggestion of a 'common good evading
antagonism' is to suggest the end of politics. From the perspective of the
political subject, lack of antagonism would suggest the lack of desire to
participate in politics. Inversely, for a citizen this would mean that there
is nothing to participate in – it is a semiotic *and* structural restriction of
political participation. And although this is a virtual impossibility (as
identities and antagonisms keep developing regardless), it was a significant
myth of the socialist hegemonic project. In this purely fantasmatic sense,
early socialists (utopian and scientific) approached an imagined 'end of
history' with the idea of a common good – only ending differently from
what Fukuyama envisioned.

Thus, the end of antagonisms and the end of politics is an anti-
democratic dream. Partnerships or other global governance institutions
cannot address *democratic* deficits by dismissing the antagonisms among
different sects of the global civil society, with narrations of win–win
solutions wherein everybody gains. Particularly from the perspective of
societies that do not consider themselves 'winners' in the existing system,
these narratives represent a dismissal of their concerns. Addressing the
democratic deficit would begin with generating platforms on which antagonisms can be articulated and possibly resolved. The following section
looks into an alternative imagery of this kind.

8.3.3 Another Utopia is Possible: Ecotopia versus End(s) of History

> They turned to politics because it was finally the only route to self-preservation.
> (Callenbach 1975 [2009]: 51)

In the twentieth century, the utopian genre produced narrations of ideal
societies, reflecting all the techno-scientific innovations of its time. While
one branch turned to technology to explain change (science fiction),
another focused on ecology, resulting in the sub-genre of *ecological
utopias*. As Marius de Geus's (1999) study of nine ecological utopias
shows, the genre is characterized (and separated from other utopias)
by the principle of *sufficiency*, following the premise of *limits* based on
the economic ideas of Schumacher and Kohr. Thus, ecological utopias

uncouple the ideal of a good society from the hegemonic discourses of progress and growth and promote a 'radically different conception of happiness and the good life' (ibid.: 210). Nevertheless, these *utopias of sufficiency* (as opposed to *utopias of abundance*) vary considerably regarding the forms of social organization, political participation, social control and individual liberties they advocate.

The assumption that political antagonism disappears in an ideal society is also present in some of these recent utopias, such as the behaviouralist utopia of B.F. Skinner (1948 [1962]), *Walden Two*. The name of the book and the community is a reference to Henry David Thoreau's *Walden* but this time 'with company'. The Walden Two community is narrated as a utopian experiment that the protagonist learns about and goes to investigate. This is a unique and somewhat isolated community in 1940s USA, but its founder expects and plans the structure to expand to other communities, and become the norm in the future within the existing political system. Yet, *within the community* there is no 'politics' to speak of. Here too property is communal, but problems are solved by carrying out experiments of 'cultural engineering'. Throughout the book, democracy is incapacitated by the founder of the community; this self-sufficient community is governed by Planners and Managers who ensure efficiency through the use of machines, and communal harmony through behavioural conditioning. With the use of positive reinforcement on the community, many of the 'outdated institutions' such as capitalism, democracy, family, religion and so forth, have become obsolete. Although *change* is continuous in *Walden Two*, this is an experimental and planned change, which completely excludes politics. Several efforts to create a *Walden Two* in real life were made, and at least two survive to this day.

Walden Two represents the endpoint of some of the current concepts in governance, with its emphasis on top-down education, positive conditioning, management and planning. The main assumption of the novel is that change can be achieved apolitically, through rational experimentation and managerial leadership. Against this behaviouralist assumption of change and the socialist idea that politics is determined completely by economics, pluralist and participatory imageries were narrated, such as Ernest Callenbach's (1975 [2009]) *Ecotopia*. Callenbach's utopia was the most influential of all *ecological utopias*, because it combined three important themes of eco-political movements: local, participatory democracy, sufficiency and anti-capitalism. An ideal society operating on the principle of sufficiency is a fundamental critique of capitalism and consumerism, and although private property is not abolished, life is communal. Ecotopia is anti-capitalistic in its logics and institutions, not because property was socialized. An active citizenry and a bottom-up, participatory democracy ensure the presence and articulation of antagonisms through various means, on various platforms and levels.

Ecotopians participate in politics as a part of their daily life, most often by 'calling the TV' (an internet-like system that broadcasts programmes and debates on the executive, judicial and legislative branches of the state), to which anyone can participate through their 'phones'. While doing that, Ecotopians do not assume objectivity, which they regard as a 'bourgeois fetish'; they simply state their positions and opinions (ibid.: 42). But *political* participation is not the only participatory process: 'Participation in the community, whether college, a living group, or an academic association, is thought to be important for all' (ibid.: 143).

Students and academics participate in the organization of the academia; each employee is a partner in the company they work at; individuals are expected to participate in all of the affairs regarding their smaller communities; the participation of users is indispensable in the commodity production process; and as one assistant-minister says: 'In Ecotopia, you will find many many things happening without government authorization' (ibid.: 21). In Illich's terms, Ecotopia is a convivial society, wherein several ways of being, living and producing the optimum results are possible. Manipulative institutions are curbed as monopolies, advertisements, overproduction, centralization and big-scale industrial production are either prohibited or discouraged.

The source of this participatory proliferation is not state regulation, or a general democratic conviction. It results from a deeply held belief that no-*body*, or no-*thing* is an individual, separate from a number of systems. In this sense, Ecotopia approaches the participatory ideal that Rahnema (1992) described as the intransitive form of the word 'participation': partaking in the course of daily life, spontaneously and without a particular objective. In Ecotopia, the intransitive form of participation, 'participation while living one's own life' or even '*by* living one's own life' is the norm: identities are constantly reflected in the way people live, participate and rule themselves.

It is not a coincidence that Callenbach's participatory utopia is an ecotopia. The eco-political movements and the European green parties in the 1970s and 1980s responded to the hegemonic struggle between capitalist and socialist political projects by refusing the 'ends of history', and regarding capitalism *and* socialism as two lanes of the same (developmentalist and ersatz-democratic) road. Instead of singling out capitalism as the only (or main) oppressing force, green parties addressed the numerous identities excluded and oppressed by the different sites and forces of the existing systems. Accordingly, grassroots and participatory democratic models have been one of the four pillars of green ideology.

The recognition of individuals as a part of a greater whole is inspired by systems theory and eco-systemic approaches to society. In systems theory, a holistic approach to ecosystems requires an understanding of numerous subsystems nested in and interdependent on each other. There is no hierarchical organization among these subsystems or among the organisms that are a part of them. Evolutionary theories overemphasize the role of adaptation, function and competition. Unlike these, the ecosystems approach argues that even when an organism appears redundant, it is not reasonable to assume that it had, or will have no function. Similarly, in Ecotopia, individuals participate in the decisions regarding various communities they are a part of. Their disagreements are voiced in various platforms, and decisions are not made consensually. Rather different approaches are allowed to solve the same problem. In Illich's terms, the system actively refrains from standardizing its policies and frustrating alternative approaches. Radical monopolies are avoided and these initiatives are often not controlled by the state. This pluralism is made explicit when the protagonist probes:

> 'Doesn't this stable-state business get awfully static? I'd think it would drive you crazy after a certain point!'
> Bert looked at me with amusement, and batted the ball back. 'Well, don't forget that we don't have to be stable. The system provides the stability, and we can be erratic within it.' [. . .]
> 'But it means giving up any notions of progress. You just want to get to that stable point and stay there, like a lump.'
> 'It may sound that way, but in practice there's no stable point. We're always striving to approximate it, but we never get there. [We] disagree on exactly what it is to be done – we only agree on the root essentials, everything else is in dispute.'
> I grinned. 'I've noticed that – you're a quarrelsome lot!'
> 'We can afford to be, because of that root agreement. Besides, that's half the fun of relating to each other – trying to work through different perspectives, seeing how other people feel about things'. (Ibid.: 33–34)

Even then, separationist and potential terrorist groups are present in Callenbach's story, that disagree with the 'root agreement' mentioned by the Ecotopia citizen Bert. These groups aim to change the government and the limited consensus it is based on. In sum, controversy is by no means restricted in *Ecotopia*. It is regarded as enriching, and a requirement of true democracy. This understanding of the root agreement (and of true democracy) is very similar to the concept of adversarial relationships in an agonistic pluralism in Mouffe's (1998) radical democratic theory:

> Agonistic pluralism [is] different from the traditional liberal conception of democracy as a negotiation among interests and is also different from the

model which is currently being developed by people like Jürgen Habermas and John Rawls. [Despite their] differences, Rawls and Habermas have in common the idea that the aim of the democratic society is the creation of a consensus, and that consensus is possible if people are only able to leave aside their particular interests and think as rational beings. However, while we desire an end to conflict, if we want people to be free we must always allow for the possibility that conflict may appear and to provide an arena where differences can be confronted. The democratic process should supply that arena.

The agonistic condition wherein conflict is an inherent dimension of politics, could guide us towards novel venues in global governance. As previous chapters demonstrated, formation of global governance institutions often results in sedimentation of various elements from competing hegemonic projects, including the sedimentation of conflict to the logics of the newly formed regime or institution. This is the main obstacle the UN's partnerships regime faces: its inherent contradictions impede the fulfilment of its many promises.

In the future the agonistic condition can be relied upon in two distinct ways. First, platforms of adjudication can be opened to the concerns of *all* non-state, non-profit actors. This would not address the democratic deficit completely, but could give civil society some leeway into challenging policies of global and transnational governance institutions. Second, new governance mechanisms, such as partnerships, can be modelled such that existing accountability and transparency standards are replaced with platforms of contestation. Generally, this would provide arenas for various conflicts to be articulated on. It would also introduce the possibility of adversarial relationships between actors with significantly divergent interests. Minimally, this would address certain conflicts in the partnerships regime. For instance, the concerns of some of the major groups can be addressed. Workers and trade unions are concerned that the UN platforms on which they previously engaged with and opposed the business actors have been lost with the invention of partnerships. Youth and women's groups expressed their frustration with the participatory promise of partnerships as their interests were in direct conflict with some projects, in which other sectors of their communities were engaged. Finally, local administrations and small farmers disagreed with the initiation of partnerships against their best interest, by national governments and agro-industry. All these contestations currently have no platform to be articulated on. Building partnerships in a radically different fashion, wherein the interests of all involved parties are discussed before initiation of the projects, could amplify the impact of the agonistic approach.

In international relations, the space for grassroots participation has been even more restricted. Partnerships were conceptualized as instruments to fill this participation deficit in global environmental governance by enabling stakeholder participation in the UNCSD as well as in partnership projects, described by Tony Hill, former coordinator of the UN NGLS, as 'the third generation of UN–Civil Society relations'. But Hill's vision or the experience of CSD partnerships over the last decade do not produce the arena for various environmental conflicts to be articulated and, at times, resolved.

In other words, the conditions for the partnerships regime to address democratic deficits in global environmental governance are not available within the UNCSD. A redefinition of their goals, rules and organizational structure would provide a necessary first step in restructuring sustainability partnerships as more democratic mechanisms of hybrid, or private environmental governance. But more importantly, if we dare to operationalize the lessons from *Ecotopia*, the partnership regime needs to be located into a system that provides the stability, so that partnerships can afford to be innovative, bottom-up, experimental organizations wherein antagonisms can be articulated and resolved, and different environmental (rather than paradoxical sustainable development) goals can be achieved according to the needs and wishes of various recipient communities. If this kind of a root agreement can be reached, everything else can remain in dispute among partners and across partnerships without jeopardizing the planet's remaining vital ecosystems but only the existing governance architecture and power relations.

8.3.4   Partnerships as Hybrid Governance Mechanisms

'Environmental politics and sustainable development has emerged as an experimental arena for new modes of governance' (Bäckstrand et al. 2010: 15). Sustainability partnerships are one such arrangement whereby new principles have been introduced to global environmental governance. Other examples of hybrid governance mechanisms (HGMs) are mitigation banking schemes, governance networks and carbon markets. They are called hybrids because they combine different rationales, steering modes, public and private sector goals regarding environmental issues (ibid.).

HGMs are also available on numerous other issue areas, including security, development and health, wherein regulatory approaches are replaced by market-based and voluntary mechanisms. Non-state actors are increasingly included in political decision-making; organizational flexibility is usually regarded as an important feature for reasons of convenience, security and urgency. When we look into the bigger picture, environmental governance has indeed been a primary area for the introduction of such institutions at the transnational and global levels, where state control is more limited than national and bilateral arrangements. By now, market-driven, privately initiated, voluntary schemes crowded the institutional architecture concerning almost every environmental issue. Terms like 'governance for sustainable development' (Lafferty 2004) or 'earth system governance' (Biermann 2007) were developed to depict the complex interaction between these numerous schemes and organizations, treaties and actors. It has become impossible to consider environmental governance without the effects of HGMs.

While HGMs are almost always introduced as a means to enhance the democratic quality of environmental governance by more inclusive, participatory processes, their democratic potential is found to have been repeatedly compromised. This can be caused by economic incentives, or being applied to processes with little policy relevance or due to an implementation deficit, or since they become a means to delegate responsibility for environmental performance to various 'partners' or consumers. Whenever there is the shadow of hierarchy, hybrid governance mechanisms are more responsive, transparent and accountable. Yet, in the context of neo-liberal globalization wherein power shifts from the political to the economic sphere, their democratic quality has been questionable; they defuse the radical potential of civic critique and legitimize global capital. At the global level, the problems are twofold. Firstly, there are very few and only fragmented mechanisms to ensure the democratic quality of HGMs. Secondly, the lack of a legal authority to petition in case of governance failures make democratic control of HGMs even more difficult. In other words, liabilities are obscured and the incentive for responsible behaviour is low. Hence, new mechanisms of governance require new mechanisms of checks and balances, specifically designed for *transnational* and *global* environmental governance.

Finally, we must consider how the scientific practices and knowledge are co-constituted by HGMs. The organization and practice of science seems to increasingly reflect a political/economic logic in which market-based criteria are used to allocate scientific resources. In his work regarding weather derivatives markets (futures markets on weather indices), Randalls (2010) suggests that HGMs promulgate this approach and transform science into an economic entity. Lave et al. (2010) note that the employment of HGMs intensified the demand for environmental scientists 'to produce applied science that can: (1) be taught as a standardized package; (2) be used by agencies to justify decisions; and (3) form the basis for new markets in ecosystems services'. Writing about carbon markets, MacKenzie (2009) describes the scientific efforts to 'make things the same' by making different gases commensurable. A similar approach can be applied to biodiversity markets (how species and habitats are made the same) and mitigation banking (how landscapes or ecosystems are made the same). This is a process through which scientific information gains applicability to market-based governance mechanisms while it loses comprehensibility, accountability, and at times its legitimacy.

To conclude, despite the intensification of HGMs, environmental indicators point towards alarming rates of increase in greenhouse gas emissions and toxicity, and of decline in habitat and biodiversity. Various such indicators are present, and they should be studied in detail in the future so as to infer the extent to which output legitimacy should be prioritized as a component of the proposed accountability and transparency framework for HGMs.

NOTE

1. It was the third largest bestseller of its time and inspired 'The Equality Colony' founded in Skagit County, Washington, in 1897.

References

Abbey, E. (1975 [2006]), *The Monkey Wrench Gang*, Philadelphia, PA: Lippincott.

Ajzenstat, S. (1997), 'Contract in *The Merchant of Venice*', *Philosophy and Literature*, **21**(2): 262–278.

Allen, W. (1992), 'Our Schizophrenic Conception of the Business Corporation', *Cardozo Law Review*, **14**(2): 261–281.

Althusser, L. (1965 [2005]), *For Marx* (trans. B. Brewster), London: Verso.

Andersen, N.A. (2008), *Partnerships: Machines of Possibilities*, Cambridge: Polity.

Andonova, L. (2005), 'International Institutions, Inc.', *Proceedings of the Berlin Conference on the Human Dimensions of Global Environmental Change*, 2–3 December 2005, Berlin.

Andonova, L. and M.A. Levy (2003), 'Franchising Global Governance: Making Sense of the Johannesburg Type-II Partnerships', in O.S. Stokke and O.B. Thommessen (eds), *Yearbook of International Co-operation on Environment and Development*, London: Earthscan, pp. 19–31.

Annan, K. (1997), 'The Address of Secretary-General Kofi Annan to the World Economic Forum', 1 February 1997, Davos, Switzerland. Available at: http://www.un.org/News/Press/docs/1997/19970131.sgsm 6153.html. Accessed: 10-2-2009.

Annan, K. (2000a), 'The Environment Millennium: The Secretary-General's Message to the Global Ministerial Environment Forum', Malmö, Sweden. Available at: http://www.unep.org/ourplanet/imgversn/ 112/annan.html. Accessed: 12-3-2010.

Annan, K. (2000b), 'Opening Address to the 53rd DPI/NGO Conference'. Available at: http://www.un.org/dpi/ngosection/annualconfs/53/sg-address.html. Accessed: 12-4-2008.

Arendt, H. (1958 [1998]), *The Human Condition*, Chicago: University of Chicago Press.

Arendt, H. (1970), 'Reflections: Civil Disobedience', *The New Yorker*, 12 September 1970: 70.

Atwood, M. (2008), *Payback: Debt and the Shadow Side of Wealth*, Toronto: Anansi.

Bäckstrand, K. and E. Lövbrand (2006), 'Planting Trees to Mitigate Climate Change: Contested Discourses of Ecological Modernization, Green Governmentality and Civic Environmentalism', *Global Environmental Politics*, **6**(1): 50–75.

Bäckstrand, K., J. Khan, A. Kronsell and E. Lövbrand (2010), *Environmental Politics and Deliberative Democracy*, Cheltenham, UK and Northampton, MA, USA: Edward Elgar.

Barthes, R. (1957 [1987]), *Mythologies*, New York: Hill and Wang.

Baudrillard, J. (2000), *The Vital Illusion*, New York: Columbia University Press.

Bellamy, E. (1887 [1951]), *Looking Backward, 2000–1887*, New York: The Modern Library.

Berle, A.A. and G. Means (1932), *The Modern Corporation and Private Property*, New York: Macmillan.

Bernstein, S. (2000), 'Ideas, Social Structure and the Compromise of Liberal Environmentalism', *European Journal of International Relations*, **6**(4): 464–512.

Bernstein, S. (2001), *The Compromise of Liberal Environmentalism*, New York: Columbia University Press.

Bernstein, S. (2005), 'Legitimacy in Global Environmental Governance', *Journal of International Law and International Relations*, **1**(1–2): 139–166.

Biermann, F. (2007), 'Earth System Governance as a Cross-Cutting Theme of Global Change Research', *Global Environmental Change*, **17**(3–4): 326–337.

Biermann, F. (2012), 'Curtain Down and Nothing Settled. Global Sustainability Governance after the "Rio+20" Earth Summit', Earth System Governance Working Paper No. 26, Lund and Amsterdam: Earth System Governance Project.

Biermann, F. and K. Dingwerth (2004), 'Global Environmental Change and the Nation State', *Global Environmental Politics*, **4**(1): 1–22.

Biermann, F., P. Pattberg, S. Chan and A. Mert (2007), 'Multi-stakeholder Partnerships for Sustainable Development: Does the Promise Hold?', in P. Glasbergen, F. Biermann and A. Mol (eds), *Partnerships, Governance and Sustainable Development*, Cheltenham, UK and Northampton, MA, USA: Edward Elgar, pp. 239–260.

Blair, M. (1995), *Ownership and Control: Rethinking Corporate Governance for the Twenty-first Century*, Washington, DC: The Brookings Institution.

Blair, T. (2005), 'Remarks at the 2005 Labour Party Conference', 27 September 2005, Brighton. Available at: http://www.theglobalist.com/StoryId.aspx?StoryId=4833. Accessed: 12-4-2008.

Bookchin, M. (1962), *Our Synthetic Environment*, New York: Alfred A. Knopf.

Brinkerhoff, J. (2002), 'Government–Nonprofit Partnership: A Defining Framework', *Public Administration and Development*, **22**: 19–30.

Bruno, K. (2002), 'The Earth Summit's Deathblow to Sustainable Development'. Available at: http://www.corpwatch.org/article.php?id= 3831. Accessed: 14-06-2008.

Bruno, K. and J. Karliner (2002), *Earthsummit.Biz: The Corporate Takeover of Sustainable Development*, Oakland, CA: Food First.

Bryer, R. (1997), 'The Mercantile Laws Commission of 1854 and the Political Economy of Limited Liability', *Economic History Review*, **50**(1): 37–56.

Buchnan, J. (2001), *Frozen Desire: Meaning of Money*, New York: Welcome Rain.

Buse, K. (2004), 'Governing Public–Private Infectious Disease Partnerships', *Brown Journal of World Affairs*, **2**: 225–242.

Byatt, A.S. (2011), *Ragnarok*, Edinburgh: Canongate.

CAI-Asia (2010), 'Private Sector'. Available at: http://cleanairinitiative. org/portal/members/partnership/member/Private%20sector. Accessed: 25-11-2011.

Callenbach, E. (1975 [2009]), *Ecotopia: The Notebooks and Reports of William Weston*, Berkeley: Heyday.

Cameron, A. and R. Palan (2004), *The Imagined Economies of Globalization*, London: Sage.

Carson, R. (1962), *Silent Spring*, London: Penguin.

Cashore, B. (2002), 'Legitimacy and the Privatization of Environmental Governance: How Non-State Market-Driven (NSMD) Governance Systems Gain Rule-Making Authority', *Governance*, **15**(4): 503–529.

Castoriadis, C. (1975 [1987]), *The Imaginary Institution of Society*, Oxford: Polity.

Centre for American Progress (2012), 'How the Rio+20 Earth Summit Could Have Been Better'. Available from: http://www.americanprogress. org/issues/green/news/2012/06/26/11797/how-the-rio20-earth-summit-could-have-been-better/. Accessed: 20-02-2013.

Cevasco, G.A. and R.P. Harmond (2009), *Modern American Environmentalists: A Biographical Encyclopedia*, Baltimore: John Hopkins University Press.

Chambers, R. (1997), *Whose Reality Counts? Putting the First Last*, London: IT.

Clapp, J. (1998), 'The Privatization of Global Environmental Governance: ISO 14000 and the Developing World', *Global Governance*, **4**(3): 295–316.

Clapp, J. and P. Dauvergne (2005), *Paths to a Green World: The Political Economy of the Global Environment*, Cambridge, MA: MIT Press.

Clark, A.M., E.J. Friedman, and K. Hochstetler (1998), 'The Sovereign Limits of Global Civil Society: A Comparison of NGO Participation in UN World Conferences on the Environment, Human Rights, and Women', *World Politics*, **51**(1): 1–35.

Cleaver, F. (2001), 'Institutions, Agency and the Limitations of Participatory Approaches to Development', in B. Cooke and U. Kothari (eds), *Participation: The New Tyranny?* London: Zed, pp. 36–55.

Cooke, C.A. (1950), *Corporation, Trust and Company*, Manchester: Manchester University Press.

Cooney, R. (2001), 'CITES and the CBD: Tensions and Synergies', *Review of European Community and International Environmental Law*, **10**: 259–267.

Cox, R. (1996), 'Social Forces, States, and World Orders: Beyond International Relations Theory', in R. Cox and T.J. Sinclair (eds), *Approaches to World Order*, Cambridge: Cambridge University Press, pp. 85–122.

Critchley, S. and O. Marchart (2004), 'Introduction', in S. Critchley, and O. Marchart (eds), *Laclau: A Critical Reader*, London: Routledge, pp. 1–14.

Curry, P. (2002), 'Nature Post-Nature', *New Formations*, **26**: 51–64.

Cutler, C. (2002), 'Private International Regimes and Interfirm Cooperation', in R. Hall and T. Biersteker (eds), *The Emergence of Private Authority in Global Governance*, Cambridge: Cambridge University Press, pp. 23–40.

Cutler, C., V. Haufler and T. Porter (1999), *Private Authority and International Affairs*, New York: SUNY Press.

Dahl, R. (1989), *Democracy and Its Critics*, New Haven, NJ: Yale University Press.

Deibel, E. and A. Mert (2014), 'Partnerships and Miracle Crops: On Open Access and the Commodification of Plant Varieties', *Asian Biotechnology and Development Review*, **16**(1): 1–33.

Derrida, J. (1967 [1976]), 'The Exorbitant Question of Method', in G.C. Spivak (ed.) *Of Grammatology*, Baltimore: Johns Hopkins University Press, pp. 157–164.

Derrida, J. (2002), *Negotiations: Interventions and Interviews, 1971–2001* (trans. E. Rottenberg), Stanford: Stanford University Press.

Dingwerth, K. (2007), *The New Transnationalism: Transnational Governance and Democratic Legitimacy*, Basingstoke: Palgrave Macmillan.

Dodd, Jr., E.M. (1932), 'For Whom Are Corporate Managers Trustees?', *Harvard Law Review*, **45**: 1145–1163.

Eckersley, R. (2012), 'Moving Forward in the Climate Negotiations: Multilateralism or Minilateralism?', *Global Environmental Politics*, **12**(2): 24–42.

Ehrlich, P. (1968), *The Population Bomb*, Cutchoque, NY: Buccaneer.

ENB (Earth Negotiations Bulletin) (2012), Summary of The United Nations Conference on Sustainable Development, 13–22 June 2012. Available at: http://www.iisd.ca/vol27/enb2751e.html. Accessed: 20-02-2013.

Engels, F. (1880 [1999]), *Socialism: Utopian and Scientific*, Chippensdale: Resistance.

Escobar, A. (1995), *Encountering Development: The Making and Unmaking of the Third World*, Princeton, NJ: Princeton University Press.

Escobar, A. (1999), 'After Nature: Steps to an Antiessentialist Political Ecology', *Current Anthropology*, **40**(1): 1–30.

Esteva, G. (1992), 'Development', in W. Sachs (ed.), *The Development Dictionary*, London: Zed, pp. 6–25.

Fannon, F. (1961 [1967]), *The Wretched of the Earth*, London: Penguin.

Ferrarini, G. (2002), 'Origins of Limited Liability Companies and Company Law Modernisation in Italy: A Historical Outline', *Centre for Law and Finance Working Papers*, No. 5. Available at: www.estig.ipbeja.pt/~ac_direito/Ferrarini3.pdf. Accessed: 14-3-2008.

Fligstein, N. (2001), *Architecture of Markets: An Economic Sociology of Twenty-First-Century Capitalist Societies*, Princeton, NJ: Princeton University Press.

Formoy, R.R. (1923), *The Historical Foundation of Modern Company Law*, London: Sweet and Maxwell.

Foucault, M. (1972), *Archaeology of Knowledge*, New York: Pantheon.

Foucault, M. (1976 [1990]), *The History of Sexuality*, New York: Pantheon.

Foucault, M. (1977), *Discipline and Punishment*, London: Tavistock.

Freire, P. (2004), *Pedagogy of Hope: Reliving Pedagogy of the Oppressed*, New York: Continuum.

Friedman, M. (1970), 'The Social Responsibility of Business is to Increase its Profits', *New York Times Magazine*, 13 September 1970: 33.

Fukuyama, F. (1989), 'The End of History?', *The National Interest*, Summer 1989. Available at: http://courses.essex.ac.uk/GV/GV905/IR%20Media%202010-11/W4%20Readings/Fukuyama%20End%20of%20History.pdf. Accessed: 14-6-2011.

Gabriel, Y. (2000), *Storytelling in Organizations: Facts, Fictions, and Fantasies*, Oxford: Oxford University Press.

Garrard, G. (2004), *Ecocriticism*, Abingdon: Routledge.

de Geus, M. (1999), *Ecological Utopias: Envisioning the Sustainable Society*, Utrecht: International Books.

Glasbergen, P. (2002), 'The Green Polder Model: Institutionalizing Multi-Stakeholder Processes in Strategic Environmental Decision-making', *European Environment*, **12**(6): 303–315.

Glasbergen, P. (2007), 'Setting the Scene: the Partnership Paradigm in the Making', in P. Glasbergen, F. Biermann and A. Mol (eds), *Partnerships, Governance and Sustainable Development: Reflections on Theory and Practice*, Cheltenham, UK and Northampton, MA, USA: Edward Elgar, pp. 1–25.

Global Sustainability Partnerships Database (GSPD), Version 2, 2008. Institute for Environmental Studies, Vrije Universiteit Amsterdam.

Glotfelty, C. (1996), 'Introduction', in C. Glotfelty and H. Fromm (eds), *The Ecocriticism Reader: Landmarks in Literary Ecology*, London: University of Georgia Press.

Glynos, J. and D. Howarth (2007), *Logics of Critical Explanation in Social and Political Theory*, Abingdon: Routledge.

Gottlieb, R. (1993), *Forcing the Spring: The Transformation of the American Environmental Movement*, Washington, DC: Island Press.

Gunningham, N. (2007), 'Environmental Partnerships in Agriculture: Reflections on the Australian Experience', in F. Biermann, P. Glasbergen and A. Mol (eds), *Partnerships, Governance and Sustainable Development: Reflections on Theory and Practice*, Cheltenham, UK and Northampton, MA, USA: Edward Elgar, pp. 115–137.

Haas, P. (2004), 'Addressing the Global Governance Deficit', *Global Environmental Politics*, **4**(4): 1–15.

Hagberg, L. (2010), 'Participation under Administrative Rationality: Implementing the EU Water Framework Directive in Forestry', in K. Bäckstrand, J. Khan, A. Kronsell and E. Lövbrand (eds), *Environmental Politics and Deliberative Democracy*, Cheltenham, UK and Northampton, MA, USA: Edward Elgar, pp. 123–143.

Hajer, M. (1995), *The Politics of Environmental Discourse: Ecological Modernization and the Policy Process*, Oxford: Clarendon.

Haldane, J.B.S. (1924), *Daedalus, Or, Science and the Future: A Paper Read to the Heretics*, New York: E.P. Dutton.

Haldane, J.B.S. (1926 [1985]), *On Being the Right Size*, Oxford: Oxford University Press.

Hale, T.N. and D.L. Mauzerall (2004), 'Thinking Globally and Acting Locally: Can the Johannesburg Partnerships Coordinate Action on Sustainable Development?', *The Journal of Environment and Development*, **13**(3): 220–239.

Hall, R. and T. Biersteker (2002), *The Emergence of Private Authority in Global Governance*, Cambridge: Cambridge University Press.

Hannah, L. (2007), 'The "Divorce" of Ownership from Control from 1900

Onwards: Re-calibrating Imagined Global Trends', *Business History*, **49**(4): 404–438.

Hansen, A.D. (2008), 'Laclauian Discourse Theory and the Problems of Institutions', Paper Presented at WISC Conference, Ljubjana, 23–26 July 2008. Available at: http://rudar.ruc.dk/bitstream/1800/3831/1/ ADHpaper Ljubljana.pdf. Accessed: 27-7-2010.

Hansen, A.D. and E. Sørenson (2005), 'Polity as Politics: Studying the Shaping and Effects of Discursive Polities', in D. Howarth and J. Torfing (eds), *Discourse Theory in European Politics: Identity, Policy, Governance*, Basingstoke: Palgrave, pp. 93–115.

Hansen, L. (2006), *Security as Practice: Discourse Analysis and the Bosnian War*, Abingdon: Routledge.

Haraway, D. (1985), 'A Manifesto for Cyborgs: Science Technology and Socialist Feminism in the 1980s', *Socialist Review*, **80**: 65–107.

Hardin, G. (1968), 'The Tragedy of the Commons', *Science*, **162**: 1243–1248.

Hardt, M. and A. Negri (2004), *Multitude: War and Democracy in the Age of Empire*, New York: Penguin.

Harvey, D. (1996), *Justice, Nature and the Geography of Difference*, Malden: Blackwell.

Hayek, F. (1985), 'The Corporation in a Democratic Society', in M. Anshen and G. Bach (eds), *Management and Corporations*, New York: McGraw-Hill, pp. 99–117.

Hays, S.P. (2000), *A History of Environmental Politics since 1945*, Pittsburgh, PA: University of Pittsburgh Press.

Held, D. and M. Koenig-Archibugi (2004), 'Introduction', *Government and Opposition*, **39**(2): 125–131.

Hill, T. (2004), 'Three Generations of UN–Civil Society Relations: A Quick Sketch'. Available at: http://www.un-ngls.org/orf/UNreform. htm. Accessed: 7-7-2008.

Hobbes, T. (1651 [1985]), *Leviathan*, London: Penguin.

Howarth, D. (1995), 'Discourse Theory', in D. Marsh and G. Stoker (eds), *Theory and Methods in Political Science*, Basingstoke: MacMillan.

Howarth, D. (2000), *Discourse*, Milton Keynes, Bucks: Open University.

Howarth, D. (2005), 'Applying Discourse Theory: The Method of Articulation', in D. Howarth and J. Torfing (eds), *Discourse Theory in European Politics: Identity, Policy and Governance*, Basingstoke: Palgrave, pp. 316–349.

Howarth, D. (2009), 'Power, Discourse, and Policy: Articulating a Hegemony Approach to Critical Policy Studies', *Critical Policy Studies*, **3**(3): 309–335.

Howarth, D. and Y. Stavrakakis (2000), 'Introducing Discourse Theory and Political Analysis', in D. Howarth, A. Norval and Y. Stavrakakis (eds), *Discourse Theory and Political Analysis: Identities, Hegemonies and Social Change*, Manchester: Manchester University Press, pp. 1–23.

Hultman, N. (2012), 'The Rio+20 Conference: A Useful Forum for External Commitments but No Transformative Vision'. Available from: http://www.brookings.edu/research/opinions/2012/06/25-rio-20-conference-hultman. Accessed: 20-02-2013.

IISD (1996), 'The Earth Summit and Agenda 21', in *Global Tomorrow Coalition Sustainable Development Tool Kit*. Available at: http://www.iisd.org/educate/learn/agenda21. Retrieved: 02-02-2007.

IISD (2001), *Summary of the First Preparatory Session of the World Summit on Sustainable Development*. Available at: http://www.iisd.ca/vol22/enb2203e.html. Accessed: 7-7-2008.

IISD (2002), *Summary of the Second Preparatory Session of the World Summit on Sustainable Development*. Available at: http://www.iisd.ca/vol22/enb2219e.html. Accessed: 7-7-2008.

Illich, I. (1968), 'To Hell with Good Intentions', Address to the Conference on Inter-American Student Projects (CIASP) in Cuernavaca, Mexico, 20 April 1968. Available at: http://www.swaraj.org/illich_hell.htm. Accessed: 02-12-2010.

Illich, I. (1970), *Deschooling Society*, New York: Harper and Row.

Illich, I. (1975), *Limits to Medicine: Medical Nemesis, the Expropriation of Health*, London: Calder and Boyars.

Illich, I. (2000), *Corruption of Christianity* (Audio Cassette), Canadian Broadcasting Corporation (CBC Audio), August.

IUCN, UNEP and WWF (1980), *World Conservation Strategy: Living Resource Conservation for Sustainable Development*, Gland: IUCN-UNEP-WWF.

Jeffares, S.R. (2007), *Why Public Policy Ideas Catch On: Empty Signifiers and Flourishing Neighbourhoods*, PhD Thesis University of Birmingham. Available at: http://etheses.bham.ac.uk/193/1/Jeffares08PhD_A1a.pdf. Accessed: 28-4-2011.

Kara, J. and D. Quarless (2002), 'Guiding Principles for Partnerships for Sustainable Development ("Type 2 Outcomes") to Be Elaborated by Interested Parties in the Context of the World Summit on Sustainable Development', Paper read at 4th Summit Preparatory Committee, 27 May–7 June 2002, at Bali, Indonesia.

Keck, M. and K. Sikkink (1998), *Activists beyond Borders: Advocacy Networks in International Politics*, Ithaca: Cornell University Press.

Kerridge, R. (1998), 'Introduction', in R. Kerridge and N. Sammells (eds), *Writing the Environment*, London: Zed, pp. 1–11.

Kleiber, M. (1932), 'Body Size and Metabolism', *Hilgardia*, **6**: 315–351.

Klein, E. (1971), *A Comprehensive Etymological Dictionary of the English Language*, Amsterdam: Elsevier.

Kohr, L. (1941), 'Disunion Now: A Plea for a Society Based upon Small Autonomous Units', *The Commonwealth*, 26 September 1941.

Kohr, L. (1957), *The Breakdown of Nations*, London; New York: Routledge and Kegan Paul.

Kohr, L. (1978), *Overdeveloped Nations: The Diseconomies of Scale*, Swansea: Christopher Davies.

Krasner, S.D. (1983), 'Structural Causes and Regime Consequences: Regimes as Intervening Variables', in S. D. Krasner (ed.), *International Regimes*, Ithaca: Cornell University Press.

Kroll, G. (2002), 'Rachel Carson – Silent Spring: A Brief History of Ecology as a Subversive Subject'. Available at: http://onlineethics.org/moral/carson/kroll.html. Accessed: 10-2-2008.

Laclau, E. (1983), 'The Impossibility of Society', *Canadian Journal of Political and Social Theory*, **7**(1–2): 21–24.

Laclau, E. (1990), *New Reflections on the Revolution of Our Times*, London: Verso.

Laclau, E. (ed.) (1994), *The Making of Political Identities*, London: Verso.

Laclau, E. (1996), *Emancipation(s)*, London: Verso.

Laclau, E. (2005a), *On Populist Reason*, London: Verso.

Laclau, E. (2005b), 'Populism: What's in a Name?', in F. Panizza (ed.), *Populism and the Mirror of Democracy*, London: Verso, pp. 32–48.

Laclau, E. and C. Mouffe (1985), *Hegemony and Socialist Strategy: Towards a Radical Democratic Politics*, London: Verso.

Lafferty, W. (ed.) (2004), *Governance for Sustainable Development: The Challenge of Adapting Form to Function*, Cheltenham, UK and Northampton, MA, USA: Edward Elgar.

Latouche, S. (1989 [1996]), *The Westernization of the World*, Cambridge: Polity.

Latour, B. (1993), *We Have Never Been Modern*, Cambridge, MA: Harvard University Press.

Latour, B. (2004), 'Why Has Critique Run out of Steam? From Matters of Fact to Matters of Concern', *Critical Inquiry*, **30**(2): 225–248.

Latour, B. (2010), 'An Attempt at a "Compositionist Manifesto"', *New Literary History*, **41**(3): 471–490.

Lave, R., M. Doyle and M. Robertson (2010), 'Privatizing Stream Restoration in the US', *Social Studies of Science*, **40**(5): 677–703.

Leopold, A. (1949 [1968]), *A Sand County Almanac and Sketches Here and There*, Oxford: Oxford University Press.

Lewis, C.S. (1953), 'The Humanitarian Theory of Punishment', *The Churchman*, **73**(2): 55–60.

Lipschutz, R. and C. Fogel (2002), '"Regulation for the Rest of Us?" Global Civil Society and the Privatization of Transnational Regulation', in R. Hall and T. Biersteker (eds), *The Emergence of Private Authority in Global Governance*, Cambridge: Cambridge University Press, pp. 115–140.

Lowes, B. and R. Dobbins (1978), 'Objective Setting: A Corporate Planning Approach', *Managerial Finance*, **4**(1): 67–79.

MacKenzie, D. (2009), 'Making Things the Same: Gases, Emission Rights and the Politics of Carbon Markets', *Accounting, Organizations and Society*, **34**(3–4): 440–455.

Maor, E. (1987), *To Infinity and Beyond: A Cultural History of the Infinite*, Boston: Birkhauser.

Marcuse, H. (1972), 'Ecology and Revolution', *Liberation*, **16**: 10–12.

Martens, J. (2007), 'Multistakeholder Partnerships – Future Models of Multilateralism?', Occasional Papers No. 29, Friedrich-Ebert-Stiftung, Berlin.

Marx, K. (1853), 'The Future Results of British Rule in India', *New York Daily Tribune*, 25 June–8 August; reprinted in K. Marx and F. Engels (1959), *On Colonialism*, Moscow: Progress.

Marx, K. (1867 [1991]), *Capital: A Critique of Political Economy Vol. 3*, London: Penguin.

Marx, K. (1939 [1981]), *Grundrisse*, Harmondsworth: Penguin.

Meadows, D.L., D.H. Meadows, J. Randers and W.W. Behrens (1972), *Limits to Growth*, New York: Universe.

Merchant, C. (1992), *Radical Ecology*, New York: Routledge.

Merchant, C. (1998), 'The Death of Nature: A Retrospective', *Organization and Environment*, **11**(2): 198–206.

Mert, A. (2012), 'The Privatisation of Environmental Governance: On Myths, Forces of Nature and Other Inevitabilities', *Environmental Values*, **21**(4): 475–498.

Mert, A. (2013), 'Hybrid Governance Mechanisms as Political Instruments: The Case of Sustainability Partnerships', *International Environmental Agreements* (Online first. DOI 10.1007/s10784-013-9221-6).

Mert, A. and E. Dellas (2012), 'Assessing the Legitimacy of Technology Transfer through Partnerships for Sustainable Development in the Water Sector', in P. Pattberg, F. Biermann, S. Chan and A. Mert (eds), *Public–Private Partnerships for Sustainable Development*, Cheltenham, UK and Northampton, MA, USA: Edward Elgar, pp. 209–238.

Miller J. (1996), *Rousseau: Dreamer of Democracy*, New Haven, CT: Yale University Press.

Mitchell, R.B. (2010), International Environmental Agreements Database Project (version 2010.2). Available at: http://iea.uoregon.edu. Accessed: 30-6-2011.

Montesquieu, C. (1748 [1989]), *The Spirit of the Laws*, A.M. Cohler, B.C. Miller and H.S. Stone (eds), Cambridge: Cambridge University Press.

Morris, W. (1891 [1970]), *News from Nowhere*, London: Routledge.

Mouffe, C. (1993), *Return of the Political*, London: Verso.

Mouffe, C. (1996), 'Democracy, Power, and the "Political"', in S. Benhabib (ed.), *Democracy and Difference*, Princeton, NJ: Princeton University Press, pp. 245–255.

Mouffe, C. (1998), 'Hearts, Minds and Radical Democracy', Interview with Dave Castle, *Red Pepper*. Available at: www.redpepper.org.uk/hearts-minds-and-radical-democracy. Accessed: 17-5-2006.

Mouffe, C. (2000), *The Democratic Paradox*, London: Verso.

Mouffe, C. (2005), *On the Political*, London: Routledge.

Multatuli (1860 [1987]), *Max Havelaar*, London: Penguin.

Munck, R. and D. O'Hearn (eds) (1999), *Critical Development Theory: Contributions to a New Paradigm*, London: Zed Books.

MWC Dictionary (1996), MA: Merriam-Webster.

Næss, A. (1989), *Ecology, Community and Lifestyle*, Cambridge: Cambridge University Press.

Najam, A. and C.J. Cleveland (2004), 'World Environment Summits: The Role of Energy', *Encyclopaedia of Energy*, **6**: 539–548.

NASB (New American Standard Bible) (1977), La Habra: Lockman.

Nelson, G. (1993), 'How the First Earth Day Came About'. Available at: http://earthday.envirolink.org/history.html. Accessed: 23-12-2008.

Nietzsche, F. (1872 [1956]), *The Birth of Tragedy and the Genealogy of Morals*, New York: Anchor.

Nixon, R.M. (1970), 'State of the Union Address, 12 January 1970'. Available at: http://millercenter.org/president/speeches/detail/3889. Accessed: 4-4-2007.

OECD (2006), 'Evaluating the Effectiveness and Efficiency of Partnerships'. Available at: http://www.olis.oecd.org/olis/2006doc.nsf/LinkTo/NT000097BA/$FILE/JT03243465.pdf. Accessed: 17-12-2006.

O'Hara, E. (2007), 'Focus on Carbon "Missing the Point"', *BBC News Online*, 30 July. Available at: http://news.bbc.co.uk/2/hi/science/nature/6922065. Accessed: 13-9-2007.

Okri, B. (1992), *The Famished Road*, London: Vintage.

Osborn, F. (1948), *Our Plundered Planet*, London: Faber and Faber.

Ottaway, M. (2001), 'Corporatism Goes Global', *Global Governance*, **7**(3): 265–292.

Partnerships Wire (2007), 'Partnerships Building Cleaner Industries for a Sustainable Future'. Available at: http://www.un.org/esa/sustdev/csd/csd15/PF/wire_May_4.pdf. Accessed: 14-6-2008.

Paterson, M. (2008), 'Sustainable Consumption? Legitimation, Regulation and Environmental Governance', in J. Park, K. Conca and M. Finger (eds), *The Crisis of Global Environmental Governance*, London: Routledge, pp. 110–131.

Pattberg, P. (2005), 'The Institutionalization of Private Governance: How Business and Non-Profits Agree on Transnational Rules', *Governance*, **18**(4): 589–610.

Pearce, F. (2012), 'Beyond Rio, Green Economics Can Give Us Hope', *The Guardian*, 28 June. Available from: http://www.guardian.co.uk/environ ment/2012/jun/28/rio-green-economics-hope. Accessed: 20-02-2013.

Phillips, L. and M.W. Jørgensen (2002), *Discourse Analysis as Theory and Method*, London: Sage.

Plato ([1984]), *The Laws*, London: Penguin.

Plato ([2006]), *The Republic*, New Haven: Yale University Press.

Polanyi, K. (1944 [2001]), *The Great Transformation: The Political and Economic Origins of Our Time*, Boston: Beacon.

Pretes, M. (1997), 'Development and Infinity', *World Development*, **25**(9): 1421–1430.

Quental, N., J.M. Lourenço and F.N. da Silva (2011), 'Sustainable Development Policy: Goals, Targets and Political Cycles', *Sustainable Development*, **19**(1): 15–29.

Rahnema, M. (1992), 'Participation', in W. Sachs (ed.), *The Development Dictionary*, London: Zed, pp. 116–131.

Rajasingham-Senanayake, D. (2009), 'Transnational Peace Building and Conflict: Lessons from Aceh, Indonesia, and Sri Lanka', *Sojourn*, **24**(2): 211–235.

Randalls, S. (2010), 'Weather Profits: Weather Derivatives and the Commercialization of Meteorology', *Social Studies of Science*, **40**(5): 706–730.

Rist, G. (1997), *The History of Development: From Western Origins to Global Faith*, London: Zed.

Robertson, T.B. (2005), *The Population Bomb: Population Growth, Globalization and American Environmentalism, 1945–1980*, PhD Dissertation, University of Wisconsin-Madison.

Rosdolsky, R. (1977), *The Making of Marx's Capital*, London: Pluto.

Rose, N. (1996), 'Governing "Advanced" Liberal Democracies', in A. Barry, T. Osborne and N. Rose (eds), *Foucault and Political Reason*, Chicago: University of Chicago Press.

Rosenau, J.N. and E.O. Czempiel (1992), *Governance without Government: Order and Change in World Politics*, Cambridge: Cambridge University Press.

Rousseau, J. (1762 [1968]), *The Social Contract or Principles of Political Right*, London: Penguin.

Rowden, R. and J. Ocaya Irama (2004), 'Rethinking Participation: Questions for Civil Society about the Limits of Participation in PRSPs Organization'. Available at: http://www.un-ngls.org/orf/cso/cso2/rethinking.html. Accessed: 17-12-2006.

Roy, A. (1997), *The God of Small Things*, New York: Harper Perennial.

Rozmovits, L. (1998), *Shakespeare and the Politics of Culture in Late Victorian England*, Baltimore: Johns Hopkins University Press.

Rubin, C.T. (1994), *The Green Crusade: Rethinking the Roots of Environmentalism*, Lanham: Rowman & Littlefield.

Sachs, W. (ed.) (1992a), *The Development Dictionary*, London: Zed.

Sachs, W. (1992b), 'Environment', in W. Sachs (ed.), *The Development Dictionary*, London: Zed, pp. 26–37.

Şahin, Ü. (2004), 'Truva Atı Olarak Sürdürülebilir Kalkınma', *Üç Ekoloji*, **1**(2): 9–30.

Said, E.W. (1978 [1995]), *Orientalism: Western Conceptions of the Orient*, Harmondsworth: Penguin.

Said, E.W. (1983), *The World, the Text, and the Critic*, Cambridge, MA: Harvard University Press.

Said, E.W. (1994), *Culture and Imperialism*, New York: Vintage.

Sassen, S. (1996), *Losing Control? Sovereignty in an Age of Globalization*, New York: Columbia University Press.

Saville, J. (1956), 'Sleeping Partnership and Limited Liability, 1850–1856', *The Economic History Review*, **8**(3): 418–433.

Schumacher, E.F. (1973), *Small Is Beautiful: Economics as If People Mattered*, New York: Harper Row.

SDIN (2004), 'Historic Statement at CSD 12', *Taking Issue*, **4**(10): 1–2.

Shakespeare, W. (1596 [1987]), *The Merchant of Venice*, in M.M. Mahood (ed.), Cambridge: Cambridge University Press.

Shepard, P. (1969), 'Introduction: Ecology and Man', in P. Shepard and D. McKinley (eds), *The Subversive Science: Essays Toward an Ecology of Man*, Boston: Houghton Mifflin, pp. 1–10.

Shiva, V. (2001), *Lecture Given at the Institute for Global Environmental Strategies*, 26 August 2001, Kamakura, Japan.

Skinner, B.F. (1948 [1962]), *Walden Two*, New York: Macmillan.

Slater, D. (1993), 'The Geopolitical Imagination and the Enframing of Development Theory', *Transactions of the Institute of British Geographers*, New Series, **18**(4): 419–437.

Soper, K. (1996), 'Nature/"nature"', in George Robertson (ed.), *FutureNatural*, London: Routledge, pp. 22–34.

Spengler, O. (1919 [2011]), *The Decline of the West*, Toronto: University of Toronto Libraries.

Srikandarajah, D. (2005), 'The Returns of Peace in Sri Lanka', *Journal of Peacebuilding and Development*, 1(2): 21–35.

Stavrakakis, Y. (2005), 'Passions of Identification: Discourse, Enjoyment, and European Identity', in D. Howarth, and J. Torfing (eds), *Discourse Theory in European Politics: Identity, Policy, Governance*, Basingstoke: Palgrave, pp. 68–92.

Stiglitz, J. (2003), *Globalization and Its Discontents*, London: W.W. Norton.

Strathern, M. (1992), *After Nature: English Kinship in the Late Twentieth Century*, Cambridge: Cambridge University Press.

Stripple, J. (2010), 'Weberian Climate Policy: Administrative Rationality Organized as a Market', in K. Bäckstrand, J. Khan, A. Kronsell and E. Lövbrand (eds), *Environmental Politics and Deliberative Democracy*, Cheltenham, UK and Northampton, MA, USA: Edward Elgar, pp. 67–83.

Strong, M. (2002), 'The Road from Stockholm to Johannesburg', *UN Chronicle*, Issue 3. Available at: http://www.un.org/Pubs/chronicle/2002/issue3/0302p14_essay. Accessed: 12-6-2007.

The Ecologist (1972), *A Blueprint for Survival*, London: Ecosystems.

The Guardian (2004), 'Pentagon Forced to Withdraw Leaflet Linking Aid to Information on Taliban', 6 May. Available at: http://www.the guardian.com/world/2004/may/06/Afghanistan.usa. Accessed: 16-11-2014.

The New York Times (2003), 'Environmental Word Games', 15 March 2003. Available at: http://www.nytimes.com/2003/03/15/opinion/environmental-word-games. Accessed: 6-8-2007.

The Times (2009), 'Tsunami Aid Windfall in Aceh Brings Sinister Threat to Foreign Workers', 26 December 2009. Available at: www.timesonline.co.uk/tol/news/world/asia/article6968000.ece. Accessed: 26-12-2009.

Thompson, D.W. (1917 [1952]), *On Growth and Form*, Cambridge: Cambridge University Press.

Time Magazine (1970), *Nation: A Memento Mori to the Earth*, 4 May. Available at: http://content.time.com/time/magazine/article/0,9171,943782,00.html. Accessed: 16-11-2014.

de Tocqueville, A. (1835), *Democracy in America*, London: Saunders and Otley.

Toms, S. (2007), 'Calculating Profit: A Historical Perspective on the Development of Capitalism', Paper presented at the 7th ECAS Conference, University of Glasgow.

Torfing, J. (1999), *New Theories of Discourse: Laclau, Mouffe and Žižek*, Oxford: Blackwell.

Torfing, J. (2005), 'Discourse Theory: Achievements, Arguments, and Challenges', in D. Howarth and J. Torfing (eds), *Discourse Theory in European Politics, Identity, Policy and Governance*, Basingstoke: Palgrave, pp. 1–32.

Truman, H.S. (1949), *Inaugural Address, Thursday, January 20, 1949.* Available at: http://avalon.law.yale.edu/20th_century/truman.asp. Accessed: 10-7-2006.

Tuathail, G.Ó. (1994), 'Critical Geopolitics and Development Theory: Intensifying the Dialogue', *Transactions of the Institute of British Geographers*, **19**(2): 228–233.

Tully, J. (1995), 'Cultural Demands for Constitutional Recognition', *Journal of Political Philosophy*, **3**(2): 111–132.

UN (1945), *The UN Charter.* Available at: http://www.un.org/en/docu ments/ charter/chapter11. Accessed: 13-11-2007.

UN (1972), *Declaration of the United Nations Conference on the Human Environment.* Available at: http://www.unep.org/Documents. Multilingual /Default.asp?documentid=97&articleid=1503. Accessed: 5-9-2008.

UN (1983), *Process of Preparation of the Environmental Perspective to the Year 2000 and Beyond*, General Assembly Resolution 38/161. Available at: http://www.un.org/documents/ga/res/38/a38r161.htm. Accessed: 8-12-2009.

UN (1992a), *Rio Declaration on Environment and Development*, UN Doc. A/CONF.151/26, UN General Assembly, New York. Available at: http://www.unep.org/Documents.Multilingual/Default.asp?documenti d=78&articleid=1163. Accessed: 24-10-2007.

UN (1992b), *Agenda 21.* Available at: http://www.un.org/esa/dsd/ agenda21. Accessed: 23-9-2009.

UN (2000), *The Millennium Declaration*, Resolution adopted by the General Assembly 55/2, 8 September 2000. Available at: http://www.un.org/mil lennium/declaration/ares552e.htm. Accessed: 13-10-2007.

UN (2001a), *Towards Global Partnerships: Resolution Adopted by the UN General Assembly.* Available at: http://www.unhcr.org/refworld/ docid/3da44afc7.html. Accessed: 20-12-2009.

UN (2001b), *UN Secretary-General's Report on Major Groups to the Commission on Sustainable Development Acting as the Preparatory Committee for the World Summit on Sustainable Development, organizational session*, 30 April–2 May, UN Doc. E/CN.17/2001/PC/ 41.

UN (2002a), *Johannesburg Plan of Implementation.* Available at: http:// www.un.org/esa/sustdev/documents/WSSD_POI_PD/English/POIToc. htm. Accessed: 3-3-2006.

UN (2002b), *Johannesburg Declaration on Sustainable Development.* Available at: http://www.un.org/esa/sustdev/documents/WSSD_POI_PD/English/POI_PD.htm. Accessed: 23-9-2009.

UN (2012), 'Draft Resolution Submitted by the President of the General Assembly: The Future We Want'. Available at: http://daccess-dds-ny.un.org/doc/UNDOC/LTD/N12/436/88/PDF/N1243688.pdf?Open Element.

UNCSD (2002a), *Vice-Chairs' Summary of the Informal Meetings on Partnerships/ Initiatives,* New York, 5 April 2002. Available at: http://www.un.org/esa/dsd/dsd_aofw_par/par_mand_vicechaisumm.shtml. Accessed: 2-11-2011.

UNCSD (2002b), *Bali Guiding Principles.* Available at: http://www.un.org/esa/dsd/dsd_ aofw_par/par_mand_baliguidprin.shtml. Accessed: 10-11-2009.

UNCSD (2007), *Partnerships for Sustainable Development.* Available at: http://www.un.org/esa/sustdev/partnerships/partnerships.htm. Accessed: 2-9-2009.

UNCSD (2008), 'Secretary-General's Report on Partnerships'. Available at: http://daccess-dds-ny.un.org/doc/UNDOC/GEN/N08/229/62/PDF/N0822962.pdf?OpenElement. Accessed: 23-9-2009.

UNCSD (2012a), 'Summary of Voluntary Commitments Registered at Rio+20'. Available at: http://www.un.org/ga/search/view_doc.asp?symbol5A/RES/66/288&Lang5E. Accessed: 20-02-2013.

UNCSD (2012b), 'Rio+20 Voluntary Commitments'. Available at: http://www.uncsd2012.org/voluntarycommitments.html. Accessed: 20-02-2013.

UNCSD Partnerships Database (2004), 'Safe Water System Program'. Available at: http://webapps01.un.org/dsd/partnerships/public/partnerships/94.html. Accessed: 25-11-2010.

UNCSD Partnerships Database (2007), 'World Nuclear University'. Available at: http://webapps01.un.org/dsd/partnerships/public/partnerships/1859.html. Accessed 25-11-2010.

UNCSD Partnerships Database (2008), 'Invasive Species Compendium Consortium'. Available at: http://webapps01.un.org/dsd/partnerships/public/partnerships/2354.html. Accessed 25-11-2010.

UNESCAP (2005), *Final Statement of the Asian Civil Society Forum on UN Reform.* Available at: http://www.seaca.net/print_template.php?aID=398. Accessed: 23-9-2009.

UNESCAP (2011), *What is Good Governance?* Available at: http://www.unescap.org/pdd/prs/ProjectActivities/Ongoing/gg/governance.asp. Accessed: 8-12-2009.

UNFIP (2006), 'United Nations Fund for International Partnerships

Report'. Available at: http://www.un.org/partnerships/YLatestUpdate 2006. Accessed: 16-6-2008.

UN Global Compact (2003), 'Report of the UN Secretary-General, August 2003'. Available at: http://www.unglobalcompact.org/Issues/partnerships/index.html. Accessed: 18-6-2006.

UNICEF (1999), *Statement of UNICEF Executive Director Carol Bellamy*. Available at: http://www.unicef.org/media/media_11989. Accessed: 11-02-2008.

UNOP (2010), 'A Selection of Partnership Initiatives'. Available at: http://www.un.org/partnerships/partnership_initiatives.html. Accessed: 25-11-2010.

USAID (2008), 'Fiscal Year 2008: USAID Annual Performance Report'. Available at: http://www.usaid.gov/policy/budget/apr08. Accessed: 3-10-2009.

Visseren-Hamakers, I.J. and P. Glasbergen (2007), 'Partnerships in Forest Governance', *Global Environmental Change*, **17**(3–4): 408–419.

Vogt, W. (1948), *Road to Survival*, New York: William Sloane.

Votaw, D. (1965), *Modern Corporations*, Englewood Cliffs: Prentice-Hall.

Wæver, O. (2005), 'European Integration and Security', in D. Howarth and J. Torfing (eds), *Discourse Theory in European Politics: Identity, Policy, Governance*, Basingstoke: Palgrave, pp. 33–67.

Walzer, M. (1984), 'Liberalism and the Art of Separation', *Political Theory*, **12**(3): 315–330.

Ward, B. and R. Dubos (1972 [1980]), *Only One Earth*, Harmondsworth: Penguin.

WCED (1987), *Our Common Future*, Oxford: Oxford University Press.

Wells, H.G. (1906 [2004]), *In the Days of the Comet*, London: Macmillan.

Witte, J.M., C. Streck and T. Benner (2002), 'The Road from Johannesburg: What Future for Partnerships in Global Environmental Governance?' in *Progress or Peril? Networks and Partnerships in Global Environmental Governance, The Post-Johannesburg Agenda*, Berlin and Washington: Global Public Policy Institute, pp. 59–84.

Wolf, K.D. (2002), 'Contextualizing Normative Standards for Legitimate Governance Beyond the State', in J. Grote and B. Gbikpi (eds), *Participatory Governance: Political and Societal Implications*, Opladen: Leske und Budrich, pp. 35–50.

World Bank (2007), *World Bank Report: Aceh Economic Update*. Available at: http://siteresources.worldbank.org/INTINDONESIA/Resources/226271-1176706430507/3681211-1194602678235/aeu_nov 2007_en. Accessed: 20-1-2009.

Yanow, D. (1992), 'Silences in Public Policy Discourse: Organizational and Policy Myths', *Journal of Public Administration Research and Theory*, **2**(4): 399–423.

Young, O.R. (1989), *International Cooperation: Building Regimes for Natural Resources and the Environment*, Ithaca: Cornell University Press.

Zammit, A. (2003), 'Development at Risk: Rethinking UN–Business Partnerships', Geneva: The South Centre and UNRISD. Available at: http://www.globalpolicy.org/re form/business/2003/risk.pdf. Accessed: 11-2-2008.

Žižek, S. (1997), *The Sublime Object of Ideology*, London: Verso.

Žižek, S. (2006), *How to Read Lacan*, New York: W.W. Norton.

Zoja, L. (1993 [1995]), *Growth and Guilt: Psychology and the Limits of Development*, London: Routledge.

Index

democracy 6, 8, 10–11, 16, 21, 52, 65,
    137, 186–9, 199, 209–10, 233,
    236–40
democratic deficit 65, 222, 237, 241
see also governance deficit;
    participation deficit
Derrida, J. 8, 14, 30
deschooling 147
developmentalism 15, 32, 45, 49–53,
    68, 121–5, 131–9, 149, 156–7,
    161–2, 166, 170–71, 179–82,
    205–6, 210–13, 221–2, 227, 239
discourse institutionalization 14, 40,
    55–6, 59, 63, 88–9, 223, 226
discourse structuration 13, 40
dislocation 18, 21, 39–40, 44, 47, 52,
    189, 220, 230
Dow Chemical Company, 93
dystopia 188
see also utopia (genre)

Earth Day 151–2
Earth First! 159–60, 162
earth system governance 243
ecocriticism 31–3
emissions 58, 64, 80–82, 93, 244
see also greenhouse gas
empty signifier 47–52, 56–7, 86–7,
    145–8, 150, 154, 157, 170, 179–80,
    224
see also floating signifier; remainder
Engels, F. 231, 235
Environmental Defense Fund 146
environmentalism 8, 15, 104–5, 121,
    124, 146–7, 151–4, 160
equivalential chain *see* chain of
    equivalence
Escobar, A. 5, 36–7, 59, 121, 132, 141
Essex School 21–2
European Union 73, 224–5

Fannon, F. 129
fantasmatic logic 45, 53, 96–9, 122–4,
    136, 186–90, 213, 229–30
fantasy 42–4, 48, 59–60, 81, 136, 138,
    141, 182, 189, 215
First World War 186
floating signifier 50–52, 149–50, 157,
    170, 180
see also empty signifier; remainder

Forest Stewardship Council 105,
    118
Foucault, M. 3, 20, 26, 39–42, 54, 57,
    59, 121, 149
Fourier, C. 230–31
Freire, P. 211
French Revolution 51, 188–9, 213
Friedman, M. 107
see also Chicago School
Friends of the Earth 147
Fukuyama, F. 6

Generation IV International Forum
    78, 81
Global Compact 65, 100, 105, 120,
    173–4
global demos, 187, 215
Global Initiative Towards a Sustainable
    Iraq (GITSI) 209
Global Sustainability Partnerships
    Database (GSPD) 15, 29–30,
    78–9, 82–5, 201–2
Glynos, J. 11, 23, 34, 42, 45, 53, 59
see also Essex School
good governance 186, 190, 197–8
governance deficit 64, 118, 120, 220,
    227
see also implementation deficit;
    participation deficit; democratic
    deficit
Gramsci, A. 21, 34, 50
greenhouse gas 64, 244
see also emissions
Greenpeace 147, 159
Group of 77 (G77) 72–3, 191

Hajer, M. 13–14, 20–21, 40–41, 55, 89,
    223, 226
Haldane, J.B.S. 143–4, 182
Hansen, A.D. 27, 31–2, 54
see also Essex School
Haraway, D. 35–6
Hardt, M. 113, 117, 186
Harvey, D. 30
Hayek, F. 108
see also Chicago School
hegemonic discourse 45–6, 49–53,
    179–81, 218, 221
hegemonic struggle 38, 45, 48–53, 57,
    180, 213, 221, 235, 239